# Environment, labour and capitalism at sea

MANCHESTER
1824

Manchester University Press

# New
# Ethnographies

*Series editor*
Alexander Thomas T. Smith

## Already published

# Environment, labour and capitalism at sea

## 'Working the ground' in Scotland

Penny McCall Howard

Manchester University Press

Published by Manchester University Press
Altrincham Street, Manchester M1 7JA
www.manchesteruniversitypress.co.uk

British Library Cataloguing-in-Publication Data
A catalogue record for this book is available from the British Library

ISBN 978 1 7849 9414 3 hardback
ISBN 978 1 5261 4369 3 paperback

First published by Manchester University Press in hardback 2017
This edition first published 2019

The publisher has no responsibility for the persistence or accuracy of URLs for any external or third-party internet websites referred to in this book, and does not guarantee that any content on such websites is, or will remain, accurate or appropriate.

Typeset by Out of House Publishing

*To Fiona McCall and Paul Howard, parents who first took me to sea and across several oceans at the age of six, and who have loved, supported and encouraged me ever since.*

# Contents

# Figures

# Series editor's foreword

At its best, ethnography has provided a valuable tool for apprehending a world in flux. A couple of years after the Second World War, Max Gluckman founded the Department of Social Anthropology at the University of Manchester. In the years that followed, he and his colleagues built a programme of ethnographic research that drew eclectically on the work of leading anthropologists, economists and sociologists to explore issues of conflict, reconciliation and social justice 'at home' and abroad. Often placing emphasis on detailed analysis of case studies drawn from small-scale societies and organisations, the famous 'Manchester School' in social anthropology built an enviable reputation for methodological innovation in its attempts to explore the pressing political questions of the second half of the twentieth century. Looking back, that era is often thought to constitute a 'gold standard' for how ethnographers might grapple with new challenges and issues in the contemporary world.

The *New Ethnographies* series aims to build on that ethnographic legacy at Manchester. It will publish the best new ethnographic monographs that promote interdisciplinary debate and methodological innovation in the qualitative social sciences. This includes the growing number of books that seek to apprehend the 'new' ethnographic objects of a seemingly brave new world, some recent examples of which have included auditing, democracy and elections, documents, financial markets, human rights, assisted reproductive technologies and political activism. Analysing such objects has often demanded new skills and techniques from the ethnographer. As a result, this series will give voice to those using ethnographic methods across disciplines to innovate, such as through the application of multi-sited fieldwork and the extended comparative case study method. Such innovations have often challenged more traditional ethnographic approaches. *New Ethnographies* therefore seeks to provide a platform for emerging scholars and their more established counterparts engaging with ethnographic methods in new and imaginative ways.

*Dr Alexander Thomas T. Smith*

# Acknowledgements

My research would have been impossible without the time, trust and generosity extended to me by the many people I met in the towns around the Inner Sound and further afield in Scotland. In particular, Alasdair MacPhail, Iain 'Bodach' MacKenzie and Billy Finlayson went out of their way to give me insight into their lives and to introduce me to others. Alasdair also read large portions of this book and provided invaluable feedback.

*Suilven* was the best companion I could hope for at sea and in port, keeping me warm and dry, powering my laptop and camera, and providing endless opportunities for tinkering and conversation. Sadly, she was wrecked on the Isle of Bute in 2011.

At the Anthropology Department of the University of Aberdeen, Arnar Árnason and Andrew Whitehouse were always patient and insightful. I will always appreciate Tim Ingold's willingness to admit me to his department and his ongoing support. I miss the vibrant and supportive community in that department. Jo Vergunst and Laura Bear challenged me as excellent examiners. I have had the considerable benefit of developing ideas with Liam Campling and Elizabeth Havice. Linda Connor has provided invaluable support and advice, and encouragement to develop my ideas.

I have benefited from the love, friendship and patience of many people through the course of writing this book. Warren Smith has been endlessly patient and supportive, and Benji had perfect timing. Joshua Brown sacrificed a lot, which I appreciate immensely. Donna Borokinni, Beth Armstrong, Rachel Harkness, Amber Lincoln and Bob Plant provided encouragement at various difficult and crucial times. Anne Harkness provided invaluable assistance and reassurance in the final stages of editing the manuscript. The team at Manchester University Press and Out of House Publishing have been a pleasure to work with.

This research would not have been possible without financial support from the Commonwealth Scholarship Foundation, the Wenner-Gren Foundation, the Social Science and Humanities Research Council of Canada, the University of Aberdeen, the Overseas Students Awards Schemes and the Inverness Field Club.

Any errors or shortcomings in this book are of course my own.

# Map

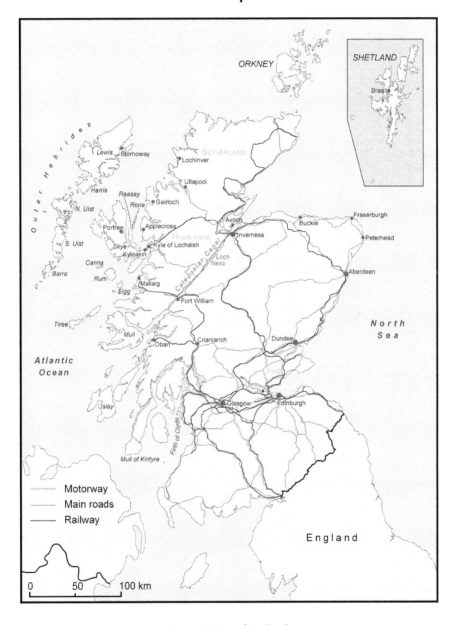

Figure 1  Map of Scotland.

# Introduction

I ate my breakfast outside in the bright morning stillness of summer in Scotland, examining the fishing boats around me, which were perfectly reflected in the water of this cosy harbour. The engine of each pickup truck echoed off the rocks surrounding the harbour with precision as men arrived down to the boat ramp to start their working day. I rowed ashore from the small sailboat I lived on to wait for DJ.[1] He greeted me with some surprise, and warmth, and agreed to take me out on the small creel boat[2] he usually worked on by himself around the Applecross Peninsula. We had met ashore in a different harbour a few months before but I had delayed visiting his home port due to the constantly changeable weather and difficult harbour entrance.

It was a beautiful sunny day, the kind of day in which the world seemed to have opened right up. The air was clear enough to see 50 miles out to the peaks of Harris in the Western Isles. Around us on three sides every intimate fold of the treeless rocky hills was exposed from the sea straight up to the summits. The water was slick and the clouds were reflected in constant motion in the sea we passed through. Once we got beyond the harbour DJ took a moment to look around and smiled. 'Sometimes when I'm out here, I think, people pay me to do this?!'

We worked hauling up and re-setting DJ's creel fleets. He operated the hydraulic creel hauler, swung the creels onto the boat, took out the prawns[3] and re-baited the creels while I stacked them in the stern of the boat according to his careful instructions. I got a break when we re-set the creels back into the water by letting them fly out of a gate in the stern, and as he motored to the next fleet (Figure 2). During these breaks, and with his permission, I scribbled notes about our conversation in the small dirty notebook I kept in my pocket.

DJ pointed out his house and his children's school just a few miles away on the Applecross shore. We could see out to Harris in the Western Isles where his ancestors had lived. We worked near the small and barren Crowlin Islands his ancestors had moved to from Harris: 'things were that bleak in Harris that the Crowlins looked better. There were 20-odd people there. I don't know how they survived.' After a spell on the Crowlins they settled in nearby Applecross where his parents were born. To the south of us was the town of Kyle of Lochalsh where his parents had moved after their marriage and where he had grown up. 'It was hard times in

Figure 2  A freshly-baited creel flying off the back of a creel boat.

Applecross then', he explained, 'the old man told me to take French and go on and get out. There was no future here.'

Other ancestors came from Raasay, the island across the Sound from us where his wife now worked. We could see up to Brochel Castle at the north end of Raasay where people had once paid their taxes to the Norse rulers of the area. DJ told me how much he admired the Vikings, 'they brought new farming, new boats, they settled here, they integrated, and they left lots of names'. He had studied Scottish and Scandinavian history at Edinburgh University, 'but it was Thatcher's time, everyone was unemployed', so he moved back into the family house in Applecross. 'There was nothing to do so I took a chance and bought a boat', he said. He was pleased that he had been able to make a decent living from creel fishing for prawns but sad that most of the coast had become a 'prawn monoculture' without the herring and whitefish[4] fisheries that had once been so important. 'We've got ourselves into a hell of a mess', he said with regret. 'We should have some of the most productive fish grounds in the world here.'

On the Applecross side we could see right up the glen that cut the Applecross Peninsula in half, 'people used to live up the glen, but the MacKenzies cleared them out to right along the shore'. Landlords had made a similar attempt on the opposite shore at Braes on Skye. But in Braes the crofters had fought back and regained the grazing land that had been taken. DJ was related to the Nicholsons of Braes, who had been arrested and gaoled in Inverness for participating in the now-celebrated Battle of Braes. On the coast just north of the glen was Sand, where a recent archaeological dig had found Mesolithic remains including large quantities of seafood. He explained that 'even when they lived in the glen, they probably always fished, even 10,000 years ago'.

We worked right up to the big yellow buoys which marked the edges of the British Underwater Testing and Evaluation Centre (BUTEC), but today there were no trials of submarines, sonar buoys or torpedoes.[5] We could see about eight other boats working around us on the water, boats from Kyle, Portree, Plockton, Applecross and Torridon, each one recognisable, familiar and distinct. I had been out fishing on some of those boats before.

Halfway through the day we had hauled and re-set four fleets of creels. DJ had ducked into the wheelhouse to move the boat to the next fleet, but then slowed the engine down and dashed back out again, exclaiming: 'Do you know, ever since you got on this boat, you have been talking about connections? Between one place and another, between people here and in Portree and in Raasay, all these names, and between different times, and that's what it's about, that's the most important thing!' I smiled, and scribbled. I felt the sea and air around me thickening with this mat of connections, a tangible tracing of history, stories and hardship, of work, and happiness and hope too.

This book is about connections and ruptures in lives lived and livelihoods earned at sea. I start with a focus on human–environment relations – how people worked in and named and changed the features of the sea they relied on. I build on anthropological landscape research to trace the mutually constitutive and productive connections between people and their environments at sea, as well as with the tools and machines that people have developed to work with and survive in these environments. I focus on people's labour as what ties environments, people and tools together as they work to make fishing grounds productive. I take a phenomenological approach that focuses on people's experience of their own labour, including the results of that labour, and the aspirations and hopes that they pour into it. As a result, this book challenges the popular conception of the sea as a hostile wilderness, a conception which 'has distorted the reality of life at sea by concentrating on the struggle of man and nature to the exclusion of other aspects of maritime life, notably the jarring confrontation of man against man [sic]' (Rediker 1989: 5). Instead, I explore the more complicated reasons why human–environment relations at sea are fraught with ruptures, tensions and contradictions, tragedy, unfulfilled hope, and even desperation. I met people who lost limbs and friends at sea. I put my examination of human–environment relations at sea in the context of broader market and class relations and show how people's contemporary experience of their own labour is structured by capitalist relations of production.

In this book, I trace the connections and ruptures in the experience of people, mostly men, mostly Scottish, as they work in the prawn and other fisheries on the west coast of Scotland. I trace the development of fishing grounds and other places at sea (Part I), people's use of tools and machines to extend their bodily senses and capabilities into the sea, and techniques for orienting themselves and navigating at sea (Part II). I show how political economy structures these experiences and histories and has created a situation of unacknowledged structural violence for people working in the fishing industry (Part III).

## 'How are you going to write about this?'

The difficulty of writing about *both* connections and ruptures was put to me at two o'clock one Saturday morning at the house of Donald and Mairi as they hosted their nieces and boyfriends, including Donald's former crewman, Charlie. Drinks were poured. The atmosphere, as they say on Skye (usually with a smile and a wink), was '*very* social'. Donald had once owned a large trawler, but had sold up several years ago. Charlie was talkative and keen to tell me about his long history of fishing and the skilled heroics he had performed along the way. With Donald listening, he described a dramatic time they shared right before Christmas some years ago. The local bank manager had just shot and killed himself after lending out more money than was being returned:

> The bank manager was a good guy and he could see when people could and couldn't pay. After he shot himself, the bank sent someone else up to start getting the money back in that he had lent out. It was January when they called everyone in, one by one.
> Now, January is *not* the time to try to start getting money back from fishermen. Prices are always the lowest. They called Donald in and told him that he had six weeks to pay off his £40,000 overdraft, or he would lose the boat. That's £40,000 *after* wages and expenses.

Somehow, they had managed. They had hired another crewman and worked around the clock. 'We landed 240 boxes of fish the last day, in a howling storm. They couldn't believe it!' Charlie chuckled, proud of the memory, hugged Donald's niece and went to get himself another drink.

Donald looked at me silently, seriously. 'How are you going to write about this?' he challenged me:

> How can you?! It's too complicated. How can you explain that a bank manager shot himself and his dog? And what we had to do on a fishing boat in January, in six weeks, because of that? How can you explain this, here, what is happening now, my beautiful nieces here at two o'clock in the morning, and the craic,[6] and Charlie here too?
> No. What you are trying to do is impossible, impossible.

Donald's warning has haunted me ever since, and he was not the only one. There were other men who also wanted to tell me their most troubling stories, usually late at night or in the pub. But at the same time as they wanted to tell me these stories, they usually insisted that I could not possibly understand them. I remember coming home, overwhelmed and weighed down, wondering what on earth I could do with all this. I could not describe the connections, the scenery and the sunshine, without also describing struggle, tragedy and death.

There was Angus (Chapter 6), who started telling me about the death of friends and workmates on cargo ships on the second day I knew him. I returned home to the boat, notes scrawled down in confusion: 'I don't know where to begin when you see someone breaking down in tears before you. What do you do? It is a heavy load to carry. I feel shaken, unsure of what to do with it.' With tears running down his face, he told me 'You don't want to know. I can't put this on you. I can't give someone else nightmares like this. It's not fair. I've seen things that no one should ever have to see, to even think about.'

There was Alasdair who, after a month of patiently answering questions about fishing and prawns and boats and weather, finally asked me why I hadn't yet asked him about deaths at sea. He told me that night about the sinking of his friend Findus' fishing boat, and returned to the story again and again over the next two years (Chapter 6). Later, he reflected that 'there is not a year goes by, I don't think, without somebody I know or know of killed at the job'.

There was John, in the pub the morning after an all-nighter, talking about the death of his friend Iain who worked on a fish farm after the new Norwegian owners and managers 'cut back the people'. Iain had ended up 'out in a tin boat by himself with a ton of feed. With a ton of feed! That's why he died!' And then, angrily, he said 'I shouldn't speak to you about this! How can you understand?! You don't understand!' He kept pushing me away, scoffing and mocking, but then always came back to speak to me again after finishing his cigarette.

The scepticism about my ability to understand the pain that people shared with me was manifest more generally in the scrutiny I was subject to, the reactions of those who felt themselves living in 'a state of siege' (Taussig 1992: 10). People Googled me to ensure the story I was telling them about myself was correct, and they let me know that. They wanted to know who was funding me and why. They knew what conferences I was presenting at and they wanted to read the papers I presented. Many assumed that my research agenda was to undermine their very existence. After one trawler skipper decided that he trusted me, he told me about another who didn't, who was 'nervous and suspicious about you and what you are doing'. He explained, 'If you are a trawlerman you think everyone is out to get you'. A young crewman, drunk in the pub one evening, accused me of being 'an ecologist here to destroy people's livelihoods' and warned me to 'be careful because it is people's lives! Think of the old guys that have been doing this all their lives, the children who are being supported!' When I was introduced as a researcher to a man who used to work on salmon farms, he introduced himself as 'one of those bad environment-destroying salmon farmers, out there polluting the lochs!' The state of siege in which people lived was manifest in their very stance towards me.

This tension and pain was not new. On my second day in Portree, Bodach pointed across the harbour to Scorr, an exposed and rocky ledge at the harbour entrance where his family had once lived (Figure 3). His great-granduncle had been born there and Bodach showed me a letter he had written back to the family in Skye after he immigrated to Australia in 1852. It started with a detailed report

Figure 3  Scorr, at the entrance to Portree harbour, where Bodach's family stayed 'starving and in slavery' after moving from Rona to Skye in the first part of the 1800s.

on the employment and wages he and other Skye families had been able to secure in Australia, and then continued with a report on the passage to Australia on the *Araminta*:[7]

> We was complaining for being so long on the passage. We were 16 weeks at sea … There was a great number of children died on this ship, but we did not lose one, and they stood well to the sea. All the children, that was on both sides of us was taken away, and our two was left, and another child that was aside us. There was ten families on both sides of us, and there was not a child left in the ten families but four. (MacKenzie n.d. [1852]: 73)

Despite this horrific experience, his great-granduncle reflected: 'It was the leading of the Almighty that encouraged me to come to this place, besides being at home starving and in slavery, as many one behind me is; and I would advise many to come if they choose to come' (MacKenzie n.d. [1852]: 74). Like DJ's family, Bodach's had moved and moved, from Raasay to Rona and then to different places around Skye, 'starving and in slavery', and then to Carolina and Australia, with members also leaving to find work in Glasgow and on board cargo ships travelling around the world.

I have taken up the challenges from Donald and the others though close attention to both happiness and pain, hope and fear, connections and ruptures, skill and its breakdown: the reward and contradictions of human labour at sea. They challenged me to understand not only what was happening in the moment but also the history that went into building that moment. I have tried to deal fully and respectfully with a form of labour that is very much maligned: that of fishermen[8] who feel that 'everyone is out to get them'. First, I describe the lively ways in which people formed and inhabited grounds and places through the process of working in them and developing what they afford to those who make them productive (Chapters 2 and 3). Second, I examine the ways in which boats, winches, nets and other tools were enrolled into fishermen's skilled techniques and how tension was manipulated in feeling and sounding the sea and extending the senses of the body into its depths (Chapter 4). Third, I describe the skilled processes of orientation as movement in the land/seascape, and the role of electronic navigation devices in facilitating this movement (Chapter 5).

Despite these skilled and productive contributions, the painful reality for fishermen is that their extraordinary efforts are often not seen by others as productive, but as destructive. A crisis in many aspects of the ocean and planet's ecosystem (Angus 2016; Clausen and Clark 2008) has squeezed fishers between the limits of the environment they rely on, the demands of the market the sell to, and the concerns of environmentalists who usually see fishers as part of the problem too (Chapter 1). It is frequently overlooked that commercial fishing is a labour process dominated by market forces that shape what fishers must do to survive but which they cannot control (Campling *et al.* 2012) – instead fishers are simply labelled as greedy and destructive. The exploitation of the sea's resources and of the people at the sharp end of extracting them are driven by similar economic and political pressures: a market whose competitive dynamics mean that people often need to catch more and more fish just to stay even, and where the consequences of not being able to keep up can be deadly (Chapters 5 and 6). The context of political economy is crucial for a full understanding of how people experienced and practised their own labour at sea (Part III).

Capitalist relations in the labour process of fishing meant it was fraught with tensions and contradictions that shaped human–environment and human–machine relations. Who was able to fully exercise their skills and in what circumstances? When did boats and tools act as smooth and productive extensions of persons and when did they maim and kill? When, and for whom, was a fishing boat a fondly regarded companion or a 'shit-bucket'? What kinds of social relations did particular navigation techniques promote? Who decided what tools were available on a boat, and based on what priorities? Through a holistic Marxist analysis, I show how these seemingly disparate questions all connect to changes in political economy, class relations, fishing techniques and relations to the environment. With this approach, I have tried to capture the pleasure and pain, the frustration and reward, the giddiness and tragedy of work at sea under capitalist relations of production.

In writing this book I was lucky to have a vigorous critic in the form of the skipper of the trawler I worked on over the course of 18 months and who I kept in touch with. He read most of this book and returned pages of commentary and additional information, which we then discussed at length. We had a creative and productive tension: I knew that Alasdair would not agree with all of my analysis, yet his feedback was always thought-provoking and useful. We both enjoyed it: as he wrote in a note attached to the front of his extensive written feedback on earlier versions of Chapters 4, 5 and 6: 'I doubt you've had the fun or enjoyment I've had reading this. More please if you think it worthwhile.' His feedback contributed significantly to my writing process. For example, in his comments on Chapter 2 he explained how the Decca (a now-obsolete navigation device) was used to find places at sea before the GPS (Global Positioning System). Our subsequent discussions about the history of navigation techniques led directly to my then-unwritten Chapter 4.

I was most nervous about Alasdair's reaction to an earlier version of Chapter 5, which contained a historical account and economic analysis of the fishing industry he had worked in for 30 years. In particular, I argue that the often lethal 'nature of the job' he described was not a 'natural' consequence of the environment of the sea, but was in a large part a result of the nakedly capitalist market pressures on those who work at sea. I was pleased that although he had plenty of criticism, my analysis also struck a chord. We sat in a pub near my flat in Glasgow, and he got quite emotional as he told me 'I don't keep track of the number of people I have lost. I guess I have been close to only a few of them'. He banged on the table, tears starting in his eyes. 'But why do we accept this?! Why do I accept it? Why does every other bastard accept it?' It was only a week later that he rang me, impatiently asking when my next chapter would be complete.

## Anthropology at sea

In this book I pursue a labour-centred analysis of human and environmental connections and ruptures at sea, based in the holistic study of humans known as 'anthropology' and using its classic approach of participant observation, or 'ethnographic' research. My analysis is influenced by anthropologist Tim Ingold's understanding of the 'human condition', as being 'in an active, practical and perceptual engagement' with their environments (2000: 42). But the environment of commercial fishers is not just made up of sea, wind and land, but also markets, machines, crises, competition and experiences of tragedy and fear. It extends from the local and immediate through history and across countries.

Participant observation through living in an area allows researchers access to a depth and breadth of experience that cannot be captured in other ways. It includes everything from conversation to 'using one's body in the same way as others in the same environment' so that knowledge 'remains grounded in a field of practical activity' (Jackson 1989: 135). I shared a 'field of practical activity' by sharing a pier, living with and working under the supervision of fishermen and seafarers. From them, I learned not only how to predict tidal movements at a particular rock, but how to get the best price for your prawns in a global market. Phenomenological methods pay close attention to the feel, the smell and the sounds of people's experiences, but are sometimes criticised for being too narrow in their approach. In this book, I use a 'critical phenomenology' which aims to 'link modalities of sensation, perception, and subjectivity to pervasive political arrangements and forms of economic production and consumption' (Desjarlais 1997: 25). This means going 'beyond phenomenological description to understand why things are this way' (Desjarlais 1997: 25). Asking people 'why things are this way' often resulted in some of the most insightful discussions I experienced during my research.

I aim to provide a contextualised and historical ethnography in this book that describes the connections and tensions that exist in place, and with other parts of the world and economy. This approach builds on Jane Nadel-Klein's book about the former fishing villages of north-east Scotland that demonstrates how 'capitalism can create and then dismiss a way of life' (2003: 1), and more broadly, on fisheries ethnographies by Gerald Sider in Newfoundland (2003) and Charles Menzies in France (2011). These connections are lived every day in almost every conversation: how else could I understand why DJ's ex-fishermen neighbours were now working on offshore oil platforms in Angola and Nigeria, or how another local man had been on the Piper Alpha oil platform when it exploded in the North Sea. Then there was the bucolic lake DJ showed me, surrounded by wetlands, with stairs and a boardwalk running down from the road to a small bird-watching hut, built by UK soldiers as practise in 'logistics and reconstruction' before they were sent to Iraq in 2003. In contrast, anthropologies of Scotland have tended to focus on rural areas (Rapport 2009: 49), often portrayed as traditional and left behind by modern society (MacDonald 1997: 8). As a result 'Scottish villages, crofters, or peasants come to be identified as backward and to stand for the Western version of the primitive' (Nadel-Klein 1991: 503). Yet, however remote these places may appear, they have been shaped by capitalism and political power for centuries.

My research centred on human–environment relations at sea, which made the best use of my own skills and experience as a professional seafarer, and provided a wealth of rich opportunities for participant observation. While many anthropological studies at sea have focused on particular uses of the sea, such as fishing, tourism or tenure rights, this book follows more broadly-conceived research into the human–environment relations of people living and working at sea (Hoeppe 2007; King and Robinson forthcoming 2017; Tyrrell 2006). Other anthropologists have examined the social and political aspects of fishers' lives, including the impact of state conservation and fisheries policies, the development of fishers' political representation, and how these articulate with other social and cultural formations such as religion and social organisation (Subramanian 2009; Walley 2004). This literature traces the connections that extend across seascapes and landscapes and challenges the popular conception of fishing communities as isolated societies and the sea as a hostile wilderness to be preserved from human influence.

The way in which social scientists have thought about the sea has changed markedly over the years. Many early anthropologists described the sea as a wholly natural 'other' that framed land-based culture and theory. The activities of fishers have been analysed as if they were foraging animals, and the sea has also been understood as an 'aquarium' that must be enclosed and controlled. A sharply different approach by contemporary social scientists has been to use the sea and water as a 'theory-machine', sometimes using metaphors based on the materiality of water which bear no resemblance to the experience of living and working at sea.

Narratives of 'oceanisation' emphasise regional oceanic connections and capitalist world systems – but sometimes 'flow' into easy but not-always-accurate metaphors about globalisation (Helmreich 2011). Stefan Helmreich notes the pervasiveness of the watery metaphor of 'immersion' for both understanding the sea and ethnographic methods (2007), but argues that it is 'a poor tool' that elides 'the question of the organisation of space, of medium, of milieu – whether of an ecosystem or a social order' (2007: 631). Likewise, he criticises authors such as Veronica Strang, Ben Orlove and Steve Caton who theorise about the materiality of water as if it is a historic and cultural given.

Anthropologists have a responsibility to thoroughly and ethnographically consider people's experience of working and living at sea, and not to be seduced by tidy metaphors of flow, fluidity and immersion that may easily arise in contemplating the physical presence of the sea. Such an understanding builds on the work of maritime anthropologists who have demonstrated that distinctive systems of meaning have arisen with human activity at sea. Such studies inevitably overflow the sea itself to follow lives, livelihoods, markets, and pressures far beyond it. The sea is only 'fluid' in appearance, as I discovered from the people I worked with who continually challenged me to include and understand the jarring and difficult disruptions, tensions and tragedies which punctuated their lives. Amidst the rising popularity of a 'new materialism' in anthropology that focuses on the qualities of materials (like water), the history of such theorising at sea offers a cautionary tale.

I worked as a professional seafarer before I began studying anthropology in 2004, and in 1997 obtained a 100-ton captain's licence from the US Merchant Navy. I worked on board various traditional fishing boats that were used for education programs in the United States, including as the skipper of a 26-meter sailing oyster dredger, which took students out on the Chesapeake Bay to learn about history and ecology. I also travelled by small sailboat through the North Atlantic: from the Chesapeake Bay up the US coast to the Gulf of Maine, and from Toronto to Newfoundland, Labrador, and across to Iceland, the Faroe Islands and Scotland.

I arrived in the Inner Sound to begin my field research in May 2006, sailing into Kyleakin harbour on a pleasant sunny afternoon. I had bought a small sailboat to live on and spent several months working to prepare it in a harbour further south (Figure 4). Friends helped me sail up the coast but the trip from Mallaig to Kyleakin was my first day sailing the boat alone – 15 miles up the coast and then through Kyle Rhea, the air crystal clear and the mountains rising massively and nakedly up from the narrow passage where the sea, propelled by the tide, raced between Skye and the mainland.

I called the harbourmaster to tell him I was arriving, and he came down to catch my dock lines. It took me some time to get everything organised and prepared for docking while the boat drifted in the harbour, and I became keenly aware of being watched. There were at least 20 yachts tied in rows along the pontoon, five fishing boats at the end, another five across the harbour, houses facing the pier all round (Figure 5). Finally, I was alongside, and the harbourmaster invited me to participate in the yacht race the next day: 'It will

Figure 4 *Suilven II*, 1977–2011. The author lived on this boat while carrying out research for this book.

Figure 5 Kyleakin harbour with Skye, the Skye bridge and Raasay in the background, and showing the Inner Sound stretching away to the North. The Crowlin Islands, the Applecross Peninsula, and the rest of the Scottish mainland are on the right. I spent a great deal of time living at the pontoon in the centre-left just in front of the houses. My boat is visible in the middle of the pontoon.

be fun!' Over the afternoon I met several other men ambling along the pier or working leisurely on their boats.

It turned out to be an excellent place to be an anthropologist: with a shop, a café and three pubs a short walk away, and two piers and a ramp that were in constant use by fishermen landing their catch and cleaning and repairing their fishing gear. There was a perpetual stream of tourists, and yachts owned locally and those from other countries regularly docked there. Each day I interacted with people on their way out to sea or on their way back in. I spent the majority of the next 16 months conducting ethnographic participant observation while living on my boat in Kyleakin, and in other harbours around the Sound. I explained to the people I met that I was a researcher interested in speaking to people who worked or spent time at sea, and that I wrote daily notes about the people I talked to and what I learned. People almost always had a story to share and were often curious about my project, what had brought me to the area, and what my own seafaring background was.

I got to know a few fishermen on the pier while they repaired their nets and creels. Three months into my research, the skipper-owner of a small trawler offered me paid work as relief crew when his regular crew needed time off. I worked on the boat with both the owner and the hired skipper for an average of about five days each month over the next year (Figure 6). This opportunity allowed me to become a skilled crew member, to develop long-term working relationships

Figure 6 The author at work on a small trawler.

with the skipper-owner and hired skipper-crew of that boat, and to interact with other fishing boat crew as they worked at sea and travelled from port to port. I also needed the money. My reliance on the uncertain income from fishing was also an important mode of participation.[9] This reliance increased when my (non-fisherman) partner became unemployed and also worked part-time on trawlers for about four months.

Living on a boat, participating in sailboat races and getting a respectable result, and making short trips around the area meant that other fishermen could see that I was competent on a boat, and I believe this made it easier for me to go out fishing with them. I also invited people onto my boat, for a cup of tea or to travel around the Sound: novices who could give me their first impressions about being at sea, but also fishermen and crews from cargo ships who could reflect on the enormous differences between the boats they worked on and mine. Staying on the boat meant I could be hospitable myself, but I also had control over my own space for writing fieldnotes and a retreat when fieldwork became too intense.

A body of water is usually shared by people from many different places on land. Living on a boat gave me the mobility and flexibility to follow these relationships, although I was constrained in significant ways by the weather and by the available harbour facilities. These constraints also provided productive opportunities for discussion with those who were familiar with the area's weather patterns and local harbours. Connections extended across harbours. For example, Bodach was from Portree but I met him during a yacht race in Kyle. He then smoothed over relations with the Portree harbourmaster and set about introducing me to fishermen and local historians when I arrived in Portree. I had met DJ, who took me out fishing that sunny morning in Applecross, at a meeting I had attended while visiting a loch further north along the coast.

I spent approximately 80 days actually travelling or working at sea on 13 boats, including four trawlers, four creel boats, a tour boat, sailboats, a lifeboat and a fish farm boat. Each boat provided a very different experience and perspective on being at sea: following different routes, for different purposes, at a different speed or elevation. The variety of experiences also provided an important reminder that the experience of 'being at sea' is much more accurately described as 'being on a boat', as it is the boat that most directly shapes one's experience of being at sea (Chapter 3).

In addition to the time I spent on and around boats, I was also a more general participant-observer in settings frequented by those working at sea, principally the pier and the pub. This gave me the opportunity to interact with people working on cargo ships, on ferries, in the offshore oil and gas industry, on fish farms, in marine weapons testing, and sailing on yachts. I conducted more formal semi-structured interviews with individuals in specific roles to whom I did not readily have access (for example, the manager of the BUTEC base, the fisheries protection officer, civil servants, the lifeboat coxswain, seafood buyers, several retired fishermen, and fishermen's partners and mothers). I also attended government consultations on fisheries, marine parks and marine energy, as well as the annual 'Fishing Expo' trade show in Glasgow.

My fieldwork was conducted entirely in English, but I took an introductory Gaelic course to assist me in understanding phrases and place names. The use of Gaelic was patchy in the area and it was only towards the end of my fieldwork that I met people who were fully bilingual.

I ended up with four kinds of fieldnotes: reflections and conversations recalled and typed directly into my laptop on the boat as soon as I was able to; jottings made in a small notebook which I carried in my pocket at all times; notes made in a large notebook during more formal interviews; and recordings of interviews. My research continued informally until 2010 as I kept my boat in the area and remained in contact with several people I worked with. I also conducted some targeted interviews between 2007 and 2010 as gaps in my research became apparent and the writing process generated new questions.

### Constraints and opportunities in fieldwork

The approach that I took to my research significantly affected who I came to know, and who I didn't. I spent the most time with fishing boat skipper-owners like Alasdair, Ruaridh and James. All three had started fishing in the late 1960s and had owned their own boats since the 1970s. James was the only one who came from a fishing family. James' father lived in Orkney and worked in a boatyard but had fallen in love with a Skye woman who had travelled to work in an Orkney hotel. James' father married her and emigrated from Orkney to Skye, and then started fishing in the newly emerging prawn creel fishery. James, his brother and other family members now owned a number of fishing boats. Ruaridh had started his working life as a bricklayer in Lochalsh but switched to fishing because the money was better (Chapter 5). Alasdair was from the west coast island of Iona and had worked on local fishing boats in summers as a school student and then while studying natural philosophy at Glasgow University. His father was the island's postmaster. These skipper-owners had the experience and authority to speak about the fishing industry now and in the past, and they were exceedingly generous and helpful to me. They had an encyclopaedic knowledge of all aspects of the local and regional fishing industry for the past 40 years (and more). These skippers were thoroughly identified with their fishing boat – they were referred to as James 'the *Iris*' and Ruaridh 'the *Accord*'.

Younger hired fishing crew usually deferred to skippers when they were present, which, on the boat or the pier, was almost always. I spent more time speaking to crew in the pub, or in moments when skippers were busy elsewhere. They were mostly 20-something young men who had varied working lives, moving between jobs in fishing, the offshore oil and gas industry, fish farms, and forestry. A few had stable jobs on one boat, but many switched from job to job quite regularly. In social situations, these younger hired crew tended to keep their distance from me, perhaps because they knew that I spent a lot of time with their employers, or maybe because my incessant questions about fishing bored them. I was also a bit wary of the intensity of the local party scene that many participated in. I encountered hired Filipino crew a few times while their boats arrived or left the pier but only once had the opportunity for a real conversation. We both glanced nervously over our shoulders, worried the boat owner would arrive and wonder what we were speaking about, and they refused my offer to meet up later (Chapter 5).

I got to know quite a number of hired skippers and a few older and more experienced hired crew like 'Buckie' John, Graeme and Charlie. They tended to have quite varied life experiences and strong opinions about the different sectors of the industry they had worked in. These men had worked in different fishing fleets all over Scotland and England, and other jobs as well. 'Buckie' John was from a Buckie family who had fished for many generations, but the rest of the family now lived in North Shields, England, and the family did not own a fishing boat. Through this group of men and in the cafés and pubs around the harbours I also met other skippers, crew, ex-fishermen, fish farm workers, offshore oil workers, fish processing workers, and some family members and partners.

I met only a few fishing boat owners who owned multiple fishing boats and did not work on them, mainly through fishermen's associations (which primarily represented boat owners), at formal government consultations, and at presentations and meetings held at the annual Fishing Expo trade show in Glasgow. They were obviously keen to ensure that their political and economic interests were represented in such forums. They were generally friendly and helpful, and clearly wanted to ensure that I represented their industry in a positive light. 'Ah well the last social anthropologist who came to speak to me ended up working for me so I'm sure I'll see you again', one told me with some arrogance. Conversely, they also reacted with highly-coordinated fury to ensure that I was not able to work for any industry body they had influence with after I publicly criticised the employment conditions of the migrant crew that many hired (Chapter 5).

Prohibitions against women going on board Scottish fishing boats are well documented (Knipe 1984). I did not expect to be able to find work on fishing boats or even to go on board them. I never met another woman working on a fishing boat (I was told of a few). I found that while everyone was aware of these prohibitions, virtually everyone claimed it was other fishermen, not them, who held such beliefs. I had never worked on a real fishing boat and had no prior local connections. I am grateful that, despite some wariness I described earlier, I was welcomed by fishing boat owners, skippers and crew with openness, warmth and curiosity, and was flattered by the respect I was offered. I had characterised my own skill and experience at sea in an early draft of Chapter 5 as 'a competent sailor but novice fisher completely unfamiliar with the area'. I received the following written feedback from my skipper, Alasdair:

> You demean your own ability. Take sentence 'a competent sailor etc.', and delete. You can not include that in your argument unless you are much more honest regarding your ability. It distorts the point you make by being basically untrue. Sorry but you can't do that …
>
> You, however, describe yourself as a novice, completely unfamiliar with the area. No novice. 20+ year small boat experience. Tickets [professional captain's and mate's licences] to what degree? Command experience and responsibility by the gallon, very fast learner, highly safety conscious, excellent skills of judgement,

> totally in step with the boat's (skipper's) two rules: 1. If in doubt, shout, 2. Don't
> panic, it turns a hiccup into a fuck-up.
>     To hide these facts as you do is insulting to you, yourself, <u>and</u> the skipper whose
> judgment of you put you there and who wrote the above. <u>Sort this out please</u>.

When discussing the chapter later, the skipper insisted that by the end of my year crewing, he would have been comfortable having me skipper his trawler.

The unexpected consequence of this acceptance by fishermen was that I became limited to predominantly male spaces. Focusing only on male aspects of fishing has been rightly criticised by feminist political economists for limiting the role that women, households and broader political economy play in analysis of fisheries (Neis *et al.* 2005). I was conscious of this potential problem and tried to overcome it by making every effort to meet fishermen's families, and also by ensuring that broader questions of political economy were included in my research. However, it soon became clear that my initial entry point through mostly male seagoing working spaces also limited my access to other areas. I did get to know the young female partner of a hired skipper, but got to see her much less after their relationship ended. Far from seeing herself as a member of a fishing household, she ran her own small cleaning business and was sometimes critical of her partner's occupation. I also developed a relationship with the mother of an ex-fisherman who worked in the oil and gas industry, whose (now deceased) husband had been a prominent local fisherman. Her insights and experience were very useful but were of course historical. With only a few exceptions, the households and families that I came to know were those of older single fishermen, or those who were retired. It seemed that many women saw me as firmly belonging to the local male seagoing working spaces (and their associated pubs) and wanted to keep me there, and out of their family lives. Although my partner came to visit several times during my research, it is also likely that most men were not keen on advertising to their partners the existence of a young, inquisitive and (apparently) single woman down on the docks.

My acceptance into male seagoing spaces was not universal. I participated in local yacht races, and in the process realised that there was a quite distinct social division between seagoing workers and fishermen, and the 'respectable' local yacht owners. These yacht owners were (sometimes retired) local managers, skilled engineers, small business owners, local elected councillors and navy officers. I had never seen them in the pub before – they went only in the afternoon after the yacht races and almost always dispersed before evening. I realised that although these pubs were busy and pleasant and seemed perfectly safe to me, they were not places where everyone would hang out. Pubs were marked as spaces for the mostly young, mostly single, mostly male persons working in manual jobs. Families and partners did not go there (except for the few that had an adjoining restaurant). Pubs were avoided by people of all genders who felt themselves of a certain (higher) local status. I believe I unknowingly ruffled a few feathers by participating in local yacht races with a pub-going local fishing skipper. We won a few races on my sailboat, and it was interpreted as significant by other locals that no one clapped when our first victory was announced.

I was surprised by the local classification of myself as part of the male manual working world, and the exclusions from family life that I experienced were precisely the opposite of what I expected. Yet being accepted into this male working environment also seemed to highlight my female-ness. On virtually every fishing boat I went out on, I was subject to playful speculation about whether I would be a 'Jonah', bringing bad luck. The one notable exception was hired skipper Graeme. When I inquired, Graeme told me that his luck was already so bad I couldn't possibly make it any worse (Chapter 3). As a woman dressed in oilskins and work clothes, I was subject to many puzzled glances and other fishermen were usually quite curious about who I was and how I had come to be there. 'Are you out making cups of tea?' they would ask to try and determine what my role was on board. I would explain that I took watches and tows, and if the skipper was around he would usually take great delight in saying that that he had spent the whole afternoon asleep in his bunk while I was catching prawns. I was regularly told 'you must be hardy!' The merits of having more women in the fishing industry and the particular skills which women might bring to it were regular topics of conversation that my presence provoked. Twice, during the day, wearing full fishing gear, on a boat tied up to a pier, I had a conversation that to me was completely surreal: 'Do you have any children?' I was asked by another 30-something crewman. 'No', I replied, to which he matter-of-factly responded 'Well if you ever want to have any, let me know'.

I found myself in a strangely contradictory situation: on one hand, marked as a (dangerously female) part of male working spaces and therefore excluded from most family and domestic spaces, and on the other hand, mainly accepted into those male spaces while being seen as remarkably female. Anthropologist Kirsten Hastrup observed that in 'parallel-cultural' situations (for her Denmark/Iceland, for me Scotland/Canada): 'the sex of the anthropologist, elsewhere so inconspicuous in relation to other and much more marked differences, becomes a primary element in the local classification of the ethnographer' (1987: 96). This contrasts with what Hastrup describes as 'an old notion in anthropology' that female ethnographers become honorary males in research situations (1987: 95). The local classification and implications of my gender appeared to differ markedly by class, with the local 'respectables' viewing me as part of (what they saw as) the unrespectable male manual working world, while local fishermen viewed me as an odd and remarkably female part of that world – although the niggling suspicion remained that as an academic and outsider I had an unknown potential to cause damage to their livelihoods.

The attention I received during my research was almost always to my advantage: people were interested in speaking to me and I was frequently the subject of their questioning, rather than the other way around. One consequence of my peculiar position was that people seemed very willing to share with me their stories of grief and trauma that were part of their working experience at sea. A sympathetic understanding of this is, I believe, a worthwhile contribution. However, the price I paid for this trust and insight was an exclusion from most family and domestic situations. That work is still to be done.

## Histories of the present

History is an important aspect of any critical phenomenology that seeks to understand 'why things are this way'. Phenomenological approaches to place 'tend to analyze experiences of place as culturally given: that is, as points of departure that are only *then* situated in history'. Instead, experience should be understood 'as a historical product constrained and recreated by fields of power' (Gordillo 2004: 265 n.5). Anthropologists Susana Narotzky and Gavin Smith propose 'histories of the present' as a way of showing how 'capitalism ... becomes a lived part of the present' (2006: 17, 12). In the remainder of this section I sketch some of these histories in the Inner Sound, the west coast and the fishing industry. I hope this gives some important context to the situation I found in 2006–2007 and that I describe in the rest of this book.

### *Histories of the Inner Sound*

Subsistence eating of seafood, especially shellfish growing on rocks along the shoreline, has been taking place on the Inner Sound for at least 7,000 years (Hardy and Wickham-Jones 2002). However, it is important to remember that the coastline is harsh, the weather adverse for most of the year, and that people were often very poor. Fishing year-round required large, safe boats that most could not afford. Once fish and seafood markets developed, they were located hundreds of miles away through difficult terrain with poor transport infrastructure. Thus, while there is a very long history of people fishing as one part of their livelihoods, the emergence of commercial fishing as a full-time occupation and 'fishermen' as an identifiable group of people on the west coast is quite recent and is bound up with the emergence and spread of capitalism and its associated cash economy, regional and global markets, and infrastructure (Nadel-Klein 2003).

In sixteenth-century east coast Scotland, fishers were generally serfs who gave landlords a portion of their catch (and sometimes labour or money) in exchange for the use of a boat, land and house – a kind of sharecropping that straddled land and sea (Coull 1996). It was with the profitable exports to Germany and the Baltic states in the eighteenth century that 'fishing became an organized industry', promoted by the British Fisheries Society and lairds of coastal estates who built specialised fishing villages along the coast according to the 'Improving' ethic of the Scottish Enlightenment (Nadel-Klein 2003; Smout 1970). Marx analysed this process as capitalist 'primitive accumulation' by dispossession, describing how in the early nineteenth century 15,000 people living in Sutherland were forcibly removed from 794,000 acres of land and re-settled on only 6,000 acres along the shore to become fishers (1976 [1890]: 892), for 'people with no land would fish and fish hard' (Nadel-Klein 2003: 34). In these Clearances, landlords replaced partly subsistence tenant farmers (known as crofters) with more profitable sheep farms, and then employed some of the newly landless 'rural proletariat' as fishermen (Cregeen 1970; Smout 1970). Strong memories of this dispossession remain. For example, the proposal to create a Coastal and Marine National Park during my field research was widely referred to as the second Clearances, due to people's fear it would remove a working human presence from the sea in a similar way that they felt it had been removed from the land.

Through these Clearances, the sea became a route through which a given area of land could be made more profitable, and through which people were forced to become occupational specialists (fishers) and participate in a cash economy. Although this process took place earlier and more completely on the east coast of Scotland, Calum MacLeod writes in his memoirs about people being forced from the west coast island of Raasay on to rocky and barren Rona (both next to Skye), and recounts that 'the people would have starved if they could not turn to the sea' (2007: 15, 57; see also Grigor 2000). These measures are remembered as having a profound effect on people's lives. For example, Bodach's family was one of those moved from Raasay to Rona to several places in Skye 'starving and in slavery' and then to Australia through the end of the eighteenth and early ninetieth centuries. Some of the people caught up in this process stayed and became full-time fishers, but most found other work or emigrated.

Through the nineteenth century, fishing merchants increasingly took on the role of providing fishing capital (such as boats and nets) previously secured from landlords. Fishers in specialised east coast fishing villages like Buckie, Fraserburgh and Peterhead paid boat-rents to merchants (Coull 1996; Nadel-Klein 2003). Most east coast fishers no longer had any access to land, but those extended families who were more successful started to buy shares in their boats, some eventually purchasing entire boats (Coull 1996). Today, ownership of Scottish fishing vessels is still registered with the government in 1/64ths, an indication of the minuscule ownership shares that some fishermen held.

East coast boat owners and herring merchants developed and dominated the herring industry. Today, almost all fisheries infrastructure is located on the east coast: faster rail transportation links to London and Europe, big ports, the main fish curers, processors, exporters and sources of finance, and the national fisheries research laboratory. Landlords and merchants never made the same level of capital investment in fisheries or related infrastructure on the west coast (Nadel-Klein 2003). Only a few specialised fishing villages were built and none was particularly successful (Smout 1970). On the west coast the Stromeferry to Dingwall railway line opened in 1870 and the Mallaig to Glasgow line opened in 1901, which meant it became possible to sell fresh lobsters and herring directly to markets in Glasgow, London and elsewhere (Figure 1). However, transport to seafood markets from the west coast still took much longer, making it harder to keep seafood fresh. Uneven development in east and west fisheries continues today, with west coast fishers tending to have fewer, smaller and lower powered boats than east coast fishers. As one west coast skipper-owner explained: 'They [the east coast] were always steps ahead of us – they had the money and the share ownership to buy big boats and equipment. We [on the west coast] were always well behind.'

'Fishing' on the west coast came to refer to two very different activities: local subsistence fishing from small open row-boats with some market selling, and the migration of west coast men and women to work in the much larger scale east coast and Irish fisheries (Nadel-Klein 2003). In the lead-up to the First World War, thousands of west coast men and women were employed by east coast herring-curers to catch and gut herring while following the fish all around the UK in a 'proletarianized, and increasingly class-conscious division of labor' (Nadel-Klein 2003: 70). Many of the thousands of migrant fishing labourers from tiny west coast villages participated in mass meetings supporting the burgeoning 1880s land reform movement while working in distant herring industry ports, evidence that their participation as migrant labourers in the herring fishery was related to their lack of access to land (Grigor 2000). In the early 1880s, Land League campaigner John MacPherson spoke to a meeting of 2,000 Highlanders working in Fraserburgh in the summer fishing, and in Shetland 'hundreds' of people from the distant west coast of Scotland working in the herring fishery 'met to demand land reform' (Grigor 2000: 63, 90, 92).

For at least 200 years Scotland has been thoroughly integrated into the global capitalist system. Scots have played important global roles as soldiers and fur traders, as settlers in distant colonies and part of a global supply of indentured labour (Wolf 1997). Scots were also wealthy parliamentarians and merchants throughout the colonies, and influential Scots Adam Smith and David Hume were philosophers of a newly emergent capitalist economy and a new Enlightenment (Patterson 2009: 22; Wolf 1997: 257). The vast majority of people living on the west coast today have an intimate and varied experience of waged labour and the capitalist organisation of work, and a long history of using waged labour to complement (or to replace) what they were able to cultivate on land or catch at sea. Since the eighteenth century, Highland men have worked on cargo ships all over the world, work that historian Marcus Rediker has argued 'foreshadowed' that of the factory worker (1989: 206). As they 'entered new relationships both to capital – as one of the first generations of free waged labourers – and to each other – as collective labourers', seafarers were 'indispensable to the rise and growth of North Atlantic capitalism' (Rediker 1989: 290). Until the 1970s there were enough Skye men working on cargo ships that they would sometimes meet for the first time in Canadian or Australian ports – 'no one had a car!' one man explained, laughing, so how would they have met each other in Skye?

Many Highlanders ended up in direct contact with emerging capitalists: in the nineteenth century many wealthy industrialists bought large sailing yachts and employed men from Skye, Lochalsh and Wester Ross to work as crew:[10] the grandfather of one Skye man I met during fieldwork worked on the Coats[11] family yacht. Some families I met had ancestors who had worked in American plantations shortly after the abolition of slavery, returning to Scotland with horrific tales of the working conditions they had endured. The building of the Caledonian Canal across Scotland, completed in 1822, employed approximately 3,000 Highlanders.

There is a long history of Highlanders from Skye and the Western Isles working in Glasgow, one of the UK's largest industrial centres (Parman 1990: 175). Even celebrated icons of the 1880s Highland land movement like Mairi Mhor spent long periods of their lives working for wages in Inverness and Glasgow. As I wrote after watching a play in Skye celebrating her life, 'to live away is part of the experience of being from here'. To this day the Park Bar and the Islay Inn in Finneston in Glasgow's west end are known as places to congregate and meet other Highlanders from back home.

The 1970s North Sea oil boom opened new opportunities for work. Although the new industry was based mainly in Aberdeen, hundreds of Skye residents took the bus or train to work on North Sea offshore drilling rigs, oil platforms or supply boats. The oil boom arrived abruptly on Skye's doorstep in the late 1970s with the construction of the massive Ninian Central oil platform in Kishorn on the south side of the Applecross Peninsula. This project employed 3,000 workers at its height and after its closure quite a few stayed in the area. Many local men and some women continued to work offshore, in the North Sea and further afield in Norway, Algeria and Nigeria. BUTEC, a torpedo and submarine testing range, was established in the 1970s in Kyle of Lochalsh, with the result that fishing was banned in some of the area. Now it is operated by the private company Qinetiq, along with many other weapons testing facilities. I was told that Qinetiq was the largest employer in the Highlands after the local government.

Salmon farms were established in lochs along the Scottish coast in the 1980s, in what many hoped would provide stable jobs for years to come. Yet although the production of salmon increased rapidly, automation and rapid corporate concentration meant that employment actually declined: one ex-fish-farm worker estimated that whereas 40 people worked on one fish farm on the west coast of Skye in the 1980s, a total of 20 permanent fish-farm jobs existed in the whole Isle of Skye in 2007. Seasonal employment on fish farms increased, with people hired onto mobile teams employed in the annual 'jagging', or inoculating, of thousands of fish per day at farms located throughout Scotland and Norway.

The result of these multiple economic and industrial transformations is that people from west coast fishing families or villages also have friends, neighbours or family members working in offshore oil and gas, salmon farms, cargo shipping or other jobs. I met fishermen who had previously worked as chefs, electrical engineers, supermarket workers, fish-farm workers, loggers, bricklayers, as fisheries inspectors, as welders, in car factories, in hotels, renovating houses, as farm hands and in seafood processing. Several had university degrees: in physics, history or agricultural economics. Contrary to the perception that fishing is a family skill handed from generation to generation, many had no previous family history of full-time commercial fishing. Fathers of fishing skippers had been employed as postmasters, joiners, policemen and factory workers. Thus most people experienced and understood fishing as work, in the sense of a generic type of waged labour, and as a way to pay their bills. In the present-day west coast, fishermen are not a separate occupational group. Young men might work in a seafood processing factory before starting work as crew of a fishing boat, and then leave for the summer 'to make good money' 'jagging' salmon on Norwegian fish farms. When the fishing got poor, young men might take training courses in order to work in the global offshore oil and gas industry, and for the next few years would closely compare their income and opportunities with friends who had decided to stay 'at the fishing'. Men working in offshore oil might fill in as crew on fishing boats between contracts, or might retire from fishing to work on a fish farm so they could sleep in their own bed at night. Those who owned their own boats had a much more permanent connection to fishing, but they were only a minority of those working on fishing boats, and they had to constantly try to recruit crew from other kinds of waged labour. People's experience of fishing was not isolated, but linked to and understood in comparison with all of these other industries, and connected with broader capitalist relations of production through its many trans-formations on the west coast of Scotland.

### *Fishing today*

The research in this book took place primarily in the commercial fishing indus-try, which has changed continuously throughout its history. The once-enormous commercial cod and herring fisheries have shrunk from their dominant position to make up only a combined 7 per cent of the value of Scottish fisheries in 2009. The inshore fisheries that occupy most of the fishing boats in the small harbours around the coast of Scotland are for shellfish (mainly prawns), which made up one-third of fishing industry value in 2009. Most fishing boats and fishermen I met were in the prawn fishery. These Scottish 'prawns' are more like a small elongated lobster and are also known to the fisheries markets as 'langoustines' or 'scampi', and to fisheries managers and scientists as *Nephrops norveigicus* or 'Norway lob-ster' (Figure 7). The Nephrops stocks in the areas around Skye covered in this book are considered to be 'exploited sustainably' in the assessments by the International Council for the Exploration of the Sea (ICES) (Ungfors *et al.* 2013: 260, 285).[12] Despite the health of the prawn stocks, other fish stocks like herring, mackerel, cod and whiting collapsed dramatically earlier in the twentieth century, and are now only fished commercially in other parts of Scotland.

The prawn fishery, which is often presented as 'traditional', only began in 1954 (Mason 1987) but grew rapidly to a first-sale value of £77 million in 2009. There were approximately 1,842 vessels fishing for shellfish in 2009, almost all of which are quite small (under 15m in length) and are dispersed around the entire coast of Scotland, especially the smaller west coast harbours. The prawn fishery has much lower levels of capitalisation than the other main demersal (or whitefish[13]) and pelagic (mainly mackerel) fleets, which make up the other two-thirds of the value of fisheries. There were 307 quite large vessels in the demersal fleet and only 25 (very large and very expensive) vessels in the pelagic fleet in the same year – in sharp contrast to the thousands of boats that once fished for pelagic herring around the coast. Most of these 330 large vessels are based in the north-east ports of Fraserburgh and Peterhead which account for 42 per cent by value of Scotland's entire landings (all fisheries statistics from Scottish Government Statistician Group 2010).

The prawn fleet is divided between trawl and creel sectors. Almost all creel vessels are based on the west coast and are under 10m in length. They fish using a

Figure 7  Prawns, also known as langoustines, Nephrops and Norway lobster.
These ones were caught by a trawler for the 'fresh' market.

baited trap left on the seafloor for days at a time and produce large whole prawn for live export to Spain, France and Italy. Product is sold to packing and export companies based in Scotland or directly to Spanish companies that send trucks north to Scotland each week (KPMG and Sea Fish Industry Authority 2004). There were three local processing companies in Skye and Lochalsh in 2007, at least two with direct links to Spanish seafood importers. The 275-vessel prawn trawler fleet produces prawn 'tails' (with head and body removed) or whole 'fresh' (neither frozen nor live) prawns sold directly to processors based in north-east Scotland, whose trucks collect landings from west coast fishing piers daily. The processors sell whole fresh prawns, frozen prawn tails, or tails processed into scampi to UK, Spanish, French and Italian markets. The UK is the largest exporter of Nephrops prawns in the world and Scotland produces about 80 per cent of the UK catch (KPMG and Sea Fish Industry Authority 2004). The research for this book was primarily with the west coast under-10m prawn trawler fleet, and to a lesser extent the under-10m creel fleet.

In 2006, when I began my research, good prices fed optimism and prosperity in the prawn fleet. A new law required seafood buyers and sellers to officially register to prevent the sale of under-the-table 'blackfish' for low prices, and there was ample prawn fishing quota.[14] However, simmering in the background were tensions caused by the ongoing marketisation of licenses (required to fish) and quota (governing the amount of fish that could be caught) and the concentration of the fleet into larger vessels in larger ports. Fishing licences were tradable and had acquired a substantial value separate from the vessel.[15] Meanwhile, the government paid to decommission (or destroy) many large whitefish boats to reduce fishing capacity; some fishermen on smaller vessels complained that well-connected industry leaders had 'made out like bandits' with money from these decommissionings, some of which was invested into smaller shellfish boats. The herring fishery, which until the 1970s had been based in ports all around the coast (including Applecross, Kyleakin and Kyle of Lochalsh), was now entirely operated out of Peterhead on the east coast by about 25 large boats, each worth millions of pounds, that owned all the quota. The crab fishery was concentrating in large vivier crab potters that worked farther offshore and stored crabs live in tanks. Their efficiency drove low crab prices down even further. As a result of these dynamics, more and more fishermen turned to chasing prawns, increasing the tensions between them. For example, creel fishermen set more creels to physically stake claim to their fishing grounds, which upset trawler crew who felt they were losing access to grounds they had historically fished. I was told of many instances of trawlers towing through fleets of creels while they lay on the seafloor and creel fishermen deliberately setting obstacles for trawl nets (such as old cars and caravans). The resulting damage (or loss) of valuable fishing gear meant that these conflicts occasionally spilled into violence ashore.

Fishermen also felt under pressure from conservationists who wanted to restrict their activities. A new Coastal and Marine National Park was proposed by the Scottish government in 2006, with the Inner Sound as one potential site, but after widespread opposition and a change in the Scottish government, it was 'kicked into the long grass' in 2008. However, from 2009 the UK and Scottish governments began designating many EU-mandated Marine Protected Areas through the UK and Scottish Marine Acts.

Tension between creel and trawl fishermen and burgeoning environmental concern about the seas came together in the Torridon Project, which resulted in trawlers being banned from an area around Loch Torridon (and creel fishing from an adjacent area) in exchange for the creel fishermen making voluntary restrictions on the number of creels they set, days they worked, and the gear they used (Nightingale 2011). That fishery was one of the first in the world to be certified by the Marine Stewardship Council's eco-labelling scheme, which was renewed in 2007.[16] It became government strategy to encourage Marine Stewardship Council (MSC) certification, and by 2009, many fisheries around Scotland, including herring fisheries and prawn trawl fisheries, had applied for, and received, this label.

One reason for the rapid spread of the MSC scheme is because of a growing mistrust of conventional fisheries management mechanisms. Another manifestation of this mistrust was the government initiative to develop Inshore Fisheries Groups, ostensibly to provide more 'community management' of fisheries. The initiation of these groups around the coast of Scotland was exceedingly lengthy and fraught because established fishing industry organisations fought to make sure that they would control these new organisations, and small-scale fishermen who felt unrepresented by existing fishing industry organisations also fought to have their voice heard (Nightingale 2011).

By 2010, the mood of boat owners and fisherman had substantially deteriorated. Fuel prices increased sharply through 2007 and 2008 (Brown 2009). As soon as they declined, the global recession hit and prices and demand dropped. Then prawn quotas were cut. To cope with these pressures, prawn trawl owners began to employ Eastern European and then Filipino crew on low wages, instead of share fishermen from Scotland, even on very small owner-operated vessels (Chapter 5). One prawn trawl skipper described a de facto policy of 'decommissioning by bankruptcy' with market pressures on fishermen increasing to an extent that forced many to sell up or go bankrupt. At the same time, more profitable prawn trawler owners launched a stream of new multi-million pound, highly efficient boats. EU Multi-Annual Guidance Programmes designed to reduce fleet size facilitated concentration: the owner of a large new boat could buy and merge the licences of two smaller boats, but the reverse was not possible. Across all sections of the industry, the numbers of boats and fishermen have decreased since 1999, but the remaining vessels have more engine (and therefore more catching) power (Scottish Government Statistician Group 2010). As an example of the pressure that this presented for small owner-operators, in 2010 the skipper and owner of the prawn trawler that I had worked on began to talk for the first time about selling up and getting out of an industry he had worked in since the 1970s.

This book reflects only a small portion of the time and generosity extended to me by so many people on the west coast of Scotland. It attempts to describe, with interest and respect, the considerable skills and warmth of a group of people who feel that they are consistently maligned and stigmatised, and the difficult pressures and situations they must cope with. I do not offer a rosy view and do not shy away from some of the more unpleasant realities I found. This book reflects a particular view and analysis which some may find challenging, but which I hope will at least provide some opportunity for reflection, for discussion and dialogue, and for a creative tension we all can learn from.

### Notes

1 Not his real name. Most names have been changed to protect the privacy of the people who spoke with me. I have not changed the names of a few people who were very familiar with my research and who wanted to be identified.

2 A creel boat is a type of fishing boat that uses pots or traps to catch prawns. The creels have a metal frame and are covered in netting. They are left attached to each other in 'fleets' on the seafloor and marked with a buoy at the surface.

3 Those working in the fishery universally refer to their catch as 'prawns', and the boats they work on as 'prawn trawlers' or 'prawn creel boats'. These shellfish are *Nephrops norveigicus*, which have two claws and look like a small elongated lobster (Figure 7). Regulatory agencies and government refer to these shellfish as nephrops. They are also called Norway lobster and marketed as 'langoustines' or 'scampi'.

4 'Whitefish' are bottom-dwelling fish, including cod, haddock, whiting and monkfish.

5  The British Underwater Testing and Evaluation Centre was established off the coast of Raasay in the 1970s by the Ministry of Defence as the UK's only torpedo testing facility. It is adjacent to an older submarine testing range and now run by the company Qinetiq.

6  'Craic' is a Scots word referring to good entertaining conversation.

7  The *Araminta* sailed from Liverpool to Geelong with 394 people on board, 191 of them from the Skye MacDonald estates. The Skye Emigration Society, formed by 'men of influence' on Skye, arranged and supported the passage of adults and families, with the requirement that they 'must, in all respects be capable of labour, and going out to work for wages' (Clarke n.d.).

8  I did not meet any women while fishing, although I was told of a few. I have used the indigenous term fisherman/men when talking about fishers in Scotland, and the gender-neutral term 'fishers' when talking about global fisheries.

9  I did check to ensure that I was not taking, or perceived to be taking, someone else's job as trawler crew. Trawlers generally found it quite difficult to find crew (see Chapter 5).

10  I was told that Portree harbour would be full of these yachts during the Highland Games and 'the Season', when the landed gentry would tour the Highlands holding parties at each other's mansions.

11  The Coats family established a textile mill in Paisley near Glasgow in 1826. The company now says that it operates in 70 countries with over 20,000 employees.

12  Fish and nephrops stocks are assessed in Divisions. This research took place within Division VIa (West of Scotland), Functional Unit 11 (North Minch) and Functional Unit 12 (South Minch). Landings of nephrops prawns by fishing boats in these areas have generally been less than the maximum landings advised by scientists (ICES 2015a, 2015b).

13  Scottish whitefish catches in 2009 were mainly of haddock and monkfish, instead of the historically dominant cod.

14  Annual EU negotiations set the total species quotas and divide them by country and fisheries management area. During my 2006–2008 fieldwork there was generally more prawn quota available than there were prawns to catch.

15  For a 10m fishing boat, a licence could range from £10,000 to £30,000.

16  MSC certification for the Torridon prawn creel fishery was suspended in January 2011.

# Part I

A metabolism of labour and environment

# 1

## 'Working the ground'

After living on Skye and working in the wild salmon fishery, in cargo shipping and operating a salmon farm, Lachie now owned a small hotel and bar on the harbour pier. It functioned as a social centre where curious tourists and holiday regulars mixed with local and visiting fishermen, men who worked in the offshore oil and gas industry, and several pensioners who had adopted the pub as their home away from home. Lachie was not a gregarious man but he was hospitable, his weather forecasts and nautical advice were consistently reliable, and there was always good craic in the bar. Lachie went out mackerel fishing most summer evenings in his small open motorboat, distributing his catch in plastic shopping bags to various regulars and visitors, and boiling up the mackerel and salt herring with potatoes to share with people at the bar. Fishing skippers coming in for a drink would often bring Lachie a few extra fish, a gesture that was usually repaid with a free pint of lager or a dram of whisky.

One long and beautiful evening in late July, I joined Lachie on one of his fishing trips. After stopping the boat in his favourite fishing spot (next to a salmon farm at the harbour entrance), he put a handline over the side and caught a mackerel almost immediately. He then put the line back in the water and gave it to me. Nothing happened. 'What are you doing there, Penny?' Lachie said in frustration, shaking his head and abruptly taking the line from my hand. 'You must work the *whole* ground, up and down.' He showed me how to jig the lure up and down while lowering it a few feet with each movement until I felt the weight hit the bottom and the line go slack, and then how to raise the lure a few feet with each jig until it eventually arrived back up at the surface. He explained how the shoal of mackerel would move up and down in the water and that we needed to make the lure cover 'the ground' in order to find them.

I had become used to the term 'ground' as it was used by the prawn fishermen I worked with and I had assumed that it just referred the deep and muddy seafloor that they fished in and constantly talked about. This was the first time I heard the term used to describe the whole volume of the sea. When I later analysed my fieldnotes, I found more than 80 uses of 'ground', describing quite different parts of the sea. What linked these places was the productive labour that took place in them. The ground was a place that afforded fishermen better catches and where they found their work to be productive. The affordances of grounds were not static and they were historically and inextricably connected to the labour expended there: fishermen re-shaped the affordances of grounds through their work and developed new tools in order to further develop the affordances of grounds.[1] The work that went into developing grounds meant that they were places with which people formed strong bonds and which came to be expressive of their personalities.

In this chapter I offer a detailed description of how fishermen on the west coast of Scotland worked their fishing grounds and developed their productivity. Anthropology was once famously described as 'philosophy with the people in' (Ingold 2002b: xvii), so I will use this practical examination to build on the broader understanding of human–environment relations developed by ecological psychologist James Gibson, anthropologist Tim Ingold, geographer Neil Smith and Karl Marx. A particularly useful basis for understanding human–environment relations is James Gibson's concept of 'affordances', which describes the 'complementarity of the animal and the environment' (1979: 127). Gibson explains:

> An affordance is neither an objective property nor a subjective property; or it is both if you like. An affordance cuts across the dichotomy of subjective-objective and helps us to understand its inadequacy. It is equally a fact of the environment and a fact of behaviour. It is both physical and psychical, yet neither. An affordance points both ways, to the environment and to the observer. (1979: 129)

The fishing grounds I discuss in this book are both 'a fact of the environment' and 'a fact of behaviour', both 'subjective' and 'objective'. Yet I also show that Gibson's understanding of affordances is not enough – that affordances can only be properly understood in the context of the whole field of relations they are a part of – what Marx described as 'metabolisms of labour'. Why are affordances developed? By whom? Seeking what material results? And who controls the metabolisms of labour that affordances are a part of? Such questions have the potential to connect an understanding of grounds to the role of political economy in their development. I see this ethnography of grounds and my theoretical understanding of the development of their affordances through labour as the foundation upon which the rest of this book rests.

## Developing grounds

Ground most commonly described an area where fishing was practised, as in, 'just north of the bridge there is a big expanse of prawn ground'. Ground was 'worked'. The ground was the worked-in and lived-in area, the area that was contested at sea and discussed on the radio, on the pier and in the pub. Grounds had particular characteristics relative to the kind of work that was undertaken there. Fishing for mackerel, Lachie's ground was the entire volume of the sea, but for most fishermen a great deal of the discussion of the ground was about the character of the seafloor as this was the habitat of the prawns and crabs which were now the focus of almost all present-day fisheries.

The sea in which these grounds are located is highly variable, patchy and changeable, partly because the west coast coastline is so complex and the seabed so uneven (Figure 8). There are underwater hills and plains and valleys, and the

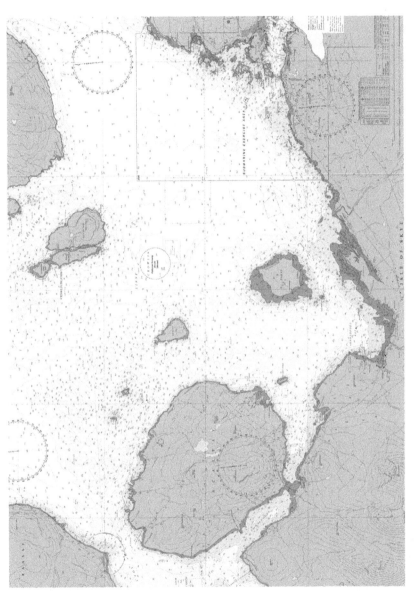

Figure 8  A nautical chart showing the seafloor at the southern end of the Inner Sound. Kyle of Lochalsh, Kyleakin, and the Skye bridge are on the bottom right. The Isle of Skye runs along the bottom and curves up to the left, and the island of Raasay is in the top left. On the top right is the Applecross Peninsula and the Crowlin Islands. Darker green areas are shallowest and white areas are deepest.

bottom ranges from weed to rocky boulders to fine silt. The tidal range in Kyle of Lochalsh is between two and five metres. When this volume of water races through the narrow passages between islands it causes four-times daily tidal currents strong enough to feel like a marine roller coaster – but in the same place the water will also be slack and (almost) motionless four times a day at high and low tide. There is a current or eddy of some speed in most of the sea, but this can range from a whirlpool to waters gently rising and falling at the head of a sea loch. Distinctive and frequently mobile ecosystems thrived in each of these areas, which fishermen explored and developed into specific fishing grounds.

Skipper-owner Yogi described how he began to develop velvet crab grounds on the advice of a Spanish seafood company which was seeking more suppliers of velvet crabs for its markets. A company representative told Yogi 'what kind of ground to look for, to go in by the kelp'. Excited, he 'took a fleet of prawn creels, shortened the ends,[2] and put them in shallow water. I couldn't even wait until the next day. I came to check them in five hours, and they filled seven boxes!' The Spanish seafood buyer, the pressures of a competitive international seafood market, the depletion of Spanish crab stocks and the crabs living among the kelp all contributed to producing this ground, but it was Yogi's work which linked these factors and ultimately produced both the ground and crabs for an international seafood market.

Yogi was reputedly the first person to fish commercially for velvet crabs on the Inner Sound.[3] After the encouragement from the Spanish buyer, Yogi deliberately began to look for grounds and develop techniques that afforded him velvet crabs, but he didn't know exactly where or how to find them. Opening up grounds was an experimental process, which was both intentional (in that it had a goal), but was also improvised (as he tried to figure out how best to catch and land the crabs). Around the Scottish coast, there have been many others experimenting as Yogi did: seeing an opportunity, finding new affordances of familiar places, producing new grounds, and working them. Ground is not simply produced by carrying out an activity in a particular place, but because a particular kind of effort in a particular place is found to have the affordances that people seek. Ground must be productive or people would not work there. Affordances are not just descriptions of the physical characteristics of a place, but emerge through particular techniques applied with specific goals in mind, and initiated by particular individuals. The affordances people seek are affected by political and economic influences and pressures. The imagined possibility and the concrete potential for developing such affordances draws people into applying their labour in a particular place whose material circumstances they combine into a metabolism which produces seafood for international markets and which defines the grounds.

Some recent anthropology of human–environment relations, skill and enskilment has focused on the immediacy of those relations and limited human intentionality to being 'immanent in the activity itself' (Ingold 2000: 352) and not at all planned in advance (Suchman 2007). Yet philosopher John Searle made a distinction between 'prior intentionality' and 'intentionality in action', and argued that even actions which are not planned in advance contain an element of intentionality in action (1983: 85, 107). Intentions also have some condition for their satisfaction

(Searle 1983: 88), in this case, finding grounds and techniques to produce fish or shellfish. Writers that have rejected the role of human intentionality have also tended to downplay the material results of human activity, instead discussing the 'materiality' and 'materials' of human–environment relations.

Yogi offers us an example of how intentionality relates to improvisation and material results. Motivated by an unexpected opportunity to make money and develop a new market, Yogi intentionally set out to find velvet crabs, but he didn't know exactly how or where he would find them. He took the advice of others and experimented with fishing gear and locations until he found what he was looking for: a combination of grounds and techniques that produced velvet crabs in exhilarating quantities. By the time I met him he had done well enough selling crabs to Spain to own two small fishing boats, a beautiful house on the harbour and a shiny black BMW. If researchers avoid the question of intentionality and material results and focus only on the interaction between Yogi, his fishing gear and the velvet crabs, they lose an understanding of how and why these grounds were developed and the significance they held for Yogi. Grounds are places where affordances are intentionally developed in particular social and economic contexts, and through often improvised actions with particular conditions of satisfaction.

### Personal relationships to grounds

Fishermen poured themselves into opening up and working grounds, which they often saw as an expression of their efforts, skills and persons. I was told, with admiration, about Graeme, a young and successful hired skipper who 'prided himself on trying to work an edge – a lot of people would just go up and down in the clean because they are too afraid of the [rocky and challenging] edge'. 'Buckie' John was a hired skipper who also prided himself on working the rocky and challenging 'edges' of grounds. He saw himself as a 'grafter' (a hard worker) who would 'go for quality' (large prawns), which meant working short tows on harder ground and lots of time spent mending 'damage' to nets. Like Graeme, 'not minding the ground' was an important part of 'Buckie' John's identity: he enjoyed the challenge of working hard and rocky ground and was proud of the effort and skill required to do so.

One fisherman had been fishing on the Inner Sound for 40 years and the strong relationship he developed with his grounds was described to me as follows:

> The Back of Kyle is his back garden. It is his cabbage patch. Do not try to fish in Pabay Corner [fishing ground] when he is about, he will show you the red light,[4] back you into a corner, and force you onto a nasty bit of ground or to haul up [your net].
>
> He is superb at that and good for him! If you go to steal brussels sprouts out of someone's garden, you should expect to get the back of the hand.

This fisherman was set in his ways and had the authority and the boat manoeuvring skills to keep others out of the grounds that he preferred to work. Graeme and

'Buckie' John were brave enough to always 'work an edge'. Such strong attachments to the grounds developed through people's histories of personally developing their affordances. These histories could flare into territorial conflict between fishermen using different techniques (such as trawlers or creel fishermen, both targeting prawns), or who were from different ports. One creel boat skipper complained about creel boats from another port, saying: 'They want the ground to be theirs only. They aggressively defend it. But I have as much right to be there as anyone else!' A trawler skipper, frustrated at finding creels blocking what he saw as his fishing ground, complained 'Next year, I'm not going to bother with the fishery officer, I'll just go straight through and clear them myself. They can't just keep taking more and more ground! We are losing ground all the time!'

Such relationships could also mean that people never came in contact with each other at sea because 'we are on different ground'. But in either case, the relationship between fishermen and the grounds they worked was strong and distinctive. Grounds afforded fishermen crabs, prawns and a livelihood, and through their history of developing these affordances they also developed personal identities and social histories in these places, which through conversations could develop into place names for these grounds (Chapter 2).

### 'Feeling the ground'

While most places became ground because they afforded prawns or crabs that were valuable in the international seafood market, some grounds were areas that were almost too hard, rocky and difficult to work, causing 'damage' to fishing gear and headaches for the skipper. These grounds were also defined through labour fishermen applied there.

The majority of productive prawn grounds were 'clean', meaning deep, flat, muddy, full of prawns and cleared of major obstacles through the process of fishing. 'The clean' was defined by its steep 'edges' and the shallower hard and rocky 'ground' that surrounded it. Hard and rocky ground was often weedy and inhabited by squat lobsters – but there was virtually no market for them so they were regarded as a nuisance. The 'edge' that lay between the clean and rocky ground was often the most challenging, desirable and contested place for small trawlers to work in. This was where trawler skippers like Graeme and 'Buckie' John would challenge each other to go 'higher on the bank' and test the limits of their skill, attention and gear. But the location of this 'edge' has changed over time according to changes in fishing gear, the effort and attention of the skipper and crew, and changes in the population and distribution of prawns themselves (largely brought about through fishing activities).

The precise location of this 'edge' was determined by 'feeling the ground', an expression that was also used to discuss the very different herring grounds used in the 1930s (Martin 1981: 229). Constant attention to 'feeling the ground' was one of the most important skills for crew to develop and was essential for the proper development of the affordances of fishing grounds. New trawler crew had to learn not only to feel, but to react appropriately by changing the boat's speed or direction in order to 'keep the trawl going'. And they had to learn to distinguish the vibrations coming through the fishing gear from the ground from the constant noise and vibration of the engine, the whine of the electronics, and the shuddering of the boat through the waves. It was important to feel when the boat was slowing down because the net was going over rougher ground and then to accelerate the engine quickly to lift the net up to prevent it from being caught on a rock or another obstacle on the seabed. If the net did 'come fast' on the bottom, it could mean stopping, hauling the net up, and the potential for serious damage to it.

The concentration required to feel the seafloor and to keep the trawl going effectively extended the body to new places, places it could not see and had never been.

Figure 9 shows skipper 'Buckie' John, a man who 'didn't mind the ground', concentrating intently while trawling over rough ground. He was feeling the seafloor through the wheelhouse wall, along the deck of the boat, up onto the steel structure taking the strain of the trawl, down 150 metres of trawl wire and finally to the hoppers at the front of the net which were bumping along the seafloor, all the while watching the depth sounder over his right shoulder. Feeling, however, was no use without interpretation and reaction. 'Buckie' John was feeling the ground with his left hand, his shoulder leaning against the chair, and his feet on the deck, but just out of the picture his right hand was poised over the engine controls ready to 'give it the handle' and push down the throttle to accelerate the engine should he feel the fishing gear 'sticking'.

Figure 9 Feeling the ground.

Crew needed an 'education of attention' (Gibson 1979: 254) in order to feel the ground and react appropriately, as 'Buckie' John expressed in frustration one afternoon: 'Iain [new crew] has been on a month and he still can't do it! He is not coarse enough on the throttle.[5] He does not pay close enough attention to catch it in time. He gets to looking at his magazines and gets distracted. I can't go below for a sleep. The most I can do is go below and cook or read the newspaper.' I was immensely proud of myself later on when 'Buckie' John teased me about being 'coarse' with the throttle. 'Who taught you that?!' he asked, shaking his head and smiling. A few months later, skipper Ruaridh 'the Accord' was showing me his old maps of fishing grounds. 'And that is where John said you gave it the handle!' he pointed out, chuckling. 'He was well impressed. He said you weren't shy at all!' Feeling the ground was an active and attentive engagement which required skilled and often forceful reaction.

Although I learned the skill of feeling the ground and keeping the trawl going, I wasn't always able to do it properly. After being away for a few months, or when I was tired or distracted, I would find myself frequently getting the net caught. 'You're not on the ball today', complained 'Buckie' John after one such morning. And the rest of the morning, no matter if he was down below cooking breakfast, or hanging upside down to put prawns in the tank, or down in the engine room, he would yell out to me 'Sticking!!!' when he felt it happen. It was almost always before I noticed.

The hard and rocky kind of ground is opened up only through the work of feeling and paying close attention to both the fishing gear and the depth sounder. During the process of writing and reflecting on these issues, I gave skipper-owner James 'the Iris' an early version of this chapter to read and discuss. I asked him how he would discover new pieces of ground. He explained: 'If you were steaming somewhere [without towing a net], and you see a bit of ground on the sounder, you remember it, and then go and have a proper look at it when you had the chance.' How did you have a proper look? I asked. 'You go and tow it', he said, bluntly. The ground and its affordances were not charted in an abstract survey, but in the process of working it, of feeling and discovering what was possible.

I asked Ruaridh 'the Accord' how new grounds were developed. He told me that when prawn trawling began in the Inner Sound in the 1970s, 'we didn't have the ground charted then. We were just told not to go within one mile of the east shore, or within two miles of the Crowlins. We just stayed on the Whiting Tow, which was clean'. A 'tow' is a part of the productive grounds where trawlers would tow their net. The Whiting Tow was originally 'opened up' to catch whiting, well before the prawn fishery began. It was a 'clean' and familiar fishing ground where fishermen could test their new prawn-trawling gear. There is an interesting ambiguity in Ruaridh's comment about not having 'the ground charted' because it is difficult to know whether he is referring to the worked-in fishing ground, or the hard and rocky ground he would need to avoid. What both forms of ground have in common is that they are 'charted' in exactly the same way – through a process of experimentation and improvisation in the process of working them. Individual initiative and attention mattered: the fact that Buckie John didn't 'mind the ground' also meant he was more likely to develop new affordances of new bits of productive ground.

The historical development of fishing techniques and fishing gear significantly affected what ground was considered 'workable'. Ruaridh explained that 'when we started with the prawn trawl, the main problem was damaging the nets and the mending – fortunately the guys in the herring fishing on the ring netters were good at it and they could show me'. Mainly, he said, you tried to stay in 'the clean' to avoid such 'damage'. At the time, they used larger nets with wheel-like 'bobbins' on them, but 'the net would catch and tear on ground'. Modern nets are smaller, with 'hoppers' (round sections of heavy truck tyre) on the bottom leading edge (Figure 10), which 'are great … they just bounce. You can go over ground with the hoppers that you would *never* get over with a bobbin'. Hoppers meant that Ruaridh could explore harder parts of the ground that had previously been off-limits, although even years later this improvised exploration required skill and close attention. As Ruaridh began to incorporate new techniques and tools into his fishing practices, he was able to develop the affordances and productivity of

Figure 10 Maintaining a modern hopper net.

the grounds familiar to him, expand the grounds he could work in, and reduce the ground he considered too hard and rocky to work.

Ruaridh's experience of being able to expand, shift and develop the grounds he worked in remains a feature of present-day fisheries. An experienced fisherman described how he got started on completely new ground a few years previously:

> When I came up here I got some readings from other people, more for hazards and wrecks than for the tows. James 'the *Iris*' gave me an old Decca[6] chart for the Back of Kyle.
>
> First I explored Portree Sound with a clean net, just going up and down the middle. Then I got the hopper net on and watched the sounder. It's a good thing to do. I should do it more often.
>
> I would watch the local boats, and then try to go where they weren't. But a lot of the time you are operating blind, opening up new ground, which is good for quality.

Ruaridh and Alasdair were constantly 'opening up new ground', using whatever tools and attention they were able to muster in their goal of developing the affordances of grounds and catching more prawns. Thus the understandings of ground on one hand as productive and, on the other hand, as unproductive and rocky, were integrated and experienced as one process in the ongoing practical efforts to expand productive ground, and avoid or reduce unproductive ground.

A person's ability to develop affordances and open up new ground is not only based on their fishing gear and the effort they put into feeling the ground, it is also based on remembering and interpreting the effects of tide, weather and light. Iain, a former hired trawler skipper, told me, 'every time you trawl, you are pushing outwards and you are opening up new ground'. He went on to tell me proudly about a deep 'hole up in Lochinver where I would tow at night, no one could understand how I did it. We got great catches there'. His ability to open up that 'hole' by finding the particular time of day it was productive was a source of pride that was still evident many years later. An understanding of the dynamic conditions of tide and season are also crucial to developing the affordances of grounds, as James 'the *Iris*', explained: 'Most have the tows now[7] but just that isn't enough, it's when you do them, the time of year, the state of the tide. It is a lot to do with the tide. If someone tries a tow at the wrong time and they don't get anything, then they think "that's not very good!" and they are away!' The extent and productivity of fishermen's ground depended on their own labour – their willingness to constantly attend to variations in light, tide and season, to feel the ground, to watch the sounder. A fisherman who did not make these efforts would have a restricted and impoverished sense of the affordances of grounds.

The constant effort to develop and expand grounds was incorporated into the everyday banter and disposition of trawler skippers. Every trawler skipper I met prided himself on towing where others had not, on finding his way through 'nasty bits of ground' and 'to wander off into corners'. Everyone wanted to 'open up new ground'. Small but significant games of one-upmanship occurred: I was warned that a fellow skipper we had arranged to tow next to to compare results 'might try to test us by going through wee tricky bits of ground. Just to see if he could trip us up!' The challenge of developing and testing the affordances of grounds shows that ground is not just a location or a set of physical attributes. It is an ongoing relationship that develops over time and through intentional and attentive labour; Searle describes 'a continuous flow of intentional behavior governed by the experience of acting' (1993: 293). Fishermen used the 'experience of acting', individually and as part of a fleet, to constantly re-adjust their actions to improve the productivity of their work.

The assessment of the affordances of grounds was an ongoing process that hinged crucially on one moment: when the net or the creel broke the surface of the water and the catch was revealed. I will turn to this material assessment in the next section.

## Making grounds productive: results mattered

Fishermen opened up grounds by assessing and developing their affordances. But how did they decide what affordances to develop, and if their efforts were successful? This assessment made the difference between the ground to avoid and the ground to return to, and whether the attention required to open up a tricky new piece of ground was remembered as an important breakthrough still discussed years later in the pub, or bitterly, as a 'waste'.

As James said, the only way to understand the affordances of ground was to 'tow it'. But what was he looking for? James would start his day with a general idea of what he was seeking: small prawns ('bulk'), or large prawns ('quality'), or to test a new piece of gear, or to train a new crew member, an easy day at the end of a long fishing trip, or a long, hard day to get some money in the bank at the beginning of a trip. He would consider all kinds of issues: prices, quota, but also how he was feeling, his assessment of the day's weather conditions and what was possible, the news he had received from other skippers, and his observations about what they were doing. But ultimately, as the skipper-owner of a commercial fishing boat selling to an international market, and as an owner with bills to pay and two crew on board, he *needed* to catch prawns. His assessment of the difference between a good day and a 'waste' would be based on these pressures. Catching a net full of squat lobsters, jellyfish or kelp was 'no use' on a commercial fishing boat. 'A lack of prawns' would put any skipper in a foul mood. A day or two of poor catches was tolerable but would inspire frantic comparison with others. But before long, paranoia, self-doubt and depression would creep in. This was the context in which intentions were formed and the affordances of grounds were assessed: a subjectivity shaped by its economic context and delicately balanced between the affordances of grounds and the market conditions in which commercial fishermen had to operate (Chapters 5 and 6).[8]

I should emphasise that the obsessive intentionality of fishing skippers did not result in or result from careful planning. Indeed, crew were frequently frustrated at the total uncertainty of work on a fishing boat, never quite sure what the skipper planned, where the boat was going, what conditions would be like, how much work there was to do, or how long they would stay out. Crew were required to adapt to this uncertainty as skippers experimented and did whatever it took to catch more prawns. Successful skippers would criticise as 'unmotivated' those who weren't willing to constantly experiment with new gear and new grounds and push themselves and their crew in an effort to catch more prawns. John Searle uses the example of a skier trying to make it to the bottom of the hill (1993: 293), which is a reasonable analogy for the intense but improvised intentionality practised by fishing skippers.

Thus the 'education of attention' of new fishermen took place in the context of searching for prawns and assessing whether that search had been successful. Intention shaped attention, which was practised in the constant work of 'feeling the ground' and in obsessively comparing one's catch with others, constantly experimenting with new gear and new techniques, and assessing the effects of light, tide and season in the process of opening up new ground. The result of each tow was critically important: were you 'catching'?

Ingold points out that it is only in the 'context of practical activity' that the 'affordances' of ground are developed (2000: 166). Objects or places 'take on their significance – or in Gibson's terms, they afford what they do – by virtue of their incorporation into a characteristic pattern of day-to-day activities' (Ingold 2000: 168). While undoubtedly true, an emphasis on 'activity' glosses over the importance of intentionality and material results. Grounds are not significant simply because activities take place there, but because they are places where these activities are productive. If a place cannot be made to produce the desired material results, the skipper would be 'away', looking for new grounds which afforded better catches.

Understanding the importance of material results also helps to explain why fishermen saw their work as actually *making*, or at least contributing to, the productivity of grounds. Crab, for example, could have a disease fishermen called 'blackspot' on their shells. At the beginning of a crab fishery in a particular place 'you had to fish those [with blackspot] out and then you would get a better quality. Crabs are like that, don't know why, the more you fish them the better the quality gets. Maybe there just isn't enough feed for them'. Fishermen felt that their actions could produce a healthier stock of crabs. Similarly, a trawler skipper told me that 'A lot of people have commented, if you come across a piece of ground with a lot of skate, first you have to fish them off, and that's when you will find you start to get a good fishing of prawns. Otherwise the skate will just hoover them all up!' Thus, a trawler's by-catch of skate was seen to increase their prawn catches. This skipper also firmly believed that prawn catches were lower in areas that excluded trawlers because creels do not catch skate, so there was no one to 'fish the skate off'. Fishermen understood their own activities in the context of and in relation to other organisms in the ecosystem in which they all participated. Trawler skippers saw themselves as intervening in ecosystems to make them more productive of the prawns or crabs they fished for.

Trawler skippers also saw their work as contributing to mixing nutrients in the sea and contributing to the overall health of the maritime ecosystem. One skipper told me: 'the seafloor is like a farmer's field, it needs to be turned over in order to release the nutrients. If that is not happening, if it is just filled up with creels – it will just go dead.' Another trawler skipper described how a creel fisherman from the same port 'works in a wee loch' and: 'Anytime there are no prawns in his creels he asks us to take a tow in there. He would get a good fishing after we churned it up, he reckoned. He would ask us to come in once or twice a month in the wintertime, after August. We would just spend one day in there and be out again.' He urged me to go speak to the creel fisherman in question: 'You go ask him about that, he'll tell you!'

While fishermen felt that prawn grounds were under a great deal of pressure, they also felt that the grounds had expanded during the 45 years of the commercial fishery. 'The prawns moved onto harder ground, that's been proved umpteen times, some of the places they are putting creels now, we wouldn't have thought of going there', said James, whose fishing experience extended back to the beginning of the commercial prawn fishery. Trawlers saw themselves as 'cleaning' grounds and tows, removing rubbish (such as car tyres and old fishing gear) and obstacles (such as boulders), making them easier to work in. Cleaner grounds had the potential to be more productive as less time was spent clearing and repairing the net, and more time spent fishing. 'Tows' were not seen as wilderness areas at all – they were areas with promising affordances that had been further developed and modified to make fishing there more productive: the fishermen's equivalent of a farmer's field.

In each case the improvements that fishermen saw themselves as making to the productivity of grounds were evaluated in terms of the success of the particular fishery they participated in, and not necessarily the overall health of the ecosystem. It would be foolish to argue that the prawn fishery has had no effect on marine ecosystems. Rather, fishermen saw their participation in the fishery as contributing to shifting marine ecosystems in directions which seemed to produce more prawns. Their labour contributed to the productivity of a 'fisheries ecosystem' – which is different from a 'wilderness ecosystem', if such a thing exists. Continuing the analogy with farming, just as a farmer's field is a qualitatively different ecosystem to the forest that may have preceded it, it is likely to be more productive of food.

Fishermen also believed that grounds *could* be overworked and overfished. However, it was usually the activities of *other* fishermen that they identified as destructive. Thus creel fishermen described trawlers as 'hammering' and 'ruining' grounds, but saw their own activities as sustainable. Similarly, trawler fishermen described creel fishermen as 'sterilising' grounds and targeting female prawns, but saw their own activities as 'cleaning' grounds, contributing nutrients and removing prawn predators. Fishermen almost always saw their own labour as making a positive contribution to the productivity of fishing grounds.

The way that fishermen saw the productivity of their labour is in sharp contrast to the way it is generally understood. Virtually all sustainable fishing schemes and fisheries management policies are framed with 'the normative subject "fishermen exploiting the seas" ' (Nightingale 2011: 124), and implicitly require that fishermen accept that their activities are destructive. This perception of fishermen's activities is frequently found in conjunction the expectation that the sea is and should remain a purely 'natural' wilderness. The pervasiveness of this view contributes to the state of siege fishermen felt themselves under (Introduction), and the frequent conflict between them and fisheries managers.

Such negative views about the results of fishermen's efforts to develop the affordances of grounds are reflected in Gibson's lament that 'human animals have altered it [the world] to suit ourselves ... wastefully, thoughtlessly, and if we do not mend our ways, fatally' (1979: 130). Yet Gibson offers no suggestions about how we might distinguish between productive and destructive human activities. Such a distinction is only possible by putting the individual development of the affordances Gibson examines in their proper context: how and why are intentions to develop affordances formed? What are the relevant pressures and incentives? What are the intended and unintended material results? What is the broader metabolism of labour that these actions form a part of, and how is it controlled?

Economic theorist Paul Burkett contrasts the labour and environmental relations of sustainable human development with that of alienated production of commodities for profit (2006). In commercial fisheries, the pressures of regional and global markets shape what intentions are prioritised, what affordances are developed, and how they are seen as satisfied. The effects of these market and commodity relations on fisheries are discussed in Chapter 5. Understanding the effect of these relations requires going beyond the focus typically used in the anthropological literature on human–environmental relations: 'engagement', 'activity', 'practise', 'lived-in', 'dwelling'. In the next section I discuss how these actions can be usefully understood as 'labour': it is people's work that ties together environments, tools and material results into ecological and economic processes. The alienation of this labour through commodity and class relations has significant human and environmental consequences.

### Labour, capitalism, environments

James Gibson's and Tim Ingold's analyses of affordances offer a useful way of understanding the development of fishing grounds, and more broadly, how humans perceive, experience and transform the environments they find themselves in, in every moment of their lives. Human actions in developing affordances are labour processes and are the basic building blocks of how humans interact with their environments, as Marx described:

> Labour is, first of all, a process between man [sic] and nature, a process by which man, through his own actions, mediates, regulates and controls the metabolism between himself and nature. He confronts the materials of nature as a force of nature. He sets in motion the natural forces which belong to his own body, his arms, legs, head and hands, in order to appropriate the materials of nature ... Through this movement he acts upon external nature and changes it, and in this way he simultaneously changes his own nature. (1976 [1890]: 283)

People shape the environments they inhabit while also relying on them and being a part of them – the body is a biological organism in constant metabolism with its environment (Ingold 2000). Throughout human history, 'both human beings and human consciousness developed from, and still depended on, interaction with the rest of the natural world. Labor was the pivot on which this relationship turned. Labor is the way in which both human consciousness and the material world interact, transforming both' (Rees 1998: 72).

Marx adopted the term 'metabolism' to describe human–environment relations from the developing understandings of respiration, biochemistry and energetics in the 1800s, and it 'includes the organism's biochemical exchanges with their environments and the regulation of these exchanges' (Foster 2000: 160). However, Marx gave the term 'metabolism' a new and more active meaning which emphasised the intentional and purposive nature of many human interactions with their environment – what anthropologist Don Donham has referred to as 'humankind in the active voice' (1999: 57). Humans not only effect 'a change of form in the materials of nature', they also realise their 'own purpose in those materials', which requires 'a purposeful will' and 'close attention' (Marx 1976 [1890]: 284).

In the development of fishing grounds, personal intentions, aspirations and their material 'conditions of satisfaction' were significant. Grounds became part of people's identities and were woven into the fabric of how people understood and related to each other and how they evaluated and thought about the places they worked and their futures. Marx's description of labour as a purposive metabolism allowed him to 'express the human relation to nature as one that encompassed both "nature-imposed conditions" and the capacity of human beings to affect this process' (Foster 2000: 158). The active role of labour in modifying environments and developing grounds was described by Marx as follows:

> Actual appropriation takes place not through the relationship to these [environmental] conditions as expressed in thought, but through the active, real relationship to them; in the process of positing them as the conditions of man's [*sic*] subjective activity. But this also clearly means that *these conditions change*. What makes a region of the earth into a hunting ground, is being hunted over by tribes; what turns the soil into a prolongation of the body of the individual is agriculture. (1964 [1858])

Human labour brings together subjective activity and material environmental conditions in the process of developing affordances through an 'active, real relationship'. The environment forms 'the conditions of man's [*sic*] subjective activity', but people also have the ability to change those conditions over time. Through both the intentional and accidental consequences of their labour, fishermen continuously modify the practical affordances of grounds, which in turns makes those grounds more useful and significant to them.

The constitution of affordances, grounds, and environments is also a social process. Ingold has criticised Gibson's highly individualistic approach to human–environment relations (2000: 167), and ecological psychologist Edward Reed takes up this point, pointing out that 'it is only in populated environments that humans learn to think about affordances and their relationships' (1996: 124). Our environments are not only 'populated' by other humans, but are also collectively transformed by them – for example, by the crew of a fleet of fishing boats engaged in a complex set of collaborative and competitive social and economic relations (Chapters 2 and 5).

These actions of humans and other organisms 'are themselves processes of regulation ... that maintain and transform the animal's relation to its environment' (Reed 1996: 93). They fit into the broader patterns of how humans have developed within and modified their environments over both very long and very short historical periods. Human–environment relations have 'always occurred under specific sets of social relations' (Patterson 2009: 222), and capitalist relations of production are just one of these 'sets'. The global scale and pervasiveness of capitalist production means that 'it is not just the immediate or the local nature of human existence that is produced under capitalism, but nature as a totality' (Smith 2008: 79). Even in the 1800s, Marx argued that the development and extraordinary expansion of human activity now means that 'the nature that preceded human history ... today no longer exists anywhere' (1998 [1845]: 46).

The key disruption in human-environment relations in capitalism is the alienation of human labour. The system rests on a 'social separation of labour-power from the land and other necessary conditions of production, and their recombination only under capitalism exploiting wage-labour for a profit' or creating commodities for sale to a market (Burkett 2009: 53). This disruption and reorganisation of the purpose of human labour and production systems creates 'metabolic rifts' under capitalism (Foster 2000). Orienting production systems with the aim of producing commodities for a profit changes what affordances people develop in their environments, how they develop them, and can change nutrient cycles by changing where the creature-commodities (like prawns) are deposited when they are used up. While Foster mainly discusses the systemic nature of these rifts, Burkett emphasises how the system is founded on the individual alienation of human labour from its environment and the metabolisms that sustain it. Of course people still relate to their environment in capitalism, but they lose significant control of these relations – at the same time as the potential scale of the changes they can effect in their environments is massively increased. Commercial fishers must catch what will immediately get a price on a competitive market, at volumes and at a cost that leaves them financially viable. They may be able to organise more or less sustainable ways of doing this, but ultimately their survival depends on market factors over which they have little control. A metabolism or an ecological relationship can be self-destructive, depending on the regulation of the relationship – how are people incentivised or pressured to develop certain affordances, and how? Who benefits from these productions, and what is taken into consideration, or not?

The existence of markets and production for profit affects the way that nature itself is produced through capitalism. Rather than debating what parts we should preserve of a wilderness that no longer exists, the important question becomes 'how we produce nature and who controls this production of nature' (Smith 2008: 88). Such an approach recognises that metabolisms of labour produce environments in many ways. For example, the labour-action of Aboriginal Belyuen has 'provided them with a way of attending to, re-enacting, and ensuring the physical, mythical, and emotional production of the environment, the human body, and the social group' – in contrast to the way that Euro-Australians have produced quite different environments according to entirely different economies and logics in the same locations (Povinelli 1993: 30, 237).

Returning to Scottish fisheries, it is possible that although individual fishermen and groups of fishermen may have very good reasons for believing that their labour contributes to the productivity of the environment they work in, the cumulative, competitive and market-incentivised effects of all persons working in that environment may result in a decline in its productivity (Chapter 5). This is the chaotic ecological regime of fisheries developed through capitalist markets and production processes, and it has real subjective consequences for fishermen. Fishermen are reliant on such fisheries, have pride in the skills and grounds they have developed to make a living in it, but also sometimes hate the job, are constantly at risk of being killed by it, and are usually held individually responsible for any damaging outcomes. This blurs the question of intentionality. People do act intentionally in their environments, but their labour and intentionality is alienated as they contend with considerable and contradictory pressures. The cumulative and collective effects of their actions may have unintended results. Engels, for example, described the 'revenge' of nature as the unanticipated but frequently destructive results of human activities organised through capitalism (Smith 2008: 88).

I have explored how humans relate to their environments through their labour and the development of its affordances, but also showed that capitalist production systems incentivise and organise the development of affordances in commercial fisheries with little regard for their sustainability. Capitalism structures how people relate to their environments, and produces nature itself, in a degraded form (Burkett 2009, Smith 2006). Studies of the ecological relations produced in capitalism are incomplete unless they recognise its role. Human labour links these global systems to individual actions, making it critical to understand how people form intentions and relate to their environments. Whose purpose is being realised in the work that people must carry out to make a living? In the next section, I will discuss how anthropologists have examined the role of human labour in relation to people's environments.

## Anthropology, labour, environments

Anthropological studies of the role of human labour in human–environment relations have generally taken place outside industrial capitalist settings and are quite distinct from anthropological studies of waged labour and capitalism. These studies of human-environment relations have tended to lean to one of two extremes: on the one hand, to emphasise the *products* of labour, often by quantitative measurement (Orlove 2002: 89–115), on the other hand, to emphasise the *experience* of labour-action (Harris 2007; Jackson 2007). Yet Donham points out that 'a simplified opposition between "material" and "cultural"' is not how Marx understood human labour, and not how anthropologists should approach it either (1999: 55). Metabolisms of labour are not simply reducible to material exchanges. They are equally not just about culture, or persons' experience: they have real material and economic aspects (Povinelli 1993: 331). A full anthropological analysis of human labour needs to include the subjective and the objective, the cultural and the material, the products and the experience of labour.

Anthropologists Michael Jackson and Olivia Harris' focus on the experience of labour has been useful in moving beyond strictly materialist and productivist understandings of labour. Jackson emphasises how labour brings humans, objects and environments into intimate, animated, reciprocal and intersubjective relationships (2007). Jackson's essay outlines 'a phenomenology of labour' to remind us that 'human minds are seamlessly and intractably linked to human bodies' and 'labor is our way back from the enchantment of things and the allure of abstraction to the transfiguring immediacy of the real' (2007: 77). Harris argues that 'the nature of work ... touches on a fundamental aspect of what it means to be human' (2007: 140). She applauds ethnography 'that privileges the lived experience of workers and the ways they give value and meaning to their activities' (Harris 2007: 156). Harris emphasises the extent to which 'work itself [is] an expression of value', rather than just 'the things that work produces' (2007: 149). Harris does lose sight of the material productions of labour: when she describes work as 'intrinsically relational' (Harris 2007: 143), she means only the relations among humans and between humans and deities (2007: 146), not the worked-in environment. Jackson argues that through our labour, material objects become alive and we relate to them as we relate to other human subjects. But both Harris and Jackson are so keen to distance themselves from an attention to 'things' and productivist understandings of labour that they minimise people's real material productions and metabolism with their environments.

In contrast, Elizabeth Povinelli's account of the labour-action of Belyuen Australian Aborigines grounds the experience of labour in its economic and metabolic interactions (1993). She argues that an understanding of labour-action is essential to a full understanding of culture, and that efforts to separate these two spheres have been damaging to Aboriginals (Povinelli 1993: 10). Unless it is acknowledged that ongoing material interaction with land forms an essential part of cultural and spiritual practises, it is very difficult for Aborigines to prove that they have rights to land-use, particularly when they have been forced to migrate due to aggressive colonial and settler activities. Separating the cultural from the economic and material means that 'economic practises' of labour-action on the land remain understood as 'moments of physical subsistence rather than central cultural and political moments in the development of human-human and human-land relations' (Povinelli 1993: 136).

Although Aboriginal Australians and Scottish commercial fishermen may appear to have little in common, there are some useful thematic links between Povinelli's ethnography and the Scottish fishermen I describe here. Both practise forms of labour that are often characterised as *extractive* instead of productive. Fishing, hunting and gathering are often thought of as activities in which particular organisms are discovered in and removed from an environment. Yet as I have discussed, this is not how Scottish fishermen thought about their own activities: they saw their labour as actually creating and maintaining productive fishing grounds. Povinelli describes the role of Belyuen labour-action in the 'process by which space becomes "country"' (Stanner quoted in Povinelli 1993: 136), resulting in the 'mutual constitution of humans and country' (Povinelli 1993: 6) because the 'health of the countryside and of human groups depends upon the mutual, positive action of each on the other' (Povinelli 1993: 31). Like the development of the affordances of fishing grounds, 'land use also creates and refashions the pre-existing features of the countryside that are then put to use'. Strong personal connections develop as well as 'places begin to body forth likenesses of people living by them' (Povinelli 1993: 146). And like Scottish fishermen, Belyuen Aborigines constantly 'challenge others to show the same level of intimate and everyday [environmental] knowledge that they possess' (1993: 33).

Cultural and the material aspects of labour are both featured in anthropologist Genese Sodikoff's ethnography of fundamentally different conceptions of labour by the indigenous Betsimisaraka and French colonists in the forests of Madagascar (2004). French colonial administrators did not recognise the productivity of Betsimisaraka practises of *jinja* (clearing and burning forest for rice and other food crops) or the intimate relations with the land it generated. They tried to change Betsimisaraka land use by enrolling them into capitalist wage labour relations to generate commodities for export, labelled Betsimisaraka as 'lazy', and their cultivation practices as destructive.

Material aspects of labour are also combined with subjective understandings of it in Orlove's study of the diaries of Bolivian villagers and their use of the Spanish term *trabajo*. He found that the most valued forms of work were those that 'most fully demonstrate the qualities of effort and productivity', in particular, agriculture and construction, activities which also 'meet the most fundamental human needs' for food and shelter (Orlove 2002: 114–115).

An attention to labour can bring to light relationships and experiences that may otherwise be obscured. The 'ritualised forgetting' of labour, says Jackson, 'may also be deliberately created as a way of expressing power' because it 'masks the context in which an object is produced' so that 'it attains a reified form that cannot be subject to questioning, and therefore imposes itself on our consciousness, as it were, not through any memory of the work that went into it or the lives that were sacrificed to create it, but simply from its presence as sheer facticity' (Jackson 2007: 75). Aboriginal labour was deliberately obscured in the establishment of the Australian settler state: it was argued that the land was *terra nullius* because its indigenous peoples did not adequately transform it with their labour (Povinelli 1993: 8–9). In Aboriginal country, as at sea, the effects of labour were invisible to those unfamiliar with it, or were wilfully and violently overlooked. The sea, and the Australian country, were made to appear as 'sheer facticity', devoid of the life and productive contributions of those who laboured in these environments. Thus, one important contribution of anthropologists is 'to make visible the productivity of indigenous people' (Povinelli 1993: 27). Marx's practical and intellectual project could also be summarised in this way: to highlight the importance of labour in producing both life's essentials and wealth, to describe how obscuring these contributions facilitated the forms of exploitation used in capitalist relations of production, and to try to overturn this situation (Patterson 2009: 151–155).

Povinelli criticises Western understandings of human labour because of the history of dispossession in Australia, and because Aboriginal Australians attribute intentionality to far more than human action: it is an attribute of the landscape and features within it, and of objects (1993: 7). Yet this criticism distorts Marx's aim, which was primarily to recognise the value and productivity of human labour (which was otherwise de-valued and ignored), and not to diminish other sources of productivity, such as the earth (Foster 2000; Marx 1976 [1890]: 134).

The ethnographies by Povinelli, Sodikoff and Orlove combine analyses of the material and experiential aspects of labour in human–environment relations. They explore people's experiences of their own labour in various metabolisms with their environments. They show that experience is materially grounded. In this book, I examine these material relations, how people experience and describe their labour within the metabolisms they are a part of, and how these relations shape both people's subjectivities and their environments.

## Labour at sea

A labour-centred analysis of human–environment relations is certainly supported by the way that fishermen described their own activities. Fishing was almost always described as 'working', in ways that emphasised productive relationships to sea-places and conditions, to fishing gear and tools, and to other fishermen.[9] Why was the term 'working' used instead of a more specifc activity-based term such as 'fishing'? Possibilities include an emphasis on the transformative and productive effort required, combined with a more alienated understanding of the need for fishing to generate income.

Fishing-work engaged all aspects of life: it was mentally and physically engaging, social, rewarding, and it described the history of people and places. Prawns were caught and grounds were produced by this work, and it described a relational, mutually constitutive and productive relationship enacted with other places, objects and people. Just as grounds could not exist unless they were worked, the existence of boats, nets, tools and ports was meaningless unless they too were worked. As anthropologist Marcel Mauss insisted, 'the tool is nothing when it is not handled' (quoted in Schlanger 1998: 200).

The most common use of 'work' in the context of fishing was in relation to sea conditions and places at sea. One fisherman told me that his fast boat meant 'we can work the limits of the weather and then get home'. Another advised that 'you can't work the Caol Mor [a channel and a tow] in a south-west [wind]'. Fishermen would talk about 'working nights', 'working shallow water', 'working an edge' or 'working close to the shore'. It was used relative to grounds, for example 'to work back and forth in one place', or to 'work right to the edge of the trawl ground', or to 'work 220 miles offshore'. This kind of usage has a long history, for example, west coast herring fishermen are quoted in the evidence to an 1864 Royal Commission saying 'we would work on any shore if there was clean ground' (Martin 1981: 141). 'Work' was used to describe a relationship with a ship or to a place: to describe someone who 'has worked in that loch ever since he started', or a boat that 'worked everywhere from the Clyde up to Fair Isle', or 'worked around the back of Skye'. It was used in reference to a boat's home port, as in 'he works out of Portnalong', or 'she [a boat] used to work out of Kyle'.

The second use of work (as fishing) was relative to particular tools or fishing gear, or the fishing boat itself. Fishermen expressed their relation to their fishing gear as 'working 500 creels', or 'working one net', or 'working handlines'. Their fathers or grandfathers 'would work drift nets in the winter and ground nets in the summer', or 'work bag nets for salmon'. The verb was also used in relation to new digital fishing gear, as in 'we work on [GPS-based] plotters'. An owner talked about his boat being 'worked by two crew', and boats also had a 'working side', where the net and catch were brought on board.

Finally, work (as fishing) took place relative to other boats and persons. A trawler skipper could be 'terrible to work beside'. When fishing was good 'everyone was working in sight of each other', and others expressed their frustration about 'working alongside foreign boats with no limits'. A fisherman could also 'work singlehanded', alone on the boat.

Like the practice of 'feeling the ground' (p.45), skilled work at sea involved actively attending to places, sea conditions, fishing gear, boats, and to other persons, and constantly interpreting, responding and adjusting one's actions in relation to them. Earlier, I described the inadequacy of 'activity' to capture the level of engagement required to fish and work at sea. As Gramsci wrote, 'man [sic] does not enter into relations with the natural world just by being himself part of the natural world, but actively, by means of work and technique' (1971: 352). Being at sea on a fishing boat was not in any way a contemplative experience, it was profoundly physically engaging. Even when sitting 'still', the continuous movement of the boat required constant muscular actions in your body. It was unrelenting. It was exhausting, it made your body ache all over, and your muscles continued adjusting and compensating for that movement even after you returned to shore. But in addition to being a skilled way of coping with being at sea, this work was done with the hope and the intention that it would be productive. A relational conception of work as a metabolism to develop the affordances of its environment meant that fishermen saw this work as actually making grounds themselves productive.

In Scotland's shore-based environments, Jedrej and Nuttall describe the strong perception by crofters that the land must be occupied, maintained and worked, rather than 'conserved' (1996: 195). Other studies have found both Skye crofters and Islay farmers think of the landscape as a worked environment. They talked about how much of it was created by human actions, and described their occupation and ownership of it as a deep social and historical relationship (Árnason et al. 2005; Whitehouse 2004).

Scottish fishermen understood fishing as 'work' undertaken in constant relation to places, tools and other persons, work which could open up grounds, develop their affordances and make the sea productive. This is not work understood as simply an effort or activity, but as something that was essentially interactive, a 'metabolism', as Marx originally described it.

### *Contradictory experiences of labour*

Marx differentiated between metabolisms of labour in [non-capitalist] 'production in general', and the specific experience of exploitation and alienation of labour
within capitalist relations of production (Patterson 2009: 147). Anthropologists
have shown that the generic category of 'work' does not exist in most languages
and cultures. Instead, different activities, such as weaving, sewing, ploughing and
hunting are described and pursued due to the value of the tasks themselves (Harris
2007: 143; Ingold 2000: 323). Ingold described this as 'task-orientation' (2000: 324).
Similarly, Orlove found that almost all of the uses of 'work' in the Bolivian journals
he surveyed referred to a more specific verb or activity (2002: 104). He observed
how similar activity-based descriptions are used instead of Spanish occupational
terms, for example, Quechua does not have a word for 'fisherman'. Such a person
would be described in phrases like 'he often catches fish', or 'he isn't at home; he
went to the lake to catch fish' (Orlove 2002: 56).

In contrast, the generic need 'to work' is a specific requirement of the way that
capitalism is organised: around the sale of labour-power. Thus:

> People who have thus sold their capacity to work, their labour-power, are conven-
> tionally defined (within the context of capitalist class relations) as 'workers', and
> the activities in which they engage during that period when their labour-power is
> under the command of an employer who has appropriated it are likewise defined
> as 'work'. (Ingold 2000: 326)

Marx described labour as a metabolism through which one's 'own purpose'
could be realised, thus the alienation of labour meant that it is not one's *own*
purpose that is realised, but another's – the person or organisation whom you
are working 'for' (see also Patterson 2009). Thus 'the product ceases to be the
objective embodiment of the individual's own personality and the distinctive
expression of his creative powers and interests ... He [*sic*] does not choose to
make it, but rather he is directed to do so ... It is never *his* product at all; he is
merely the instrument of its production. In a word, it is *alien* to him' (Schacht
1970: 85, his emphasis). This alienation could happen through waged labour (as
Ingold describes above), or alternately, through the process of selling the goods
one produces to a market, according to the demands of that market (Schacht
1970: 87; Chapter 6).

I did not find such a clear distinction between 'work' and task-oriented activities
undertaken for their own merit in coastal Scotland – which is not surprising given
the long history of capitalist labour and market relations there (Introduction).
'Work' was understood *both* as alienating work for wages (or market selling), *and*
as relational and metabolic tasks undertaken in relation to places, boats and persons. Sometimes both experiences were a part of the same activity. As Sodikoff
observed in Madagascar, different understandings of labour 'existed not in sharp
contradistinction, but in tense complementarity' (2004: 371).

With the exception of short evening trips like Lachie's at the beginning of this
chapter, fishing in Scotland is entirely commercial. Prawns and fish are sold to

make money, which is then used to pay for the expenses of fishing, crew wages and the profits that accrue to the boat owner. For most, fishing was one option for making money amongst various others. In the context of market competition and decreasing seafood prices, waged labour relations are replacing the historical 'share' system of payment on Scottish fishing boats, and sharpened the class divide between boat owners and crew (Chapter 5). Fishermen were not just alienated from their labour, they were alienated from their catches. They rarely ate the prawns they caught in enormous quantities, and it was difficult to buy them in most fishing villages. The fish people did like to eat – the herring, cod and mackerel which historically had been caught in small boats off the coast – was available for most only through the supermarket, imported from the east coast or further afield. More than one fisherman told me they hated prawns and the prawn fishery – yet a 'lack of prawns' would make them even more depressed. Out fishing with Dickie on the *Iona*, I asked him why he had chosen to fish for prawns. He sighed, and then patiently replied: 'You have to understand that the fisheries we have now have to do with the fisheries in the past. It is not by choice that we are at the prawns, but we were forced to them because everything else ran out.'

The contradictory experiences of labour under capitalism meant that it could be experienced in very different ways at the same time and in the same person's experience. The linguist Valentin Volosinov argued that 'a word in the mouth of a particular individual person is a product of the living interaction of social forces' (1986 [1929]: 41). The use of the term 'work' in coastal Scotland reflected some of these contradictory forces, often experienced as different aspects of the same activity. Work described metabolic relationships to places and things, *and* labour that was alienated for wages and for the market. The contradictory meanings of words like 'work' 'are in a state of constant tension or incessant interaction and conflict' (Volosinov quoted in Holborow 2006: 14), which is part of the contemporary subjective experience of work.

It is thus misleading to characterise a single 'Western notion of labour', as Povinelli and Harris do. Indeed, they offer precisely opposing analyses. While Povinelli argues that the West positively valued labour and deemed it to be necessary for claiming property and land (1993: 6), Harris understands it to be given wholly negative connotations, linked to slavery (2007: 138, 157). Both authors leave the reader with the impression that the Western view of labour has been relatively stable over time, and that the differences between this view and indigenous views are the proper subject of anthropological study. But within the 'West', experiences of labour are conditioned by class relations and are multiple and contradictory (Donham 1999: 38). Both Povinelli's and Harris' assertions about Western understandings of labour are based on philosophical and historical analysis, and not on ethnographies of work in the 'West'. But as anthropologists, it is important that all of our assertions about peoples' experience and understanding be subject to ethnographic investigation, including those of 'Westerners'.

After examining ethnographies of work in the 'West', Ingold concludes that 'we are not Westerners, nor are we really non-Westerners; rather we are human beings whose lives are caught up in the painful process of negotiation'. Ingold argues that anthropologists frequently displace the tensions and contradictions of modern capitalism 'onto the relation between our society and the rest of the world', in the process making sweeping statements about 'the West' which are not ethnographically grounded (2000: 338).

This book examines established anthropological topics such as human–environment relations and skill, but also considers how these are shaped through market and class relations: the often 'painful process of negotiation' that Ingold refers to. The increasingly alienated relationships among fishing boat crew, between crew and the boats they work on and the environment they work in, and between boat crew and shore-based owners (Part III), does not change the fact that fishermen have a real and ongoing metabolic relationship with the sea that they mediate through their labour. The production of grounds continues – however, these changing social relations affect the kinds of grounds and the kinds of prawns that are produced through this process.

## Labour and human–environment relations

What can a focus on work and labour bring to an understanding of human–environment relations? It draws our attention to the immediate relations between people and their environments, and their own role in developing the affordances of those environments and making them productive (Chapter 3). It also draws our attention to the tools and techniques used in the labour process, and how these techniques extend relations to other grounds, places and people (see Chapter 3 and Part II). It allows us to see how these relations can be alienated and are shaped by political economy over time (Part III). It can build on analyses of skill and human–environment relations but more explicitly draw attention to the social and market relations that affect the ability to practise skill (Chapter 6) and which affect relations to the environment and ecological processes (Chapter 5). Finally, it brings to light the ways in which humans inhabit and produce what may otherwise appear as 'empty' land (Povinelli 1993: 203), or for that matter, 'empty' sea. Just as Povinelli argued it was impossible to understand how land becomes country without an understanding of labour-action, it is impossible to understand how the sea becomes grounds without the active and attentive labour of fishermen.

An emphasis on labour is one way of focusing on the continuity of human life and processes across land and sea which avoids the environmental determinism of viewing the fluid sea in contrast to the solidity of the land. Human labour plays a critical role in opening up and working grounds, tools and boats, but the people who rely on this labour for their livelihoods must do so according to the rules of capitalist market relations in order to stay afloat economically. The 'reification of capital' obscures the role of human labour in the 'unbroken process of ... production and reproduction' (Lukács 1972 [1922]: 181; see also Jackson 2007: 75). I have argued here that an understanding of this production and reproduction needs the subjective experience *and* the material metabolism of labour at its core.

Marx famously contrasted the activity of bees with the human architect who 'builds the cell in his mind before he constructs it in wax' (1976 [1890]: 284). Povinelli criticises this understanding of human labour, arguing that 'hunter gatherers neither fix in their mind alternate images of the ecological landscape, nor permanently fix upon landscapes their labour' (1993: 25) – and the same could certainly be said about fishers. However, the Marxist analysis of human labour offered here emphasises the second part of Marx's quote which is usually neglected, that 'man [sic] not only effects a change of form in the materials of nature; he also realizes his *own purpose* in those materials' (1976 [1890]: 284, my emphasis). This focus on people's 'own purpose' in their labour does not mean that every action requires a fixed plan or 'alternate image' formed in advance. Ethnographies of labour should take seriously people's 'own purpose' in their labour, and what struggles may exist around these purposes. Such inquiries will inevitably run into the 'struggle over what will count as productive activity and what that activity can produce' (Povinelli 1993: 27), whether it takes place in Australian 'country', Malgasy forests or Scottish fishing 'grounds'. Capitalism itself can be seen as a project to redefine what counts as productive activity, how productivity is assessed, and in particular, to re-shape people's 'own purpose' in their activities. These purposes shape the affordances people seek from their environments, and the broader metabolisms they participate in. Environments themselves are produced through these metabolisms in variously degraded or sustainable forms. The meaningful places generated through these processes at sea are explored in the next chapter.

## Notes

1  I do not distinguish any significant difference in the meaning of 'work' and 'labour'. However, I generally use the indigenous term 'work' in ethnographic description and 'labour' when referencing the literature.

2  The 'ends' are the ropes at each end of a fleet of creels which lead to a buoy on the surface.

3  The first recorded commercial catches of velvet crab in Scotland were 1985 (Highland Shellfish Management Organisation 2004). In 2009, 2,762 tonnes of velvet crab with a value of £6.1 million were landed (Scottish Government Statistician Group 2010: 23).

4  If you can see the red (port side) navigation light of another boat, you must give way to it. Sometimes skippers deliberately manoeuvred 'to show the red light' to another boat.

5  The throttle is the 'handle' that controls the speed of the engine.

6  The Decca is an obsolete form of electronic navigation using radio waves from stations based on shore (Chapter 4).

7  By 'have the tows' James means that they have them plotted on a GPS chartplotter (Chapter 4).

8  An assessment of the importance of intentionality and material productivity in non-market and non-capitalist situations is unfortunately beyond the scope of this chapter. Material productions are clearly an important aspect of labour in non-capitalist situations (see for example Povinelli 1993), but market relations also have a significant effect on how intentions are formed and productivity is assessed.

9  I found approximately 100 instances in my fieldnotes where 'work' or 'working' referred to 'fishing'.

# 2

## From Wullie's Peak to the Burma
### Naming places at sea

I finally crawled into my bunk at midnight after checking and re-checking my gear to make sure I hadn't forgotten anything I would need for a five-day fishing trip in February. My alarm went off at 3.05 a.m., and I grabbed my boots, oilskins and the bag I had packed and struggled up to the pier. Headlights on the deserted road showed Alasdair, the skipper, arriving to take me to the fishing pier on the other side of the harbour. I tried to look as perky as possible. 'Good afternoon!' he greeted me, cheery and amused at my grogginess.

At the fishing pier, the tide was low. This meant climbing down a skinny 7m metal ladder carrying whatever wouldn't survive being dropped onto the steel deck of the boat far below. The fishing boats were rafted together four deep on the pier and this was now the busiest place for miles around. Engines were already revving, lights were on, steel doors clanging, docklines splashing down into the water and Bo'sun the dog was enthusiastically running from boat to boat licking anyone he could find. A spell of poor winter weather had kept the fleet tied up but now there was a break and word of 'a good fishing' up north. Our engine started with a warm roar, and then the skipper turned on our GPS chartplotter, depth sounder and radar, which chirped and beeped as they warmed up. After checking all the lines were on board, the engine roared in reverse, forward, and reverse again, as the skipper narrowly but artfully missed the other impatient skippers also manoeuvring around in this small space between piers. Within ten minutes almost all the boats were away, charging under the bridge on a flood tide, wheelhouses lit only by the glow of LCD screens.

'We'll tow up to Wullie's Peak before we turn south and head for Portree to land',[1] explained Alasdair. 'Who is Wullie?' I asked. 'I don't know', said Alasdair, 'It's just what it is called'. On the electronic chartplotter, I scrolled north from the small ship icon indicating our position and asked Alasdair to show me exactly where he wanted me to wake him up, and where he wanted to make our first tow of the day. Either Alasdair or the relief skipper, John, had already marked the underwater hill of Wullie's Peak on the chartplotter (Figure 11).

Wullie's Peak is one of many places that are part of trawler fishermen's working practices and everyday conversations, yet are completely invisible from the sea's surface and not related to any place on shore. Many of these places are the

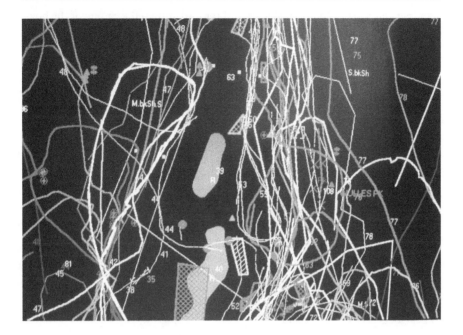

Figure 11 Wullie's Peak on the GPS chartplotter, on the right-hand side about halfway up.
The coloured lines are the GPS-plotted traces made by the trawler while it was towing.
Circles, crosses, triangles or hatched areas represent obstacles on the seafloor. Numbers
indicate the depth of the water.

fishing grounds I discussed in the previous chapter, or are places within these
grounds. In this chapter I will closely examine how these places are formed
through fishermen's working practices and conversations. For now, I will
return to our journey, heading north to Wullie's Peak eye-wateringly early one
February morning.

The skipper made sure that I was properly oriented and knew where to take
the boat, and then headed down to his bunk to get some more sleep. For a few
hours I was alone in the wheelhouse, steaming through the 'black dark'. My eyeballs ached and cups of tea didn't seem to help. With the light from the many LCD
screens reflecting off the windows I couldn't see anything beyond the wheelhouse
I sat in. If I stuck my head out the side window I could look ahead to see the
stern lights of other boats receding into the distance, and look behind to see the
green and red navigation lights of still other boats catching up with us. Every ten
minutes or so the chartplotter with our position marked in the middle silently
re-centred itself. Every 15 minutes I checked the radar screen carefully, staring
at the dancing green specks on the screen to see if they would solidify into a boat
or an island or some other hazard. This did not help my aching eyeballs. After
an hour, it felt like the outside was barely there – it was just me, the tracks on
the digital chartplotter, and the dancing green specks on the radar. I opened the

window and took deep breaths of air and reminded myself that one of the boats a few miles ahead of us was making its first trip after almost sinking in a situation just like this: steaming out to shoot the net very early one morning, the crew possibly staring at the chartplotter until cross-eyed, feeling sleepy, and possibly closing their eyes just for a minute, and then the concussive BANG! of a solidly built wooden boat slamming into a familiar cliff at full speed (Chapter 6).

I managed to stay awake. At about 6 a.m. the sky started to lighten. It was perfectly grey and calm. I put the kettle on and woke Alasdair to tell him that we were south of Wullie's Peak and ten minutes away from where he wanted to shoot the net (Figure 12).

Five months later I discovered how Wullie's Peak had been named. I was out on a prawn trawler with skipper (and part-owner) James 'the *Iris*' and his crew Charlie 'Bucket' and Hector 'the young fellow'. James had been fishing full-time since 1966, but two years ago his fishing boat was the first in 30 years to be ordered brand-new by a Portree owner. James' father and uncle had moved to Skye from Orkney, and had been among the pioneers of the prawn fishery in the 1960s and 1970s. James was a friendly and easygoing man who relished 'good craic', and seemed to spend most of his working day on the telephone and radio speaking to other fishermen. Near Rona, a few miles south of Wullie's Peak, James smiled and chuckled as he told me the story:

Figure 12  Wullie's Peak.

Wullie 'the *Sincerity*' used to steam to that peak every morning to shoot his net. He worked out of Gairloch. You would shoot the net and start just south of the peak because it was shallow right out to Staffin. When you would call Wullie on the radio to say 'Where are you this morning?' It would be, 'Oh, I'm at the Peak'. *Every* morning!

He was here for 15 years around the 1970s, and then he retired. The boat was sold and it ended up in Ireland, that would have been '82, '83.

Wullie was from Fraserburgh and was one of the many east coast fishermen worked mainly on the west coast, keeping their boats in Gairloch, driving through on a Sunday night, and driving home again on a Friday or Saturday (see Knipe 1984). Despite the fact that he was not from the west coast and did not live there permanently, Wullie's work and his participation in the community of west coast fishermen earned him a legacy in place which extended over 30 years to those who had never heard of him.

In the 1970s when Wullie was starting his mornings 'at the Peak', prawn trawling was a new fishery. It had started experimentally on the east coast of Scotland in the 1950s and gained momentum and new markets in the 1960s. Some west coast fishermen started fishing for the new prawn markets using creels in the 1960s, and then east coast fishermen like Wullie started to explore and 'open up' new west coast prawn trawl grounds. Around the Inner Sound, Portree fisherman Johnny Ferguson on the *Silver Spray* was the first to convert to trawling in 1971 (although he was killed in a car accident soon after), followed by James' father and uncle, Tommy and Alfie Corrigal, on the 'the *Iris*' in 1973. Wullie, the Corrigals and their contemporaries[2] were experimenting with new prawn trawl fishing gear and regularly 'blootering'[3] their nets on as-yet uncharted hazards on the seafloor. Together these men 'opened up new ground', developed techniques for working it, and a new vocabulary to talk about it.

Wullie's Peak was a place generated within a specific occupational community through a particular form of work, at a particular point in history. As the prawn fishery was developed in the late 1960s and 1970s and the fishing areas around the coast of Scotland were transformed into productive prawn grounds, Wullie's Peak was created during the meandering radio conversations that took place a few miles off the coast and stretched on long after sunrise. This place had power: 25 years after 'the *Sincerity*' was sold to Ireland and Wullie stopped working these grounds, Wullie's Peak was still a destination for hopeful fishing skippers and crews steaming out to sea in the black dark.

The example of Wullie's Peak shows that the creation of significant places does not need a multi-generational history, and it does not even need the people involved to be from that area. Fifteen years of working these grounds and talking about them with other fishermen were enough for them to be named for Wullie. The creation of places is 'not contingent on some primordial quality that place has in and of itself', rather 'the power of place, that is, its capacity to inhabit us, stems from the practice of social relations, as well as its historically experienced transformation' (Retsikas 2007: 969). Places are created through the conversations and social relations generated in the process of transforming them into meaningful and productive grounds.

## Places at sea

If the creation of places is not dependent on their 'primordial' qualities or people's long histories of residence, how do we explain the emergence, shifting and disappearance of particular meaningful places at sea? Anthropology has recently experienced a 'fluorescence' (Strang 2006: 148) of writing about place, landscape and human–environment relations – a turn away from its textually-focused Writing Culture period to a more materially-engaged exploration of human experience. Studies of place have primarily been phenomenological in inspiration (Feld and Basso 1996; Tilley 1994), with a focus on experience and sensory engagement, and the literal incorporation of material world into body (Strang 2006). Other studies have examined the contested politics of places and the 'tensioned landscapes in movement' they are a part of (Bender 1993: 5). Geographers such as David Harvey (2006) and Doreen Massey (1994) have examined the political economy of places, emphasising their interconnectedness and the effects of capitalist relations. In this chapter I seek to examine both the phenomenological experience of places and how these experiences have been affected by changing seafood markets, ecological, social and language change, and militarisation of the coast. I will show how these forces and experiences are reflected in the way that places are named, remembered and forgotten.

Ingold highlights the importance of people's practical and material engagements with places as follows:

> A place owes its character to the experiences it affords to those who spend time there – to the sights, sounds, and indeed smells that constitute its specific ambience. And these, in turn, depend on the kinds of activities in which its inhabitants engage. It is from this relational context of people's engagement with the world, in the business of dwelling, that each place draws its unique significance.
> (2000: 192)

At sea, the 'relational context of people's engagement' is particularly important. The limitations of the human body means that it is unusual for people to have a completely unmediated engagement with the sea. People almost always experience the sea from the vantage point of a particular boat. The same place at sea is experienced very differently depending on if one is 'dwelling' on an oil tanker or in a canoe, or if one is engaged in a sailboat race or in catching prawns. Thus the 'specific ambiance' of places at sea changes considerably according to the kind of engagement that particular boats are designed and used for, and people's role in those activities (as skipper or as cook for example), in addition to changes due to weather and tidal conditions. The fact that the surface of the sea has few immediately distinguishing features means that a particular form of engagement is usually necessary to locate a specific place, and that the same location can be experienced in jarringly different ways. As Ingold says, it is the activity that one is engaged in that is crucial to the experiences that places afford.

To the casual observer, the photograph in Figure 12 is very disorienting: there are no markers to show you are at Wullie's Peak, or to distinguish Wullie's Peak from the adjacent 'Trodday Tows'. Specific navigation techniques can be used to find Wullie's Peak, for example, using marks on the shore, compass bearings, radar or a GPS (Chapter 4). But an understanding of these techniques does not explain how Wullie's Peak became a destination in the first place. It is not just the *kind* of activity that takes place in a geographic location that makes a significant place, but the affordances of that place and the way in which people are able to develop them to satisfy their own intentional activities. It is not just the 'ambiance' of places in the course of particular kinds of engagements that makes them significant, but the productivity of places in relation to the intentions of people who carry out work there. If Wullie had never caught prawns at the Peak, he would not have continued to go there '*Every* morning!' for 15 years.

The link between specific forms of activity and the experience of places at sea has been described by other anthropologists working in a wide variety of locations: on board a scientific research vessel off South America (Goodwin 1995), in a lagoon in the Solomon Islands (Lauer and Aswani 2009), and in the coastal Canadian Arctic (Tyrrell 2006). Goodwin describes a 'convergent diversity' of method and intention that means that scientists on the same ship 'probing exactly the same patch of sea, each will in fact see something quite different there' (1995: 246). In the Roviana Lagoon, it was 'context-specific activities' and the 'outcomes of everyday human activities' that generated knowledge, with expertise demonstrated through 'fishing prowess' (Lauer and Aswani 2009: 323, 318). Desirable 'mana' was demonstrated through 'a person's or thing's efficacious qualities manifested in tangible outcomes' and 'concrete results' (Lauer and Aswani 2009: 324).

Anthropologists have also demonstrated how new places are created through movement. In Indonesia, anthropologist Kostas Retsikas demonstrates that the 'correspondence between persons and place' is 'not rooted in deep histories of sedentary habitation … rather it is predicated on short histories of mobility' (2007: 983), with movement to a new place resulting in new persons and places at the destination. In Mexico the historical processes of 'place making and place breaking' were similarly related to migration (Amith 2005). At sea in Scotland, it was not migration but the labour of movement itself that created significant new places. As Ingold argues, knowledge about places proceeds through movement (2000: 229). For example, a 'tow' is both a movement and a place. It is how trawlers tow their nets, it is where trawlers tow their nets and it is the name for trawl grounds they have found to be or made to be productive. Many named places I will discuss in this section (such as the Sound of Music, the Wall of Death, the Whiting Tow, the Caol Mor and the Crowlin) are tows that have become places through the process and labour of towing there.

In the following sections, I will show how the labour of developing affordances and creating places is a thoroughly collective and conversational social process. At the same time, these places have a subjective importance to individuals. Places were formed as a result of intensely local work but are also linked to global social history. Finally, I will discuss what happens to places when their affordances are changed or are lost.

## The collective development of affordances

Places were created and became significant through the development of their affordances with new or adjusted fishing gear, the attention of the skipper, and the social networks and communication practices which facilitated the collection of information over large areas of the coast. The transformation of places over time in an 'environment of joint practical activity' (Ingold 2000: 167) is critical to understanding them; phenomenology's focus on the immediate present can obscure such historic and dynamic relationships. The collective development of environmental affordances was critical to the development of human history and societies, the human body, and human consciousness itself (Patterson 2009: 222; Reed 1996). This is an ongoing social process: 'people and places are dependent upon each other for their physical and social life' (Povinelli 1993: 197).

The sociability of prawn trawling blossomed during the first tow, after the dark and dangerous loneliness of steaming out to the grounds. Fishermen tried to carry out the first tow just as the sun was coming up. This tow was almost always the most productive, with the number of prawns caught usually declining during the day – although sometimes the catch improved in the last hours of daylight. At 57° north, days are very short from November to January, but on the longest day of the year, in June, the sun rises at 4.30 a.m. and sets after 10 p.m., with at least an hour of twilight on either side. Fishermen would often work from 3 a.m. until 10 p.m., and then go back out at 3 a.m. the next morning. Most inshore prawn trawlers operated with only two or three crew, and without refrigeration their catch had to be landed within one or two days. In order to get some rest and to sell the prawns, the boats needed to tie up overnight – which then added travel time in the morning or evening between the harbour and the fishing grounds.

Trawler skippers spent most of their waking hours on board sitting and steering the boat from a chair in the wheelhouse, usually with the assistance of an auto-pilot. All of the trawl skippers I knew spent a vast amount of strategic and intellectual time on the telephone and on the radio (Figure 13).[4] As one skipper told me 'If you are trawling you *always* have to be thinking about where the prawns are and how to get them'. As their gear was always moving, skippers had to constantly assess where and when they could find prawns, and use every means at their disposal to do this. They were constantly interpreting small clues from their fishing gear and from the actions of other fishermen. They sorted through their accumulated experience to try and understand the changing effect of tide and light. They watched the depth sounder and chartplotter carefully, and spent a great deal of time speaking to others. As Povinelli describes for the Belyuen, there is a

Figure 13  Skipper on the phone while carefully watching the GPS chartplotter.

'constant querying of why an event occurred ... local people's strategy is to note all events, comment on their possible significance ... and then wait and see if some connection develops' (1993: 32).

'The first tow of the day is a sentinel, and you have to get it right in order to have a really good day', explained Alasdair. While an experienced and reliable crew member might be trusted to take the boat from the harbour to the place of the first tow, the skipper almost always took the first tow himself while the crew went back to sleep. The first tow was a time for observation, reflection and discussion of the weather, the engine, the trawl, the actions of other fishing boats and, most importantly, the possibilities for a successful day's fishing. Skippers took the opportunity to check in with the other boats around them, to get the news from the previous night (who landed how much and where) and the morning (where others were fishing compared to the day before, and what this might mean about the relative performance of prawn grounds yesterday). This is the time of day that Wullie would be 'at the Peak' and chatting away on the radio to the other skippers around him. Alone in the wheelhouse with the sun rising, at this time of day skippers also talked just to keep each other company, until it was time to 'go put the kettle on' and have yet another cup of tea. A few hours later, they woke the crew, ate breakfast, and then net was hauled up, emptied and re-set – a clattery, complicated and potentially dangerous process which took at least half an hour.

Once the catch was on the deck, the skipper immediately tried to assess how much they had caught and how successful the tow had been. They needed to make an immediate decision about where to trawl next, taking into account both their own catch and what they had learned during their first round of morning conversations. Skippers' reactions to the results of their first tow could range from giddy delight to a mood dark enough to silence the chattiest crew and make them creep gingerly through the wheelhouse. On boats with two or three crew, skippers would often assist in sorting through the catch, but this could also affect their ability to steer the boat and strategise about where to go next. If the catch was particularly good, they wanted to determine why, and do everything they could to replicate that success. If the catch was poor, they tried to determine if the problem was with their own fishing gear, or if everyone in the area had the same problem. Skippers constantly used all their social connections to try and evaluate the productivity of fishing grounds.

After the catch from the first tow was assessed the phone really started ringing. Many skippers spent the next hour on the phone rigorously comparing catches and speculating where the best and worst catches could be found, and why. I kept track of this process one morning and, by 9 a.m., the skipper of the boat I worked on had gathered information on catches and sea conditions directly from ten boats and indirectly from about ten others, all from different (though nearby) ports along the coast. This information covered a 60-mile stretch of coastline, and was from enough sources that he could cross-reference to ensure it was reasonably accurate. That same morning, there was a long north-west sea swell running. When I mentioned this, the skipper absent-mindedly replied, 'Yes, no one can figure out where it is coming from'. I was taken aback as we were the only ones on the boat. Yet we were part of a workplace spread out across the sea's surface, and the fishing fleet was a 'community of practice' integral to the skills of the individual trawler skipper (Pálsson 1994).

All fishing boats carried a VHF radio, usually tuned to the channel fishing skippers used for collective discussion, which everyone else on that channel could hear. Skippers could switch to another channel, but it was understood that everyone would listen in on all radio conversations, no matter what channel they were held on. The VHF radio was a place for raising general complaints or indirectly broadcasting information to other skippers. It was a common way to air complaints about seafood buyers. One particularly religious skipper read a bible passage on the VHF at 10 a.m. every morning that he fished. Mobile phones were more private – although skippers complained bitterly about other skippers they suspected of using a mobile phone scanner to listen in on conversations. News about the best catches were shared only by text message.

It was not simply the activity of fishing, but the material results of that activity that mattered desperately to these skippers and made the difference between a good and a bad day – similar to the need for fishers in the Roviana Lagoon to be 'mana' (Lauer and Aswani 2009: 324). The catch was initially measured in the crew's first count of how many baskets of 'bulk' were caught in the tow, information that was immediately shared with the skipper's close allies. Once the crew sorted through the catch, the number of baskets of each size of prawns and the number of stones[5] of small prawn 'tails' were carefully tallied (Figures 14 and 15). Masters of mental

Figure 14 Sorting the catch or 'picking prawns'. Seaweed and unwanted organisms are pushed over the side of the boat through the small holes in the shelter. Prawns are then sorted into different baskets according to size and the smallest are 'tailed'.

arithmetic, skippers would then convert that volume into weight and multiply by price to get an approximate value. Even after a long absence, when I encountered a fisherman in the grocery store or on the pier and inquired how they were doing, their reply of 'poor, poor' or 'not too bad' did not refer to themselves or their families, but to the state of their catches. I have no doubt that participating in a commercial, competitive single-species fishery did influence this constant emphasis on the results of their fishing. Yet the fact that both Povinelli (1993) and Lauer and Aswani (2009) report a similar focus on the results of subsistence hunting and fishing activities indicates that the material result of activities is critically important across a wide variety of human activity. What is different is that while Belyuen Aboriginals and people living around the Roviana lagoon emphasised *what* they caught, Scottish commercial fishermen emphasised the *value* of what they caught. The implications of this focus on value are explored in Chapters 5 and 6.

The carefully-pitched banter between skippers continued through the day, and it would not be unusual for skippers to speak to each other four or five times a day. On board the *Iris*, the skipper James spent the entire day speaking on the telephone or radio. As I sat in the wheelhouse after shooting the net in the morning, I realised I would have to plan ahead and jump in with my questions during any gaps between the continuous stream of radio and mobile phone calls. Nonetheless, James was nostalgic about a time when 'everyone spoke to each other' in the 1970s

Figure 15  The results of one tow sorted into baskets of large
and medium prawns and tails.

and 1980s. He explained, 'It was more fun then. There was a lot more communication on the radio. It was a much more interesting job, better craic! There's certain
ones, now, that will speak all right. But some, you won't hear from them for a week,
until their catches are poor. Then, they will call you wondering how you are doing!'
Considering how much I had seen skippers talking to each other, I was astonished
that James considered this level of communication to be impoverished. 'Why don't
people speak as much now?' I asked James. 'Everyone's worried that someone will
get a prawn or two more than them', he replied. James felt that the pressure of competition had ruined the sociability of being at sea.

Skippers were part of a 'community of practice', but it was also a competitive
community which included many members who were calculating how to gain the
most information they could while revealing the least to others. One new crew
member told me about the complete concentration his skipper had on this task:

The skipper was constantly gathering information. During the day, it was by
phone. If he wasn't ringing some other boat, they were ringing him. The mobile

phone played this damn song really loudly, and you would hear the ringing over the whole boat. You would hear the song in your head even when it wasn't ringing, that's how much it went off. I would hear it in my sleep!

If someone rang him, it was usually because they were trying to get information from him. So first thing, he would immediately ask them how they were doing. If there was going to be an exchange of information then he wanted to be getting his fair share.

The same skipper would often speak to the skipper of the boat I worked on. One day I woke up from my nap to find my skipper irritated and muttering. Frustration mixed with dry humour as he reported that:

> Graeme called with 20 questions, 'How many prawns do you have? What are their names? What are their shoe sizes?' Then he says, 'Oh! Call waiting! Sorry I've got to get that!' And he hangs up without sharing anything!
>
> I will have to remind him that it is a two-way street. For him it is all about sharing when you are doing poorly, then he tends to clam up if he is doing well. I'm irritated but I'm trying not to be.

This feverish gathering of information only took place among a limited group of fishermen: in this case the skippers of small prawn trawlers, who shared a common activity, purpose and grounds. Only on rare occasions did prawn trawler skippers speak to the skippers of prawn creel boats, even those from the same village. In contrast, trawler skippers who had never met could spend significant amounts of time speaking to each other, and in many cases might know each other for years by radio before actually meeting in person.

In Chapter 1, James explained that the only way to have a 'proper look' at ground was to 'tow it'. However the information gained through tows was always put in the context of observation, discussion and analysis of everyone else's tows: human labour was 'collectivised' and took place in 'populated environments' (Reed 1996: 124) characterized by friendship, mutual aid, frustration, endless speculation, scrutiny and lies. Place names arose from the discussions that took place in and about these populated environments.

## Naming places

A significant part of the constant communication among trawler skippers was an intense scrutiny and discussion of each other's actions in relation to places in fishing grounds:

> Graeme keeps calling me. He is having a canary because he doesn't know what Ruaridh is doing. Two days in a row now, Ruaridh has been up to the Caol Mor in the morning, and back to the Crowlin in the evening.
>
> It must be working because he has done it two days in a row. And it's on the ebb [tide] he is at the Crowlin, and that has got John going too because he thinks that the Crowlin is no good on the ebb. Maybe I will nip by later this evening to see what Ruaridh is landing.

The Crowlin and the Caol Mor are both 'tows': places named because trawling there is known to be productive. Ruaridh was a well-established fisherman who Graeme, John and this skipper all respected and spoke to on a regular basis. The definitive answer to the other skippers' questions was how many and what size of prawns Ruaridh was actually landing – information which he evidently was not sharing. This would be determined through a deliberately casual and friendly visit that evening, a visit that would no doubt be further discussed and analysed.

In these conversations, there was a constant balance between observation, discussion, collaboration and deception. Information about dangerous hazards on the seafloor was regularly shared by skippers, but they also might report a particularly good fishing spot as a hazard to keep others away. I asked one skipper what he would do if he got an exceptionally good catch: 'Well, I would get on the radio and tell lies, and then I would call Graeme and tell him the truth. But people would be able to see you working back and forth in one place, and eventually they could tell.' The shared conditions for satisfying the intentions of prawn trawler skippers meant that they interacted their environment in similar ways, and talked about it constantly. All of these conversations were rich with place names whose location and meanings were developed by trawler skippers themselves. The Crowlin and the Caol Mor tows are good examples: both are also names of nearby officially recognised geographic features (the Crowlin Islands and the Caol Mor narrows and the Crowlin Islands between the islands of Raasay and Scalpay). However the usage of these names by trawler skippers was quite distinct from the official features the names were taken from – instead they referred to the tows that trawler skippers had developed nearby.

I identified over 50 names for sea-places used over approximately 30 miles of the Scottish coast around the Inner Sound. I have chosen just a few to discuss in this chapter. None of these places are readily marked by islands, rocks or other terrestrial features. Such names are a feature of other fisheries seascapes. In northern Canada, anthropologist Martina Tyrrell describes how 'Arviarmiut talk endlessly about the sea' (2006: 232) and 'through long-term use and habitation the sea becomes filled with meaningful named places that are a part of the ongoing conversations among Arviarmiut' (2006: 225). However the Arviat names refer only to immediately visible features such as rocks, sandbanks and islands. Writing about the ring-net herring fishery in Scotland, historian Angus Martin produced pages of place names at sea and maps of them around the Mull of Kintyre in southern Scotland (1981: 244–252). He hypothesised that 'the process of naming was probably advanced ... by the fishermen's unfailing curiosity to know where a successful crew had hauled a catch. Thus: "Where did ye get them last night?" – "Oh, MacNair's Tree", or "The Flat Rock", or "South o' the Deer Shed"' (Martin 1981: 140). Martin's explanation links the themes I have explored: the sociable work practises and conversations involved in developing productive grounds.

Marx described language as 'practical, real consciousness' (1998 [1845]), and his work in this area was developed by Valentin Volosinov and Lev Vygotsky and summarised more recently by linguist Marnie Holborow (2006) and Ingold (2002a). Holborow explains that language '*arises* from the social demands and needs of the material world and also, through human cooperation and activity, *contributes* to the transformation of that world' (2006: 6). This is a fairly precise description of the ways that place names arose out of the practical activity of working collectively to develop the affordances of fishing grounds, and are an important tool in the process of being able to discuss this work and carry it out. These place names mark what is important and notable in an environment shared by a group of people as they seek common affordances, and allow them to work collaboratively in these places (Patterson 2009: 82–83, 168–169).

This account of how places acquire names through the development and discussion of their affordances is in contrast to that of Chris Tilley. In his account, names 'transform the sheerly physical and geographical into something that is historically and socially experienced'. 'Without a name', Tilley continues, there is only 'a raw void, a natural environment' (1994: 18). Names relate to their environment as a 'description' and 'create landscapes' (Tilley 1994: 19). In the labour-centred and Marxist account I have explored here, place names are developed haphazardly but consistently in the process of working collectively in an environment, developing its affordances and talking about it. While an affordance could possibly be developed by an individual, a name for a place where that affordance could be found was only necessary if the place was discussed and shared. Names emerge from the need to carry on a conversation about these places, to scrutinise and discuss the actions of others in them, and to gather as much information as possible to inform one's own decisions in relation to the environment. They emerge through radio and telephone conversations that start before the sun comes up and continue long into the night.

There is only a very small and slippery distance between a conversation, a story and a name that 'sticks'. In James' account, the naming of Wullie's Peak was part of a conversational working story that was picked up and repeated by enough other skippers at the time that it stuck. I experienced this transition once myself. I was speaking to a historian from Mallaig about place names at sea when he informed me that 'Mallaig men' all call Camustianavaig 'Bicycle Bay' because that is where pelagic skipper James Manson once caught a brand-new bicycle in the boat's net. I suddenly remembered Alasdair telling me a story months earlier about catching a brand-new bicycle in the net in that bay while he worked for that skipper. He no longer worked in that fishery, and was probably unaware that his experience, that story, had become a name that circulated among the pelagic fishermen of Mallaig. Experiences were discussed, stories were told, and the most memorable, amusing and resonant stories were repeated in enough conversations to name the places that they featured.

Naming is also a form of appropriation essential to the mobile activities of trawler (previously, ring-net) skippers, a way of maintaining their presence in and connection to a place from which they were usually physically absent. The easy way in which Graeme, Ruaridh, John and Alasdair discussed the features of the Caol Mor and the Crowlin clearly showed that they regarded these places as 'their' grounds, no matter where else they happened to be – a connection I will discuss in the next section.

## People and places

Places were named through the collective and conversational process of developing fishing grounds, and were also intimately connected to individuals and their subjectivities. The Peak became Wullie's through his work there, and through the 'good craic' and playful radio conversations he shared with other trawl skippers working in the area. The fact that this peak was Wullie's also told you something about the man: in a community of trawler skippers in which risk-taking was often glorified he was a man of habit, the sort of man who would take time 'to speak' because he wasn't worried 'that you would get a prawn or two more than him'. No doubt he was teased about being at the Peak '*every* morning!', but despite that he persisted for 15 years. That was enough for the place to be named after him and for him to be remembered in this place. Thus part of the 'sediment of relatedness' (Povinelli 1993: 137) that is generated through working in an environment are names that stick to places that reflect and reinforce individual subjectivities through collective discussions.

Subjectivity describes the complex relationship between people's inner states and their lived experience (Kleinman and Fitz-Henry 2007), and in this case, their experience of working in and transforming places. Places do not just reflect persons, but people also incorporate significant places into their subjectivities. This was the case for the Wall of Death, a well-known tow in the Back of Kyle located on a steep, rocky bank. The name emphasised the difficulty of towing there, an achievement that was a source of pride for some skippers. The Wall of Death was named for a popular Scottish fairground attraction where motorcyclists ride around the inside of a bowl which rises to perfectly vertical walls, while the audience looks down on them from above. As skipper 'Buckie' John described, it took effort and skill to successfully trawl on hard and rocky 'edges' like the Wall of Death. You had to use a heavy hopper net (Figure 10), you needed to tow a little faster to keep the gear lifting up off the ground so it would not catch on boulders, and you had to pay very close and constant attention to the depth sounder to stay at the right depth and be ready to head down the bank as soon as you saw the red thickening on the screen. You had to keep a sharp watch for floats marking creels set on the seafloor, and the bank was steep enough that in your three-dimensional imagining of the precise location of the trawl net on the seafloor (Chapter 4), you had to account for the fact that your net would be sliding down the side of the bank as you towed it. You also had to be prepared to mend the damage to your net that might result from working in such a place. Not everyone had the patience, attention, or wished to take these risks. When we trawled at the Wall of Death, 'Buckie' John would usually tell me stories about more experienced trawler skippers who had given up trying to tow there. One man 'tried to follow us on the Wall of Death with his big heavy gear, and he got stuck right away', and the other 'got a boulder and stopped towing on the Wall of Death. He got so many fasteners [snags] he would have to haul his net back two, three times in a tow'. In contrast, John seemed to enjoy and even relish the challenge.

When I asked James 'the *Iris*' about how the Wall of Death was named, he told me:

> Murdo, 'Loopy,' he might have christened the Wall of Death. He would tow up there and was always blootering his nets. After one time too many he said 'that place is just the wall of death!' and the name stuck. That would have been the 1980s sometime.

'Loopy's' frustrated comment, possibly over the radio, possibly on the pier, was repeated by other trawler skippers in the area with enough frequency and amusement that it stuck.

Skipper Alasdair had worked on the west and east coasts of Scotland and explained that 'You'll find these crazy names for tows all over, and they are all like that. Everyone knows them. There are probably several Walls of Death around Scotland'. For example, there is another Wall of Death 'at the back of Rum',[6] an island south of Skye. The various Walls of Death shared some of the same characteristics: they were rocky and difficult to work and therefore required particular skills and attention. Those who made the effort to work there took special pride in their achievement. These places were marked and remembered by the particular experience of working in them, and the ability to work there marked a particular kind of person. Many of the place names given to tows by fishermen reflect, celebrate and lament the labour and difficulty of working them. Alasdair told me how 'he had once spent a whole evening discussing the frightening names that fishermen give to places, and re-naming them with nice names like Primrose Valley and Sunny Delight'. This amusing exercise in the pub only reinforced the fact that such names never stuck because they did not resonate through the experiences and subjectivities of different skippers, repeated again and again as an accurate or amusing description of what it was like to work there.

In Chapter 1, trawler skipper Ruaridh described the transformation of previously inaccessible areas of the seafloor into prawn grounds with the development and use of hopper nets, and it was precisely places like the Wall of Death that were created through the process of 'opening up new ground' with these new techniques. As Retsikas put it, the relationships between places and persons directly reflects the development of social relations in the course of transforming a location, in this case the Wall of Death, into productive prawn grounds (2007). Within these social contexts it is individuals that do this work of transformation, and thus the names and places that arise through this process also reflect the development of individual subjectivities.

## Places are not just local

Places were created by work that also connected them to other places and new forms of social, economic and political organisation. The naming of Wullie's Peak was directly linked to the establishment of a fleet of small prawn trawlers based around Gairloch and Skye, which only arose with the opening of a new market for prawns and new local capital investment in fishing boats (see Chapter 5). Legislative change was required as well: trawling had been banned in waters less than three miles from shore since the 1800s, but in 1984 the rapidly expanding international market for prawns persuaded the UK parliament to abolish this restriction in the new *Inshore Fisheries Act (1984)*. The Wall of Death, the Crowlin and the Caol Mor are all inside this previously banned area. Many trawlers did work in the banned area, but the furtiveness required to fish illegally meant that they just stayed 'in the clean'. After 1984, the number of small prawn trawlers around the Inner Sound increased significantly, as did the time that people spent working, or attempting to work, places like the Wall of Death, the Crowlin and the Caol Mor. Shifting external political and economic relations regulated the access that people had to these places and the punishment or rewards they could expect for developing their affordances.

Places could also incorporate global social and military history, for example, 'The Burma', a tow located north of Wullie's Peak. James 'the *Iris*' chuckled as he told me: 'they called it The Burma because it was as flat as a pancake and you were always picking up boulders! It was named because of the British prisoners of war in World War II, they had to build a road.' Was there anyone from Skye who was imprisoned in Burma? I asked. 'There was one', James said, suddenly somber, 'but he's been dead 30 years now'. Like Wullie's Peak, the naming of The Burma was a kind of shared joke amongst trawlermen, and you could tell from the way that 'flat as a pancake and always picking up boulders!' rolled off James' tongue that it was a saying he had repeated many times. The naming and discussion of The Burma was good craic. It was not hard to imagine James, or maybe Wullie on the radio: 'Ach, I'm in The Burma picking up boulders again.' James' description of The Burma had a cruel but humourous resonance for trawler skippers. Picking up a boulder in your net was one of the most frustrating and destructive mishaps for a trawler. The boulder could be too heavy to winch to the surface, making it very difficult to recover your expensive net. If you were able to bring the boulder to the surface, the process of trying to empty it out of the net was difficult and dangerous. Once you managed to get rid of the boulder, your net would be damaged, whatever you had caught would be completely pulverised and worthless, and the whole day was likely wasted. The irony was that a flat area is the last place you would expect to pick up a boulder – they were usually caught on steep, rocky banks. A fishing ground that was 'flat as a pancake and you were always picking up boulders' would be a special kind of unexpected purgatory.

The Burma reflects the international work experience of many people living in the Highlands, usually either as soldiers or working on cargo ships. It is one of a peculiar diaspora of places which seem to be named for their association with the Second World War campaign in Burma, including a hiking path near Inverarish on the island of Raasay (Figure 16), a disused section of railway near Claremorris, Ireland, a mountain-biking trail near Aviemore, Scotland, a street in Norwich, England, a small town in Western Australia, and a road leading to Jerusalem.[7] These places are part of a diaspora that does not share blood or origins, but is identified with a common human experience. Thousands of people from around the

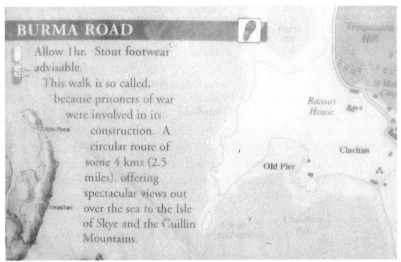

Figure 16  Signs for the Burma Road hiking trail on the island of Raasay.

world were forced to build the Burma Road and the experience was so seared into social memory that the Burma Road now extends across at least four more countries. There is an additional wrinkle: the Burma Roads of Aviemore and Raasay were reputedly built by German prisoners of war imprisoned in these locations by the British 40 years earlier in the First World War (Draper and Draper 2005: 79, Figure 16). I do not know how or why these paths were re-named after the Second World War, but their naming also recognises the pain of captive German soldiers – a recognition by the people of Raasay and Aviemore of the Burma Road burning in their midst.

'What was The Burma called before the Second World War?' I asked. James replied, 'Before World War II, it would only have been Fleetwood men out there – people from here didn't have the boats to go up there'. Before the Second World War, only large company-owned whitefish trawlers from Fleetwood (near Liverpool in England) would have worked in the exposed waters north of Skye in the area now known as The Burma. At that time, people from Skye would have been fishing for herring or lobsters or whitefish closer to the shore on much smaller and less expensive boats. None would have had the engine power to tow a trawl net and it was only for trawlers that the particular characteristics of The Burma's seafloor would have held such ironic resonance. Hence there was a sharp break in how the geographic location now known as the Burma was understood and experienced. It was only when a Scottish prawn trawler fleet was developed and began working north of Skye in the 1960s and 1970s that The Burma, as it is presently recognised, emerged out of skippers' ambling radio conversations.

Gordillo argues that 'places are eminently *relations* between social actors and that these relations dissolve these places' appearance of fixity' (2004: 6), a far cry from Tilley's description of place names as culturally significant descriptions of the raw material of the landscape. I have described places emerging through the labour of developing their affordances, the conversations that take place during this process, the way in which these conversations are incorporated into individual subjectivities and repeated, and the political and economic frameworks that regulate access to a place and make its affordances more or less desirable. These are not just local relations: searing events of social global history are also incorporated into people's experience, subjectivities and conversations, and can become part of how people think and talk about a particular place. In the next section I will discuss what happens to these relations when the affordances of places change.

## When affordances change

I have shown how places are created through the development of their affordances. But what happens to places when their affordances change due to environmental changes, or changes in human economic and social organisation that affect the affordances people seek? The places I have described so far were created quite recently, but humans have found their livelihoods at sea and on the shores of the Inner Sound for at least 7,000 years (Hardy and Wickham-Jones 2002). In this section I will examine these processes of transition: first, how shifting fishing and military practises affected the former Sound of Music tow, and second, the consequences of environmental and social change.

While the names of many tows emphasise the labour, difficulty and danger of working them, the Sound of Music was an exception. James 'the *Iris*' smiled as he remembered:

> The Sound of Music was all deep water, 100 fathoms, with a size of prawns! Big prawns! It was a circuit, you would go round and round it. Used to be you could tow right from the Raasay light to Applecross, between the Crowlin and the range terminal building.
>
> It's full of creels now but it never used to be. Twelve, fourteen year ago we were all at it. There was a time you could get at it but then the creels came in, it was just the way of it.

James remembered the Sound of Music, but it was not a place name used by skippers in 2006–2007. Trawler skippers can no longer work there. The Sound of Music would have been to the north of what is now known as the Caol Mor tow, and was immediately to the south of the closed area of the BUTEC torpedo range.[8] It was not until I sat down to match up my notes from speaking to James with a chart of the Inner Sound that I realised that I had been in the same location as the Sound of Music, several times, with working fishermen, and had never heard them use the term. The area once known by trawler skippers as the Sound of Music is now reserved exclusively for creel fishing, and contains fishing gear from at least ten creel boats from Applecross and Kyleakin. This deep water is a desirable and contested ground. It is adjacent to the BUTEC range, which purportedly contained huge 'government prawns'. Here, the creels were laid so closely that everyone had to shoot their fleets north–south, and there was virtually no room to move them. This transformation occurred after the introduction of the creel-only buffer zone around the torpedo range in the 1970s, and the rapid expansion of the prawn creel fleet (distinct from the trawler fleet) after the development of the live prawn market and new techniques for export in the 1980s (Chapter 5). The distinct working practises and social networks of creel boats and trawlers mean that once trawlers were unable to fish in this area, it ceased to be the Sound of Music.

I should emphasise that prawn trawler and prawn creel fishermen are often from the same villages, tie their boats up to the same piers, and drink in the same pubs. Many people have work experience in both sectors of the industry. The differences in their relationships to place are entirely due to the different labour processes and social relations that creel and trawl fishing required.

Creel boat fishing required constant work on deck and on your feet which meant there was no time for the ambling radio or telephone discussions of trawler skippers (Figure 17). Most trawler skipper conversations revolved around trawler catches on trawler grounds, and information from creel boats was mostly irrelevant to their work. The result was that trawler skippers would almost always speak to other trawler skippers when at sea. If trawler and creel skippers spoke to each other at sea it was usually a short and often tense conversation to resolve a particular dispute, even if they regularly worked alongside each other.

Figure 17  A skipper and crew at work on the deck of a creel boat.

Trawler crews lived on their boats for periods of time[9] and often travelled from port to port. For example, small trawlers working out of Kyle of Lochalsh would also regularly berth in Portree, Gairloch, Rona, Portnalong and Isle Oronsay. Although these places are no more than 50 miles apart, it meant that trawler skippers and crew form part of an extended network of fishers from different ports that regularly saw and spoke to each other. A few trawlers would travel down to Fort William to cross the Caledonian Canal and work out of Lossiemouth or Buckie on the Moray Firth, and a few would travel further north to Gairloch and Lochinver. Rafted up on the pier at night, trawler crews would often visit each other on their boats, swapping stories that traced detailed histories and geographies of particular boats or skippers encountered in ports up and down the coast in such intricate detail that I could not keep up. Information about near and distant places was also exchanged through old Decca charts, or a USB memory stick. The result was that trawler skippers were often familiar with the coast and fishing fleets of large portions of both the east and west coasts.

Although in the 1960s and 1970s creel boats would travel up and down the coast to fish, this is now very rare. Prawn creel boats now usually start and end each day in their home port, so their fishing-related social networks are generally based in their home port. Instead of speaking to each other at sea or socialising on their boats, creel boat crews will speak to each other on the pier, or in the pub after work, or occasionally at meetings of fishing associations. The result is that creel boat crew socialise and speak to other creel boat crew from their home port far more than trawler crew, and trawler skippers often spend far more time speaking to trawler skippers from other ports than they would to the creel boat crew with whom they shared a pier.

While some creel boat crew characterised trawlermen as 'social misfits', and others saw trawling as 'not a life', trawlermen often did not recognise creel boat crew as being proper fishermen and described creel fishing as 'a dead boring job'. The divisions between these groups were reflected in their distinctive views of the environment and what constituted a proper relationship to it; each saw their own activity as contributing to its productivity, and the other group's activity as diminishing it (Chapter 1). These divisions were matched by a scrutiny of outsiders like me and a discussion of who we were allied with: after spending a few days working on a local trawler I went to a pub that was frequented by creel boat crew. 'Are you going to put a [trawl] winch on the back of your yacht?' one creel boat skipper teased. 'You'll be doing some inshore trawling on your yacht tomorrow, will you?' said another. I had not told them where I had been, and I had been working on a trawler out of a different port, but word travelled quickly and they wanted to test where my allegiances lay.

The distinct working practises and social networks of creel boat crew and trawler crew led to James' fondly remembered the Sound of Music tow not being recognised at all by creel boat crew. Some creel boat skippers argued vehemently against the very existence of such places. 'There are no such thing as recognised tows, they are always changing!' said one creel boat skipper angrily in the pub one evening. 'What does a "tow" mean? Any piece of ground you have trawled once? And how is anyone else to know?' Another creel boat skipper worried about setting his creels near the Crowlin because 'there is an aggressive attitude [from trawlers] that we shouldn't be there, that there are established tows. But there is no such thing, legally! They want to get in by 25–30 fathoms of water! They keep talking about some whiting tow from the 1970s!' This creel boat skipper found it patently absurd that a tow fished for whiting in the early 1970s could mean anything to anyone today. In contrast, experienced trawler skippers not only knew the tows but the boats that had originally worked them – for example, the now derelict *Flowing Stream*, formerly the *Heritage*, which until 2009 was slowly sinking at the Kyleakin fishing pier. The Whiting Tow was the same place trawler skipper Ruaridh 'the *Accord*' described in Chapter 1 as the first place he began trawling in the Inner Sound.[10] Not only were the working and conversational practises of creel fishermen different, but the use of creel gear did not require the naming practises used by trawlers. Creel fishermen leave their fishing gear at sea, with individually marked buoys at the surface of the water (Figure 18). Thus the marker-buoys of creel fishermen became a geographic reference that was a visible part of the seascape, particularly in the busy areas where fleets of creels could not be moved very often. Such buoys also became a visual reference for trawler skippers, marking the top of a bank or the edge of a tow. When creel gear is not moved very often, there is less need for the kind of collaborative speculation and

Figure 18  Creel buoys on the surface. Each buoy marks one end of a fleet of up to
100 creels on the seafloor below.

assessment of grounds that trawlers constantly engaged in, and which reinforced
and constantly generated new place names.

James remembered the Sound of Music as an idyllic place to trawl in, but for
creel boat crew in 2006–2007 the experience of working this ground was quite different. With more boats entering the fishery and existing boats buying more creels,
space was at a premium. 'I would say that it is chaos, that is the best word for it', said
one creel boat skipper. Another switched to fishing for crabs, explaining 'There's
no room. It does my head in. You move it [your fleet of creels] and someone is in
behind you'. If fleets of creels are set too close together on the seafloor they can
become tangled, particularly if there is a storm. If two fleets of 100 creels with half
a mile of rope between them become tangled 150 metres away on the seafloor, sorting out the problem was a dangerous headache (Figure 19). The creels would be
hauled up to the surface in a tangle, which was usually under a terrific strain. If a
piece of rope caught your body while you were untangling it, it could pull you into
the water and down to the seafloor. It might be necessary to cut your line or someone else's line, and then it would need to be tied back together again – unless of
course you wanted to send a clear message to the other fisherman by leaving him to
find and fix the cut line himself. In addition to the problems with tangled gear, the
overcrowding of creel grounds was a source of anxiety to concerned creel skippers
who wanted to be able to move their gear and give the ground 'a rest'.

The Sound of Music now exists only in the memory of older trawl skippers, and
this location is now experienced as a very different place by the creel boat crew

Figure 19  A creel fleet pulled to the surface with the rope connecting
it to other creels tangled.

who work there. There continued to be a constant low-level battle between creel boats and trawlers at the southern edge of the old Sound of Music. As one creel boat skipper explained:

The last three years what we have done is cut the tow in half. Last week they snuck in. The trawlers were able to get in here because even though we've blocked this ground, last week we left a wee gap between here and the Crowlin boys. We keep creeping further and further south, into deeper and deeper water. I use my old creels down here, just in case!

Things have changed. Five years ago, I wouldn't have gotten my creels in here, they would have been demolished by the trawlers. What's happening here – it is not that we are more militant – but who are they to tell us to get off the ground? There is no commercial, ethical, moral, or environmental argument you can use to support that! My father, my grandfather fished here.

I remember an east coast trawlerman from Burghead telling another local fisherman where to put his creels. I was just next to him and I could look ashore and see the school ground where my son was. And here is a man who has destroyed his own fishing ground, and now he has come over here telling us what to do!

The concrete struggles between social groups over who will access fishing grounds means that places change, and are replaced. Working history is evoked by both sides in the emotive battle to maintain access to grounds and to transform them into one's own worked-in place. This contested history is meaningful because it draws on the affordances people have developed to survive and provide for themselves in the past, and the kinds of persons and places formed through this process. As Povinelli noted, 'place holds memory insofar as its use is remembered. Further, memories are seen as a product of work like other products' (1993: 146).

The Sound of Music was created with the growth of markets for trawl-caught 'fresh' or tailed prawns and the growth of a fishing fleet to catch them. The militarisation of the local sea area and the development of the creel-caught 'live' prawn market led to the loss of the Sound of Music, and to this a location becoming a different place. Creel fishing entailed much less chatty working practices and the pressure from a large number of creel boats working in the area have made working this ground a much more stressful experience. James remembers when this place was the Sound of Music, but that is not a name that resonates through the experience of the fishermen working there today – or is even remembered by them.

## 'The lochs were teeming with fish then'

Places changed due to changing state military practices, market demands and fishing techniques, and they also changed according to ecology, social organisation and language. I spent ten months working on fishing boats and asking people about place names at sea before someone finally told me about the existence of a whole earlier set of places which were no longer in use. John Angus had first gone to sea on cargo ships in 1949, and then returned to become one of the pioneers of the prawn creel fishery in the 1960s. In the early 1970s he had been one of the first in the area to convert to the trawl, and he fished until he retired in 1998. He and his wife warmly welcomed me into their home, and plied me with tea and biscuits. We talked for hours, enjoying each other's company. But when I asked him about the origins of place names such as the Wall of Death, he bristled, and said sharply: 'That was the east coast boats. They made those names up because they couldn't say the Gaelic ones. They couldn't say Caol Rona, so they just called it the Blind Sound.' The rebuke was sharp enough that I dropped the subject.

The next week I was in the bar of the Pier Hotel with Calum and Rab after we returned from checking the salmon net. We had been doing this for over a month, but it was only now that Calum told me about the Gaelic sea-place Tobair na Or, which we had passed every day. It was 'in the deep water off the north head of Portree harbour. You would go out there to fish for haddies on sma' lines [a basket of line and hooks], in a wee open boat. You would leave the lines out there overnight, and come back for them in the morning'. Notebook in hand, I asked Calum how to spell the name of that place. He laughed out loud at the absurdity of my request. I asked him what the words meant, and he shook his head and shrugged. Still chuckling, Calum consulted Finley the bartender, who had more Gaelic.

Finley declared a '*tobair*' to be a well, but he had to get out his Gaelic phrasebook from behind the bar to decide how to spell it. We decided '*òr*' must mean gold, and everyone agreed that 'Well of Gold' sounded like a feasible name for a good fishing place. Finley also advised that it would be said Tobair an Òr, not Tobair na Òr. By this time, everyone in the bar became involved in the speculation. Perhaps òr was in fact òrd, a hammer, as one of the points of land at the harbour mouth was often called 'the hammer'. Perhaps there was a well on the shore it was named after. Calum's older brother Donald was quizzed when he came in, but he couldn't remember any more details. Donald did tell me about another place called 'Ploc an As', on the opposite shore of Portree harbour, about 200 yards from the flagpole. You would go there to catch trout and grilse'. Again, no one was sure what Ploc an As meant, or how to spell it.

I asked Bodach about these sea-places. He was a fluent Gaelic speaker whose father and uncle actively participated in the open-boat handline fishery in Portree, very likely at the Ploc an As and Tobair an Or. Bodach took an interest in history and the Gaelic language and occasionally went fishing himself, but he said that he had never heard of the existence of such names, never.

I travelled down the coast to see Johnny 'Beag'[11] in Braes. Sitting out in front of his house on a sunny afternoon, binoculars in hand, he could see the whole sweep of the sea from Loch Sligachan, and across to Raasay and through the Caol Mor to the Crowlins. He had lived in this house for 86 years. Most of his working life had been spent as a lorry driver, but he had always found time to fish. He told me that when he was a boy:

> There were loads of fish, years ago, there was mackerel, saithe, haddies – there is not a haddie to be found round this area now – cod, and pollock, and flatfish, skate, flounder, all that, there was loads and loads, the lochs were teeming with fish then …
>
> Loch Sligachan was famous for herring, it was a small, small herring but it was very, very tasty, the Loch Sligachan herring was very tasty, and then further, Camustianavaig Bay, and even in that Balamenach Bay,[12] that was a bigger class of herring, but och, the place was teeming with herring, even when I was a youngster.

I asked him if he liked eating fish, and Johnny answered, with relish: 'I like a good mackerel. There's nothing like it in my way of thinking.' When I told him I had caught some the other day he suddenly perked up. 'Were they any size?' he asked, suddenly much more interested in our conversation. Not really I said, maybe one was. Johnny sighed and slowed back down as he recounted:

> We used to get them [mackerel], well, around here they were about that size [gestures expansively] and nice and fat! But I just caught three on the line this year, and they were tiny wee things, 6–7 inches long. I just threw them back.
>
> They seemed to come in the west coast of Skye first before, it was usually in the month of August, that's when they used come in here, to this shore, in shoals. But lately, they don't seem to come at all, the past two or three years they have been very, very scarce.

The fish represented more than just food, however, as Johnny 'Beag' explained, they maintained a whole network of social connections:

> It was just traditional to give a fish to a neighbour. If you didn't have a boat, and if you weren't out fishing, you would always get a fish from whoever was out fishing. And very often fish was that plentiful that somebody would come to your house, 'Do you want a fish?' 'Oh no thanks, so and so was here 10 minutes ago with a fish'. You couldn't get rid of the fish! There was nobody to take the fish! It's a different story nowadays.
>
> *Does anyone bring you fish nowadays?*
>
> No. Very, very few. People, young folk don't know how to do fish nowadays, they just go to the supermarkets, it all quick foods and the rest of it they wouldn't know how to do herring. [Pause] It's all different.
>
> *Do you get much fish from the supermarket now, or do you not eat much fish?*
>
> We don't eat much fish at all. The odd ... We've got the local fish merchant in Portree, we get nice fresh fish from them.

When I asked Johnny about the places they would fish, he remembered a few. Apart from the salmon and herring in Loch Sligachan, he told me, 'well, away out there [he pointed], that was the Clarach, that was a Gaelic – I don't know what that meant – and then there was Poll Doine, that was the deep pool away out towards Scalpay, Poll Doine'. The Clarach, he explained, was 'all good for fishing, cod and everything, skate, all types of fish'. At Poll Doine, 'that's where you fished for, well anything of course, but it was noted for haddock'. Would many people these days know these names? I asked 'Well, even I don't know them!' he exclaimed, 'but young folk wouldn't have a clue what I was talking about if I mentioned one of them'.

I continued to ask people about these Gaelic names but only learned a few more. I tried to bringing a chart to the older people I met but of course that never worked, as it was not how these places were located in the first place (Chapter 4, see also Cohen 1987: 123). The few Gaelic places that people told me about only highlighted the vast gaps that existed between them. Not only had the affordances of these places changed drastically, the language used to discuss them had too. Some mainland and Skye fishermen can speak Gaelic, but I only ever heard English radio conversations.[13]

It is not that no one is working in the specific locations which were once described the Clarach, the Poll Doine, the Tobair an Òr/Òrd or the Ploc an As. But their most important affordance, as a place to reliably catch fish, has been lost. Significantly different kinds of work, seeking different affordances, and using different work practices are now carried out there. Without actually going out on a boat with Johnny 'Beag', it is difficult to locate precisely the Clarach and the Poll Doine, but these locations are now most likely considered to be a part of the Caol Mor tow. The Tobair an Òr/Òrd is probably very close to a large salmon farm, and along with the Arche Mhor (a name given to me by another fisherman) is most likely a part of what skipper James described as 'the Circuit', a tow for prawns around the mouth of Portree bay. The Ploc an As is now filled with moorings for yachts and as Donald told me, there wouldn't have been a trout there for years.

In 2006–2007, someone going to catch fish on a handline from Portree would not go to the Tobair an Òr or the Arche Mhor. I was instructed on how to catch fish in Portree on two separate occasions by men who remembered these Gaelic place names and regularly went fishing. First, you took your boat out to the salmon farm and watched the automatic feeding tubes to see which of the ten cages was being fed with food pellets. Then, noting the direction of the tidal current, you tied your boat to the downstream side of that salmon cage. You had to be careful to position your boat far enough away from the cage so that your fishing line did not get hooked on any of the anchor lines for the cages, and you had to be especially careful to avoid the yellow CCTV cable glimmering faintly below. And, as Lachie admonished me in Chapter 1, 'you must work the *whole* ground, up and down', and you had to bring home enough mackerel to share with those who weren't out fishing themselves.

Clausen and Clark (2005) have used the concept of metabolic rift to describe the contemporary 'ocean crisis'. Johnny 'Beag' describes this ocean crisis vividly: he tries to go out fishing, but the fish are 'very, very scarce', no one remembers the places which used to be 'teeming' with fish, and instead of fish being the product of an evening at sea or a neighbourly gift, they must be bought from a merchant. For people who remember the fishing places where there are no longer any fish, these places are not simply in the process of being forgotten, but places whose memory marks a sharp difference between the past and present, and a deep sense of loneliness and loss.

The absence of the fish themselves and changes in fishing markets and techniques have meant that people now seek different affordances from the same locations, which have now become different places. These places may still be half-remembered, but new place names now feature in the conversations about these locations, and fishermen discuss and speculate about new features relevant to the new affordances of these new places. As Dickie explained (Chapter 1), people are 'at the prawns' now 'because everything else ran out'. The history of fishing in the Inner Sound is not just a history of persons contesting access to specific places, but the histories of these places are the histories of constant ecological change (which fishermen have played a role in), the development of different affordances in response to the needs of global seafood markets, and wholesale language and cultural change. As Dickie admonished me, history is important.

## Conclusion: labour and the production of places

The history of places at sea is not just the history of activities conducted in particular locations. The histories of the places created and maintained through work at sea, and the memory of their re-placement, provides a detailed history of the forms of work, social relationships and kinds of persons that have made their livelihoods at sea in the Sound. It draws in the history of the whole development of fishing in Scotland, the destruction of the whitefish and inshore herring stocks, the rise of prawn markets and prawn fishing, the developments of technologies to work and extend human perception into the sea, the acceleration of the international economies of trade in seafood, the participation of people in distant wars, and the replacement of one language and set of economic and social relations with another.

The anthropological literature on place has emphasised that it is associated with the practice of particular activities (Goodwin 1995; Lauer and Aswani 2009) and with movement from one place to another (Amith 2005; Retsikas 2007). I have tried to build upon this literature to show that the creation and naming of places is tied closely to the labour of developing the affordances of places. Activity is important, but it is also closely tied to intentions and results. Movement is also important, but it is the labour of movement and in movement rather than just re-location that I emphasise here. Place names are not descriptions of a location or its features, but emerge from conversations among groups of people about their working experience (which can incorporate global events) in the process of developing and transforming the affordances of a place, and in ways that resonate through their subjectivities. Rather than a location, places are relations (Gordillo 2004), and the same location can become a different place over time or for different groups of people. The emphasis on the specific relations between humans and their environments brings another issue to the fore: the techniques and tools actually used to work in these places and make them productive. In Part II of this book I will turn to the discussion of the techniques for working at sea, extending the body into the sea, and orienting oneself at sea.

## Notes

1  'To land' means to sell to a seafood buyer.
2  James listed nine trawl skippers who had boats working out of Gairloch at that time. Eight were from the east coast (Peterhead, Buckie, Fraserburgh (The Broch), and Avoch (Achie)). One boat was from Gairloch (Fred on the *Stroma*).
3  'Blootering' a net means to seriously damage it on some obstacle.
4  In contrast, the crew tend to spend long hours in factory-like conditions processing the catch. This chapter will primarily focus on skippers. See Chapter 5 for a discussion of the experience of crew.
5  A stone is 14 pounds or about 6.35 kilos.
6  'At the back of' meant the ocean-exposed side of an island.
7  Thanks to Alasdair MacPhail for pointing this out. The road was built by Israeli forces during the 1948 Siege of Jerusalem.
8  The establishment of the BUTEC torpedo range completely closed 130 square miles to fishing, and a buffer zone around it was reserved for creel fishing only. The range is the only part of the sea completely closed to all fishing in Scotland.
9  On the small coastal trawlers I was familiar with, crew usually live on board from two to ten days at a time. The exception were crew from Eastern Europe or the Philippines who lived the boat for the duration of their contract (from 6 to 12 months, Chapter 5).

10 Although he had trawled for many years, Ruaridh had started out as a creel fisherman, and remembered 'losing hundreds of creels in a night to the herring pair trawlers' like the *Heritage* in the area around the Whiting Tow in the late 1970s.

11 Gaelic word meaning 'small'. Pronounced 'bake'.

12 Loch Sligachan, Camustianavaig and Balamenach Bay are within a four-mile stretch of coastline. The fine-grained distinction between herring from different bays was common amongst people of Johnny's generation.

13 Fishermen from the Western Isles are reputed to regularly speak to each other in Gaelic.

# Part II

## Techniques and technologies

I have discussed how places, grounds, people, conversations, social history and markets are linked through the labour of developing affordances. But what, practically, does 'labour' involve? In the next two chapters I will explore this question through a detailed ethnography of the techniques and technologies people used to work at sea.

The next two chapters are structured through an understanding of 'techniques' developed by anthropologist Marcel Mauss, which includes 'technologies' but is not limited to them. Mauss described 'techniques'[1] as 'the whole range of material practises, objects, and skills devised and used by human beings in their interaction with their surroundings and with each other' (Schlanger 1998: 193). Techniques are 'effective' in getting results from the point of view of the practitioner, and 'traditional' in that they are learned, acquired and transmitted from person to person (Mauss 2006 [1935]: 82). Techniques are social, they are 'a tactic for living, thinking, and striving in common: they are above all means and mediums for the production and reproduction of social life' (Schlanger 2006: 20).

In the context of this book, techniques are the specific labour processes people use to understand and develop the affordances of the environments they work in, or to satisfy other intentions. In writing this book, I found this was the most effective way to understand the role of technologies in extending people's bodily perceptions into the sea and orienting themselves within the seascape. Technologies were clearly important, but they could not be separated from an understanding of how people used them, and why.

Mauss included studies of practical techniques in his anthropological writing: he saw them as an essential part of how social life was produced and reproduced. This was in contrast with strands of anthropology that saw their real object of study as 'culture', described as 'the *idea* behind the artifact' (Kroeber and Kluckhorn 1952: 65). Many other anthropologists have since complained that techniques, technics and technology have remained marginal to anthropology (Aporta and Higgs 2005; Bray 2007; Ingold 2000; Lemonnier 1992; Sigaut 2002), which anthropologist Francesca Bray ascribes to an 'antimaterialist aversion' within anthropology (2007: 43). François Sigaut suggests that this problem is not unique to anthropology but is characteristic of the intellectual milieu of societies with 'an élite exempt from at least some manual tasks' (2002: 420). As Ingold concludes, 'it is time to restore technique to its rightful place alongside economy, politics, religion, and kinship as a proper object of social anthropological inquiry' (2000: 322).

Mauss understood techniques much more widely than the present understanding of 'technology', describing his own 'fundamental mistake of thinking that there is technique only when there is an instrument' (2006 [1935]: 82). He considered the techniques for performing particular tasks to be an essential part of humanity's history, and as 'the means ... a society possess to act upon its milieu' (Mauss 2006 [1927]: 52). Techniques include the movements of the body itself, tools used in the process, the interaction between the body and its surroundings, the experience of this process, and how these are integrated into social life and structures more generally.

Methodologically, techniques should be understood in terms of 'the purpose they serve' (Mauss 2006 [1935/1947]: 114), and the wider practices into which they are integrated. In his ethnography of hospital porters, Nigel Rapport describes 'new technologies being brought within the ambit of established relations and practices' (2003: 40). Technology and techniques do not exist separately from people's lives: 'I incorporate these diverse objects into the current of my activity without attending to them *as such* ... if anything links them together, it is only that they are brought into the same current, that of my work' (Ingold 2000: 407). While studies of 'technology' tend to start with an object, an understanding of techniques begins with an understanding of how and why people have developed and integrated objects into their lives through the practice of various techniques.

Apart from a few proponents (Bray 2007; Dobres 1999; Ingold 2000), Mauss' approach to the study of techniques is largely unknown in the Anglo-American world (Schlanger 1998: 192). It is mainly archaeologists, historical anthropologists, and those interested in hunter-gatherer societies who continue to apply his approach. In many cases, the study of techniques has also become narrowly and technically focused on the documentation of *chaînes operatoires* and 'action on matter' (Lemonnier 1992: 2). Unfortunately, most anthropological research on computerised, electronic and 'information' technologies does not draw on this history of the anthropology of techniques,[2] recreating 'the ethnocentric divide which supposedly separates primitive "techniques" and modern "technology"' (Schlanger 1998: 192), a division which Sigaut has described as 'meaningless' and 'poorly informed' (2002: 452). The anthropological literature on 'high technology' has preferred to look at the relationship between humans and technology through models of 'cyborgs', techno-science and consumption. This literature tends to see 'technology' as something qualitatively new, rather than comparatively examining *how* people have pursued their objectives using different techniques in different times, places and societies. Mauss' focus on technique offers a method to overcome the artificial barrier often placed between 'old' and 'new' technology.

Material culture studies is the other main branch of anthropological inquiry into technology. It has been criticised by Bray for its 'excessive culturalism' (2007: 47). The very term 'posits the existence of "non-material culture"' as a higher category, representing 'ideas that have been made material, and natural substance that has been rendered cultural' (Thomas 2006: 15). Instead, archaeologist Julian Thomas argues 'culture is better understood as ways of doing things; practises of engagement' (2006: 22).

Mauss rejected the influence of political economy in the development of techniques (2006 [1935/1947]: 98), but in the chapters that follow, I will demonstrate how the exercise of techniques is embedded in political economies and class. Therefore, I also draw on Donald MacKenzie's labour-process analysis of technology which starts with Marx's inclusion of 'instruments' as one portion of the labour process, and examines how the valorisation process of capitalist production affects the technologies that are produced and used (1996).

Techniques are developed in the course of work to satisfy intentions, and are the specific forms of the broader metabolisms of labour I have described that link places, tools and persons. A focus on techniques emphasises how people, objects and environments shape each other, how those relationships develop, and the crucial role of practical human agency and labour in these processes. There are techniques for feeling the ground, 'keeping the trawl going', for working a fleet of creels, for monitoring the work of other fishermen, for extending one's senses into the oceans' depths, and for orienting oneself in one's environment. There are thousands of metres of wire, miles of rope, hundreds of variations of trawl nets, GPSs, chartplotters, sounders, winches, engines, generators, power tools, radars, radios, entire fishing boats, and many other objects incorporated into these techniques. What needs to be recognised is that it is not these objects, but the labour on these objects, that provides the glue that holds the systems together and produces prawns for international markets.

In Chapters 3 and 4, I will look at the techniques for extending the body's perceptual abilities, range of effective work and orientation at sea that have been developed and integrated into fishing practices. I will return to the broader political economy that these techniques are embedded into in Part III. I hope that such an approach can help me to avoid 'the enchantment of things' that Jackson warned of (2007: 77; Chapter 1) in a context where the sheer amount and complexity of 'things' is often overwhelming.

## Notes

1  Most of Mauss' writings on techniques were only recently published in English (Mauss 2006).
2  See for example Aporta and Higgs (2005) and Suchman (2007).

# 3

## Techniques to extend the body and its senses

For those who work at sea in the North Atlantic, 'being at sea' is more accurately described as 'being on a boat'. While bodily immersion in frigid sea water may be an accidental and usually lethal consequence of working on a boat, people working at sea kept a very sharp division between the experience of being *on* the sea and being *in* the sea. This points to the crucial role of boats and other machines as the places and objects which are most directly inhabited while working and living at sea.

Talking to Alex one day, I suggested that he might enjoy sailing with another fisherman who had a small dinghy. Alex was a successful young fishing skipper with almost 20 years of experience of working on the water. He replied forcefully 'I don't think so! That is just too fucking close to the water for me. They had the thing capsized too! No thanks. Not fun for someone who can't swim'. Didn't his school have access to a swimming pool? I asked. He replied:

> I went to the pool with my school, but in Primary 7 the pool manager got pissed [drunk], sitting in the office, not watching, and a kid in my class drowned. We were all in the pool at the time. We saw them pull his body out, all blue, and then trying to do mouth to mouth on him. Then they schooched us away.
>
> I was enjoying the swimming all right until then, but I was not very keen after that. A bunch of kids were called up to testify in court. The manager shot himself before the trial started. It was a big deal.
>
> I didn't get in a pool again until I had to do the water safety course for my [fishing] certificate. They wanted me to jump off this board that was up two ladders. Not fucking likely! A guy pushed me off. I had him up off the floor by the neck, I almost clocked him one. I probably would if I met him in the pub now. It was right where they pulled the boy out of the pool. The other guys explained, and the boy[1] said that he was sorry, but I told him '"Sorry" isn't fucking good enough!'

Alex had begun working on fishing boats as a teenager, less than ten years after this traumatic event, and was now a skipper who prided himself on staying out at sea and working through gales severe enough to cause much bigger boats to seek refuge in port. When I first met him, he proudly showed me a newspaper clipping about his experience of drifting on a large trawler for days without engine power, battered by a storm well offshore from the Scottish mainland. I went to see the small indoor swimming pool where his schoolmate had died and he had been pushed into the water, and to me it looked infinitely safer than the sea Alex worked on regularly. Alex directly associated immersion in water with the potential for a sudden and traumatic death. Yet, for over 20 years, Alex had managed to maintain a total separation between the experience of being *in* the water, and that of working *on* a boat. People's relationships to their boats were also complicated. Based on Alex's story, you could conclude that boats are places of safety and refuge in a hostile environment. While this was true, at other times and for other people, boats are also places of injury, trauma and death, places to escape from, and places remembered with anger and bitterness.

In this chapter I will examine the techniques people used to work effectively at sea using boats and many other tools and machines. I will examine the techniques people used to extend their bodies and perceptual abilities deep into the sea, the importance of controlling and delicately manipulating these extensions, the caring relationships of maintenance boats and machines required, and finally, how the relationships to boats and machines are affected by class and social relations of ownership.

## Techniques for extending the body

Compared to the sea they work in, the body of a fisherman is a tiny, insignificant thing. Moreover, most of the work of catching fish or prawns occurs far below the boat, in an environment fishermen cannot see and have never directly experienced[2] and in which human survival was usually impossible for more than a few minutes. Effective work at sea requires an extraordinary extension of the body's perceptual abilities and the range at which a person is able to work. Following Mauss' approach (Part II) I will trace how fishermen have developed techniques for sounding and feeling to extend both their perception and their range of effective work, techniques which have incorporated things ranging from piano wire to fishing nets to digital depth sounders and powerful engines. These techniques have not just involved tools, but also forms of social organisation like the fleet's endless discussion of weather and catches (Chapter 2) and techniques for orienting themselves in and navigating through their environment (Chapter 4).

A tool 'extends the capacity of an agent to operate within a given environment', but this is not just a mechanical process (Ingold 2000: 315). An 'inert' object becomes a tool after being enrolled in a technique and in terms of 'what it affords for a user' as a 'whole person'. A tool is 'animated by intention' and 'mediates an active purposive engagement between persons and their environments' (Ingold 2000: 319). Jackson describes this process as 'intersubjective' (2007: 295) and cites Marx's description of an agricultural worker experiencing tools and the soil as 'a prolongation of his body' and as 'the objective body of his subjectivity' (1964 [1858]: 89, 92). It is through such techniques that 'human beings make their limits recede' (Mauss 2006 [1927]: 53). The far-reaching consequences of this process are described by philosopher Clive Lawson: 'in accommodating new technologies into everyday ways of doing things our sense of our own place in our world changes … the extension of human capabilities transforms what it is to be human' (2008: 59). The intimacy of relations of extension, the satisfying experience of transforming the way in which the world is experienced and what it affords, and the frustration and alienation that may be experienced in this process also shape human subjectivities.

The comfortable way in which people's bodies were extended through multiple tools and machines is demonstrated in Figure 9. Skipper 'Buckie' John was poised between feeling his fishing gear and the seafloor with one hand, watching the electronic depth sounder over his shoulder, and reaching for the engine controls with the other hand. Experienced Icelandic skippers

> speak of knowing the details and the patterns of the 'landscape' of the sea bottom 'as well as their fingers'. This indicates that for the skilled skipper fishing technology – the boat, electronic equipment, and fishing gear – is not to be regarded as an 'external' mediator between his person and the environment but rather as a bodily extension in quite a literal sense. (Pálsson 1994: 910)

The boat and its gear was used to physically and electronically extend the perceptive powers of the body deep into the sea, which could be known as one knows one's own body. The rest of this chapter will explore the ways in which 'new' high technology devices are embedded in broader techniques and forms of social organisation that attempt to solve 'old' problems at sea, and how people's experience of such devices is embedded in and deeply affected by social, class and market relations.

### *Sound, vibration, feeling and sounding*

Extended perception rested upon techniques for sounding and feeling – techniques which drew upon a combination of hearing, whole-body feeling, ultra-sonic machines, digital visual representations of sound, and the power and vibration of internal combustion engines and hundreds of metres of steel wire. Fishermen developed their own complex visualisations of what the seafloor and their fishing gear looked like as it worked, but in this process they regarded direct vision into the sea as the least useful of their senses. One successful young prawn skipper gave me his copy of the videos that scientists made of prawns on the seafloor, explaining that it was no use to him. Another skipper who had previously worked diving for scallops told me there was nothing he saw during diving that was of use in fishing for prawns. Considering the emphasis that is put on seeing marine creatures in popular understandings of the ocean – in aquariums, on whale-watching expeditions and on marine biology television programmes, I found these dismissals of the utility of sight underwater surprising.

The use of sound in order to orient oneself or to locate other objects or organisms at sea began long before the development of electronic depth sounders. One man described to me how in thick fog going through the narrows of

Loch Hourn, his father would shout out the wheelhouse window and use the echo of his voice bouncing off the cliffs to tell where he was. This kind of human echolocation is not unique to the sea; for example, John Hull has described the use of echolocation by those who are blind, gaining a form of sight out of sound (2005: 324).

Writing about the history of the herring fishery, historian Angus Martin describes how fishermen listened intently for the *plub* of a single herring jump on dark silent nights, men with hands cupped to ears, young boys 'castigated repeatedly until silence became, for them too, habitual', and the preference for boats built with smooth planking that was quieter in wavelets so you could hear the herring more easily (Martin 1981: 164). On days when they were fishing close to shore and 'the weather was too loud for herring to be heard', fishermen held a pole in the water to feel for herring and to assess the density of shoals (Martin 1981: 172). In the summer and autumn, phosphorescent phytoplankton became more abundant. A sharp bang of a metal anchor on the wooden gunwale of the boat would send vibrations through the water and the herring would start, producing a flash in the phosphorescence that was termed 'answering the anchor' (Martin 1981: 164). The flash, or deep-down glow, of an ' "answering" shoal' was used to determine the size of individual fish, the species, and how many were in the school (Martin 1981: 164–166). The incessant knocking of anchors sounded the sea much like modern depth sounders:

> Ye wid sweir there wis two or three shipbuilding' yerds working', anchors goin' the whole night, chappin', chappin', the whole night. It wis a wonder there wis a herring lef above at aaa'. Quietness tae [till] the burnin' [phosphorescent plankton] came in the waater, an' as soon as the burning came in the waater, a man furrid [forward on the boat] wi' his anchor. (Martin 1981: 166)

The ambiguity between modes of sensory perception used by fishermen was expressed by Hugh MacFarlane, who explained that 'They *felt* wan jump [a herring], they winna hear it'. These fishermen would use the expression to 'feel herring', when, as Martin describes it, 'the obvious meaning was "hear", "smell", or "see" ' (1981: 172).

In the 1930s boats started to work in deeper water and Scots adopted from Swedish fishers the technique of using a 'feeling-wire' to find herring. The wire was made of twine, later piano wire, with a weight on the end, and would be held on the thumb or fore-finger (Martin 1981: 228). With experience the wire could be used to estimate the depth and density of a shoal of herring, and to distinguish different species of fish. 'Wiring – that was the worst job! No one wanted it. It was cold standing outside and holding the wire on your finger!' recalled John, once a young crew member on the herring boats out of Kyleakin. When the person wiring 'felt them thick' he would call the skipper (Martin 1981: 229). 'Feeling' the herring was accomplished with ears or hands or a finger, using a pole or a wire, and sometimes 'seeing' the land meant listening for a shout echoing off a cliff. These modes of sensing extended across media and combined the senses – the pole and the wire reaching beyond and far below the surface of the water, the bang of an anchor transformed into a flash of phosphorescent organisms startled by the herring around them.

In the air, hearing is usually accomplished through vibration within the ear. But in the water, sound is vibration felt with the whole body (Helmreich 2007: 264). Sounds or vibrations are also transmitted through other solids immersed in the sea – like the hull of a ship – to be heard and felt by those living and travelling on boats floating at the surface. The crew of old whaling ships describe hearing sounds of the ocean and its creatures eerily echo through the hull of the ship. The vibrations felt through fishing gear and the motion of waves formed through friction between air and water are felt as motion detected by the inner ear, or nausea in the stomach. These motions and vibrations are also heard, sometimes as the humming of tension and speed, sometimes as the crashing and clattering of objects tossed about by waves.

Techniques for sounding now incorporate electronic depth sounders. Users experience sounders as 'seeing' and even 'feeling' the seafloor. The transducers of electronic depth sounders send pulses and clicks through the water, which travel to bounce off solid objects and return. Sound measures time, which a small computer converts into distance and displays as light in a moving pixelated image on a screen (Figure 22). As Figure 9 shows, the resulting images were interpreted as the person felt the vibrations of tensioned fishing gear and combined these into a vivid three-dimensional imagination that was constantly tested and adjusted through the process of trying to catch prawns.

Sounders were not widely available to fishermen until well after the Second World War. A fisherman described using his first depth sounder in the 1970s as a kind of revelation, because 'You could tell, *off* the shore, where there was hard rock on the bottom'. The most important quality of the sounder for Scottish fishermen was to identify different seafloor ecologies.[3] Techniques using depth sounders have significantly expanded the kinds of fishing gear that can be effectively deployed on the seafloor, the kind of work that can be done there, and the affordances that can be developed.

Virtually all fishermen use their depth sounder continuously to interpolate the affordances of the ground they are working on and what they see on the display, a process I described in my notes:

> We are hauling creels and a few come up empty. Kenny leans in to check the depth sounder and sees that the depth has just changed. 'Shit! We lost the edge, what was I doing there?' he exclaims. He is constantly leaning in to check the sounder when there is a particularly good or bad haul, to interpolate between the catch he is seeing and the state of the bottom at that place.
>
> When the time comes to throw the creels back in, he zooms in on the sounder display so the seafloor is magnified. The boat swerves back and forth slightly as he tries to keep 'on the edge', at the precise depth and bottom type he has found to be productive.

Knowledge is developed through the process of cross-referencing the sounder display, catches and human effort and attention at each moment of work. The appearance of the seafloor on the sounder has become an important part of how the bottom is interpreted and described. 'Furry sand' was named because it looked thick and fluffy, and weed 'looked puffy' on the screen. Visual descriptions were used to describe information gathered through sound, like the 'echo' which is visible on the screen but describes an audible phenomenon.

Machines and electronics were integrated into other senses in the process of working effectively. As I wrote in my fieldnotes after my first day on a fishing boat, 'You are watching the chartplotter, the speed on the GPS, and the sounder all at once, and trying to feel the boat'. Being able to integrate, interpolate and act on bodily and electronic information from these various machines was a real skill, and one that I found difficult and disorienting. I wrote about my confusion while underway on a trawler one pitch-black night:

> It always strikes me how little you can see of anything outside of the wheelhouse in the dark. Charging through the night at speed, I feel blinded, with electronic-only senses. I find it very disorienting.
>
> When I try to explain this to John, he just points to the radar and tells me to use that. But all these screens – the chartplotter, the radar, the depth sounder, the world – are at different scales and different orientations and I have not yet learned to interpolate between them.

Kenny spoke of his admiration for a former skipper, 'a *good* fisherman ... I learned more from him than anyone else. There were 12 screens in the wheelhouse, he taught me how to interpret them'. The visual representations of different aspects of the environment on these screens were not straightforward, as the information they displayed required skilled interpretation.

The experience of using a depth sounder could cross over into direct feeling, which I experienced in a visceral way one evening. Dusk was falling, and after a rewarding day on his fishing boat and in the local village (Introduction), DJ generously led me out of the complicated harbour entrance on his small motorboat. After following him for what seemed like ages, DJ glided to a stop and asked me what my sounder said. I told him the depth, and he responded:

> Well, that should be you fine there. Just keep heading out. See the light on the Crowlins? Head for that just now, and just make sure you give Ardalanch Point a wide berth. It's that dark mass in front of you.
>
> What you will see on your sounder is the bottom will drop away to about 80 metres, and then it will come back up really sharply. Don't worry! It will just level out at about 20 metres.

The rocks and land were now disappearing and merging into the blackening sky. I carried on through the darkness. If I turned on a light on the boat I would be blinded. I watched the bottom fall away, and then its heart-stopping rise. The thing I most wanted to know was where the bottom was because I wanted to keep it away. I stared at the depth sounder intently. I started to imagine with dread what I would do if I ran the boat aground just now, on a falling tide with a gale coming up tomorrow, and then I had to tell myself to stop. More than anything, I felt like a person feeling along a wall in the dark, reaching out to touch something in order to hold it at a safe distance. But it was the sounder I was feeling the seafloor with. Despite the ethereal and digitally processed sound waves that connected me to the seafloor, for that hour at least, it was as if I was reaching out to touch it.[4]

Experientially, there was no radical distinction between what is 'felt' through the boat or seen on the sounder screen, just like the old herring fishermen who '*felt wan jump, they winna hear it*' (Martin 1981: 171). It was the attentiveness of one's whole body which allowed one to 'get in' to challenging ground, or feel the bottom at night. As Pálsson describes: 'The skipper's universe is very different from that of his colleagues of earlier decades, but what shows on the screens of the radar, the computer, and the fish-finder is just as much a "natural sign", directly sensed, as birds in the air or natural landmarks' (1994: 918). The techniques fishermen used to extend their bodies to sound and feel the depths, to work in and develop the affordances of places they cannot see and have never visited, combined multiple forms of perception. This full sensory attentiveness is perhaps parallel to a blind person, for whom 'the body itself has become the organ of sense' (Hull 2005: 326), but in this case it is a body extended hundreds of meters beneath and many miles across the sea's surface. The long-standing challenge of extending the body's perception entailed the creative development of various techniques that incorporated diverse kinds of tools, but which always relied on the attentive labour of fishermen to carry them out.

### The familiar sea

The extension of the whole body's perception into the sea meant that the familiar working space of the boat was also extended into the sea. Larger items, especially fishing gear, were regularly stored on the seabed for later use, sometimes marked with a buoy or on the GPS chartplotter, often just remembered and retrieved by dragging a small grappling hook across the seafloor. It was not unusual for a net to be 'run off' the winch and left on the seabed for later retrieval, and this was common practice in the 1970s and 1980s in order to evade fisheries patrol boats.[5] Wreckage or boulders caught in the net might be dumped 'behind a peak' or under the bridge – areas where they were unlikely to interfere with fishing. Things to be reused were tucked in out-of-the-way areas, to prevent someone else from finding and making use of them.

The sea was also a source of potentially useful objects which would be kept and reused if they came up in the net, typically, clothing, tyres, fishing gear and buckets. One fisherman frequently wore a red fleece jacket that had come up in the net 'in Colonsay waters', proudly telling others that its only defect was a sticky zipper. Anything that was not immediately useful would be put back, as you would no doubt catch another bucket or tyre before you needed one. Fishermen caught an extraordinary variety of things in their nets: an MG sports car, a small aeroplane, a bicycle in perfect condition, mines, waste disposal tubes from submarines, a mini-submersible (sold back to the Ministry of Defence (MoD)), parts of wrecks, wine and liqueurs (drinkable), tins of food (unopened), a door latch (later used on a dog house), a ship's bell, sonar tubes being tested by the MoD, miles of fine wire used on torpedoes, old engine blocks, steering wheels and lanterns. All of these things were discussed and many were cleaned, admired and reused. Some were simply returned to the sea after some struggle. All contributed to the sense that the sea was a repository of useful things which could be retrieved, moved about, stored and found again later. The sea was not a hostile wilderness but a humanised extension of other workspaces where the 'remains of a previous action are themselves re-interpreted as a sign of [an] … active and productive relationship with the countryside' (Povinelli 1993: 331).

Alex, who earlier in this chapter reacted so forcefully against the possibility of bodily immersion in the sea, also regarded the area under the sea's surface as his extended workplace. Despite his strong aversion to getting into the sea, he prided himself in knowing the seafloor well enough to work the most difficult ground, and he also thought nothing of leaving his fishing gear at sea for later retrieval. A case in point was his treatment of some extra wire used to tow the trawl net behind the boat. This type of wire is heavy, cumbersome, very long and quite difficult to wind onto a spool and to store on land. Instead, Alex left it stretched out on the seafloor before offering it to another fisherman who said he could make use of it. I helped the skipper retrieve that wire, and we found that a section of it was missing. Speculation immediately began over who had been 'at it' and stolen some of the wire. The possibility that it was simply lost at sea was not considered. The sea was a far too familiar and well known place for things simply to be 'lost' there.

Fishermen's familiarity with the sea and its movements not only extended into its depths but across hundreds of miles of coastline. Out trawling one day, I asked the skipper if our net was far enough from the creels marked by a nearby buoy to avoid them becoming tangled together. He asked me 'Well, what direction are the wind and tide?' I was taken aback. He explained:

> The tide is tricky up here. Although it floods from the south to the north, from the Irish Sea up the coast, all that water for the Sound and the lochs can't get through Kyle Rhea [between Skye and the mainland], so some of it has to come around the top of Skye. The Minch [north and west of Skye] is narrow up there so it pinches the water and at the top end of Fladda you get the current going almost east–west towards Rubha Reidh.
>
> So the creels are likely to be a touch closer to us than the buoy but if you look back at the wires your gear is well over to the other side of the boat so you are well clear.

A buoy in the water cannot be assumed to lie above what it marks on the seafloor as the tidal current drags the rope in different directions and the wind also pushes the buoy in its own direction. I wrote in my fieldnotes: 'He clearly sees the world as made up of forces, changing, opposing each other. His first assumption is that the appearance of things is not how they really are.' What seemed like a question of local detail about a nearby buoy and creels drew in a sweeping account of tidal forces and water movement from the Irish Sea along the entire coast of Scotland and then around specific islands.

Ingold emphasises the importance of immersion in the world for the sensory perception of it (2000: 153). Yet the intimate knowledge of the sea I describe here was not gained through immersion but through a wide variety of extended electronic and mechanical techniques used in the process of working and trying to catch prawns. Helmreich criticises the use of 'immersion' metaphors in ethnography, instead inquiring into 'the work that needs to be done so that signals can link machines and people together' (2007: 633). Despite the lack of direct bodily contact with the sea or immersion into it, the development of extended techniques for feeling, sounding, sensing and manipulating tools under its surface and down to the seafloor changed fishermen's 'sense of our own place in our world' (Lawson 2008: 59) and what was possible within it.

### Extension and over-extension: the delicate balance of control

Fishing gear was not just a tool for catching fish, it was also a tool for perceiving and understanding the environment. Because the results of fishing mattered so much (Chapter 1), a great deal of fishermen's visualisations of the underwater environment they worked in was about their fishing gear. Fishermen worked at enormous depths, with large and heavy gear, which made the tensions, weights and forces involved in operating this fishing gear immense. This gear also had to be carefully set, monitored, adjusted and maintained over time. The skilled, attentive and experienced operator had to learn to anticipate, understand, deflect, manipulate and control the tensions and forces in this gear instead of simply being subjected to them. As I learned, these extended operations all rested on a fine and potentially deadly balance.

Trawl nets were towed on bar-taut wires that extended 100 metres down to the net on the seafloor (Figure 20). The boat's roiling turbulent wake gives some indication of the forces involved in dragging the net through the water and over the seafloor. Trawl nets depended on the density and resistance of movement through water in order to give them shape. Without the tension between movement and resistance, the net was simply a useless lump, or worse, a hazardous mess. Crucial in the process of shaping and tensioning the net were the trawl doors, which had to be fabricated and maintained in a delicate balance so that they worked like kites to spread the mouth of the net open. Even on the smallest trawlers the doors consisted of hundreds of pounds of steel, but after a year or so the balance on them was almost always ruined and they stopped spreading the net properly. There was nothing obviously different about a set of doors that no longer worked, and it was also impossible to observe the net in action to see if the doors were doing their job. The skipper had to be able to tell from their experience of feeling and gathering clues from the net as it was working, observing minute patterns of wear, and regularly towing alongside and comparing their catch with others in order to tell

Figure 20  Looking from the boat into the sea along the wires attached to the trawl net.

if the doors had stopped being effective in maintaining the tension needed to keep the shape of the net (Figure 21).

The use of resistance and tension to do work underwater also required considerable imagination and experience. Fishermen frequently gave me detailed accounts of how nets worked (or didn't), what they were shaped like when they were working, and hotly debated the effects of particular adjustments. Yet the only opportunity available to fishermen to see the shape of their gear was to go to a flume tank: a kind of swimming pool with a moving bottom where nets could be tested. As Alasdair pointed out, this was no substitute for fishing on real grounds as there were 'nae prawns in a flume tank, and a pretty looking shape might never make a penny catching fish!' From 1976 to 2006 the UK fishing development body Seafish operated a flume tank in Hull, England, but I only met one person who had actually visited it. The knowledge that fishermen had about the functioning of their nets was not gained through watching them work, but through their experience of working with and feeling the tensions and resistances necessary to keep the net going under various circumstances: as James said, to 'tow it'.

Figure 21  Towing next to another fishing boat to compare catches and evaluate the net.
This boat sank after running onto a small island, luckily with no loss of life.

The techniques for working with tension – of understanding and shaping, of adjustment and compensation – appeared relatively smooth and controlled. It was several months before I understood the delicate balance upon which these apparently smooth operations rested, and the constant potential for disaster. These relationships of movement and resistance could easily go wrong with immense tensions needing to be deflected and manipulated in order to avoid catastrophic failure and to bring the situation back under control.

The ability to avoid and deflect these sudden upsets and reversals was literally a life-and-death skill, demonstrated to me late one afternoon out on a trawler. I was working on deck sorting the catch. The skipper turned the boat sharply, and the boat heeled dramatically as I tried to hold and catch the sliding, falling prawns. Then the net stuck on the seafloor and, alarmingly, the boat heeled over even more, and the sea lapped over the deck. The skipper stopped the engine and allowed the boat to drift back so the wires went slack, and then accelerated and 'made a run for it'. The door jerked free from the seabed. Relief turned to a new anxiety when we realised that the wires leading to the net were not straight and parallel as they should be. Oh dear. We tried towing the net for a little while to see if the wires would straighten but they didn't. Something was not right. We hauled the net 100 metres up to the surface and we could see that the whole net was twisted 180 degrees or more and could not be recovered in that state. Just by looking, it was clear that what needed to happen was to lever one door over the other, and let it all shake out. This, however, was an impossible task involving hundreds of pounds of steel and wire dangling above the surface and into the sea, the kind of attempt in which hands could easily be crushed and bodies thrown off-balance or overboard if the wires, doors or net sprung in an unpredictable direction.

The skipper took his time, and thought through what to do. He used a clever sequence of using smaller lines to take the strain, slackening the wires on one side, and tightening others with the winch, a process which gracefully transferred tensions and used existing weights and inertia to solve the problem. No human body would have had the brute force to do that job itself. He had only the weight of the net and the force of the winch, so he had to use those forces to his advantage rather than trying to work against them. Even if you did have the brute force to untwist or unjam something, you wouldn't want to be that close when it let go.

The net was safely untwisted in about 20 minutes. I was impressed. 'That was nothing', said the skipper, 'That was dead easy'. Later he explained that what likely happened was that the inside trawl door had fallen over with the top edge outwards as we turned and the tension came off it (a door falling inwards is usually fine, he explained, you can pick it up no bother, but outwards can cause problems). Then, when the strain came back on both wires as we straightened out, the fallen door flipped over and then dug in to the seafloor. Once we jerked the door free, the rest of the net flipped over. 'You can only guess at what might have happened', he said, 'but it would have been something like'.

The first thing that the skipper had told me when I came on board was 'if in doubt shout, and whatever happens, don't panic'. In any moment of pressure or potential crisis, he had the disconcerting habit of putting on the kettle and having a cup of instant coffee and a cigarette. 'Panic-merchant' was a disparaging term. When confronted with difficulty, the most important thing was to keep calm, think carefully about the problem, and use your understanding of the forces involved to deflect it. This would allow you to stay in control, to be able to continue monitoring and adjusting the extended forces you had put to work instead of suffering the potentially devastating consequences of letting those forces take control of you.

Learning how to stay in control of your body and the boat itself was critical to becoming skilful at sea. Pálsson has described the process of 'becoming skilful' as a recovery from seasickness, of 'getting one's sea-legs' while being 'actively engaged with the social and natural environment' (1994: 901). The key transition I observed novices having to make was how to anticipate, understand, deflect and control the motions, tensions and forces involved in working at sea instead of simply being subjected to them. Control is important in relation to human relations to machines more generally, as, 'the ways in which we experience our relationships with both persons and machines will depend upon the degree to which we feel in control of these relationships, as well as the degree to which these relationships are felt to augment rather than diminish our own sense of well-being' (Jackson 2002: 336). I made a point of inviting novice crew onto my boat at the pier and underway. Their first experience of being at sea was a loss of control, an inability to predict or understand the bewildering actions of the machines that surrounded them and which they relied on completely. Children would jump onto a stable looking boat at the dock and then shriek when they felt this huge thing move beneath the weight of their small bodies. The eyes of adults would widen and their grip would tighten at the sudden unsteadiness. An offer of a cup of tea might be declined, and then accepted, and then left half-drunk as they looked uneasily out the window and made their excuses to leave. This motion was felt throughout the body, the unsteadiness becoming hesitancy and nervousness, possibly a complete lack of will to do anything (common during seasickness), and then the body may completely reject the experience as if it were a kind of poison along with whatever half-digested food may be remaining in its stomach.

In this new and bewildering environment the first step in enskilment was to regain some control over one's own body and its immediate surroundings, by anticipating and compensating for the constant motion. The boat shifts under your weight as you step on board, your grip tightens, and your body shifts its balance in response. The boat steadies and you lean back to your original position and soon you are reacting to every movement without thinking, muscles constantly working. You feel every other boat that goes by, every person that walks down the floating dock, every wave that slaps the hull slaps you too, every alteration in course, every sudden jerk in the fishing gear, the cargo shifting, the crane swinging, the wind gusting, a sharp tidal eddy: each one of these things is felt, each one is interpreted and reacted to. Every boat is different: although I was an experienced sailor, I found the motions of a trawler completely unpredictable and unnerving on my first trip. Likewise, a man I knew who had worked at sea for 40 years on cargo ships was almost comical in his awkwardness on my own small boat.

Jackson's emphasis on control (and its potential loss) also offers the beginnings of an understanding of catastrophic failure, particularly when it involves skilled operators, as he says 'technologies … hold the potential to sustain our lives or end them' (2002: 335). Skill may be acquired for many years but shifts in market pressures and class relations could cause skilled operators to over-extend themselves, to lose control and to be overcome. Control was necessary to bring extended operations back from the brink of disaster – but relations of ownership and market pressures could prevent people from being able to properly exercise this control (Chapter 6).

Controlling large and complex machines could also be exhilarating. One man who worked for a large multinational company on an oil rig described to me his first experience on a sailboat: 'I was in the pub three years ago and Robert asked me if I would go sailing with him. I went out and I loved it. It was amazing. I loved it. Why, to harness something that powerful – it's amazing.' He spoke with a passionate intensity and I knew that he looked forward to sailing races as a highlight of his time off work. His excitement indicated to me that the experience of 'harnessing' a 'powerful' machine was radically different from other experiences he had of working with machines on the oil platforms.

What makes this relationship of control over a powerful machine possible is that both fishing boats and sailboats are machines designed around the skipper's body and perceptual abilities. On a fishing boat, the sounder, navigational equipment, engine controls and any other instruments for monitoring the trawl or ship are arrayed around the skipper's chair within easy reach (Figure 9, Figure 13, Figure 22). The chair is a kind of nerve-centre from which the skipper senses and controls the boat through their body. The chair itself is considered so important that its make and model is listed in the one-page summary of the specifications of each new fishing boat built in the past year in the annual publication *Fishing Vessels of Ireland and Britain* (Linkie 2006). Skipper Alasdair remembered that his chair was given to him as a present when he re-built his boat's wheelhouse. The result of these human-centred human–machine relations was that skippers (but only skippers) with disabilities or other special needs were able to adapt the most important aspects of the boat's operation to their own bodily needs, and carry on like everyone else. One respected and successful skipper of a local trawler had a congenital condition which restricted the mobility of both legs and both arms. I was told about the skipper of a pelagic fishing boat who 'had his arm ripped off in a winch accident. He had hardly been in the hospital when he checked himself out, flew straight to Norway where he was getting a new boat built, and had them completely rearrange the wheelhouse so he could do it all one-handed'.

Fishermen developed techniques for extending their bodily perception and effectiveness that incorporated boats, engines, fishing gear and electronic navigation

Figure 22  Instruments laid out within easy reach of the skipper. From left: A depth sounder, a GPS chartplotter, a basic GPS, the logbook, the engine throttle, VHF radio, engine gauges and steering wheel.

tools to work in and develop the affordances of fishing grounds. These techniques incorporated digital machines and other high technology into their intimate knowledge and naming of places (Chapter 2) which meant the sea was not regarded very differently from any other space they worked in – so long as you kept your own body out of it. These extended techniques involved the manipulation of immense forces, tensions, weights and pressures. The ability to manipulate tension and to maintain control of machines was crucial for effective and safe working at sea. The ability of people to control the interface between themselves and their machines and to adapt machines to their own needs strongly affected their subjective experience of these relationships. Three further questions follow. Under what circumstances were machines designed according to the needs of human bodies? What human bodies were they designed for, and why? And once a person entered into a relationship with a machine, did they have the ability to maintain that machine and adapt it to their needs and aspirations, or was this form of control estranged to another? These questions will be addressed in the rest of this chapter.

## Care and maintenance of tools and machines

Maintaining some control of the extended tools and fishing gear used to work beneath the surface required constant attention, care and labour. Over time, the care and maintenance of a machine could transform the machine itself and its affordances, as well as people's abilities and subjectivities. But not everyone was in a position to develop such attentive and transformative relations with the machines they worked with. As I will discuss in the next section, crew and skippers who did not own boats had very different and quite alienated relationships to them.

Mauss argued 'the boat … is a machine' (2006 [1935/1947]: 103), and the skill of feeling linked the body to the ship and extended it into its wider environment through the ship. Fishing crew did not directly feel the seabed, they felt it through their fishing gear and boat. Crew did not directly feel a passing wave, they felt the ship's reaction to it. The skill of feeling and interpreting motion, tension and vibration, and learning what to do about it, is at the core of many seamanship skills – on everything from fishing boats to sailing yachts to cargo ships. 'You must listen to the boat, it is talking to you through the seat of your bum, the soles of your shoes. You must develop a feeling for this', Alasdair reflected.

Teo was a skilled sailor who owned a small yacht and cultivated the skill of feeling with a particularly intense concentration. Only four years after learning how to sail, he began to win sailing races, much to the irritation of more established local sailors. Teo explained that:

> Sailing is like meditation with feedback. People don't understand what I mean by that. You have to concentrate all your effort and energy and focus in one place. And then in a race, there is feedback, you can challenge yourself and you know if you did a good job. I did a lot of new age stuff, Buddhism, meditation, and it is all very nice but when it comes down to the crunch *you don't know if it is working.*

Teo made sure he steered the boat at precisely the right angle to the wind, that he felt the sluggishness when the boat slowed down and adjusted the sails or his steering minutely until he could feel it accelerate, ensured his movement on the boat was graceful so that its momentum was not suddenly jarred, and watched the water, sails and the boat intently for clues of any variation in the wind speed or direction. He was constantly working in a reciprocal engagement with the boat, sensing its movements and trying to figure out how he could best engage the boat with the wind and currents it moved through. A rhythm of motion was internalised when sailing, especially the angle and motion of the boat relative to the wind and waves. The slightest variation in this rhythm needed to be attended to. Teo told me with pride that 'sailing is for myself, for my concentration, just me and the boat'. Teo's boat was in many ways the 'objective body' of his confident, skilled and effective subjectivity. Sailing his boat, as an immigrant to Skye whose first language was not English,[6] he was able to assert his own skill and knowledge of the area's winds and tides over those who were far more established there.

The attention Teo paid to the process of sailing is representative of the constant tinkering and work that any boat required to work effectively and safely at sea. The importance of constant attention to the boat is described by Adam Nicolson in his autobiographical book about a six-month trip up the west coast of Britain and Ireland with professional seaman George. At the end of the journey, George reproached Adam for his casual attitude during the trip, saying 'This is about seamanship, Adam. Seamanship is about taking and carrying the risk. The Risk with a capital R ... I carried it for week after week, second-guessing the next thing to go wrong. You never shared it, you never came in there with me.' Nicolson glibly responded 'I think it is impossible to share it', to which George replied cuttingly, reflecting on his years of seagoing experience with hundreds of other crew members, 'I have never not shared it before' (Nicolson 2004: 175–176). In his concluding passage Nicolson reflects 'What was seamanship? Keeping other people alive ... Attention to detail, nurturing the ship, resourcefulness; and more importantly, an ability to catch a kettle before it falls and to look after people and things before they need it' (2004: 180). Maintenance, 'looking after people and things before they need it', is a perpetual state of care, attention and anticipation essential to seamanship which must be collectively shared in order to be effective.

The result of these caring relationships of maintenance can be a highly personalised and rewarding relationship between people and their boats. Visiting another person's boat often involved a detailed tour of recent projects, plans for future improvements, and apologies for ones that were not yet complete. When I met Calum, a retired fisherman on Raasay, he was proud and eager to show me the work he had done on his yacht. Without any prompting, I was given a detailed tour of the engine, the heater he installed, the sink, the new toilet, and the cupboard in which he built in perfectly fitted holders for bottles he liked to drink and the cups he liked to use. 'It's not how everyone would want it, but it's how I want it', he explained. I understood exactly what Calum meant: I re-designed and re-placed most of the ageing wiring on my own boat and from then on the simple acts of turning on the light and ensuring the boat's batteries were properly charged gave me great pleasure and satisfaction. I photographed my wiring job and showed it off to anyone who could bear looking at it (Figure 23). Many people

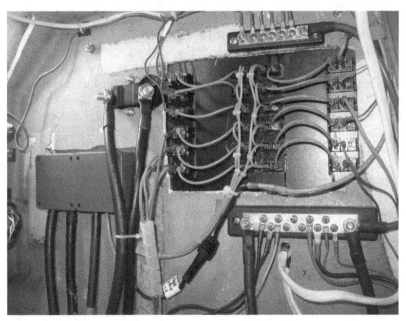

Figure 23 The wiring job I completed on my own boat. Above are the new switches and panel I installed, and below is the wiring on the back of them.

I met who owned yachts seemed to spend virtually all of their time on their boats working on them and not actually sailing. As one yacht owner told me quite happily on a sunny day in early May, 'We are all down here working on our boats all the time. By the time it gets to September we will just about have done the work for the spring!'

The benefits of having a boat to work on and pour oneself into were subjectively important and affected all aspects of people's lives. Calum incorporated his boat into his social and family life: he used it to visit family members in different parts of Scotland. James was another yacht-owner who invested a great deal of time working on and tweaking his boat. He explained to me: 'Having a boat kept me sane. It has been my bolt hole, my place to get away, to think about something else.' James incorporated his boat into the coping techniques he used to deal with stressful family and work obligations. Teo, Calum, James and other boat owners found great satisfaction in engaging with their boats in a constant process of maintenance and tinkering to transform them into places they were proud of and comfortable in, and to maintain their subjectivities and their personal relations with others.

The importance of attention, feeling and care also applied to engines. Engines created a new sensory experience that began with the Industrial Revolution which 'crosses sensory thresholds in so far as it can be simultaneously palpable and audible, visible and audible' (Trower 2008: 135). Their 'sonic habitus' (Feld and Brenneis 2004: 468) and incessant rumbling vibration was felt through the whole boat, pistons firing, alternator spinning, gearbox turning, propeller spinning, the sea astern gurgling and turbulent. The noise and vibration were constant and unrelenting, but its regularity made any variation instantly remarkable. Kenny once told me that when he was working on trawlers, 'I could sleep on a razor, through any kind of noise, except if the net came fast. I was in an aft bunk and I would hear the cavitation against the hull and would wake up instantly'.[7] My own boat acquired an algal infection in its diesel fuel which meant that its filters regularly became clogged and stopped the flow of fuel to the engine. Before the engine actually stopped there would be a long period where the rhythmic pattern of its cylinders firing would vary slightly as the fuel supply became irregular, and the engine would slow down and then suddenly speed up again before it finally spluttered to a halt. It was a routine problem which I knew how to fix: it simply required the filter to be replaced and the fuel system bled of air. But in poor weather, or when night was falling, or when I was alone on the boat, such a problem could become much more difficult to solve. I became totally sensitised to any change in the engine's noise, and the slightest variation would cause a twisting pit of apprehension and concentration in my stomach. I even became sensitised to the variations in other people's engines. When working on another fishing boat I noticed a change in its engine's rhythm, and pointed it out to the skipper. He scoffed at my apprehension, only to tell me sheepishly a few days later that his fuel had developed the same algal infection and, like me, he was now constantly listening intently and changing fuel filters at the most awkward times and places. The state of my own fuel filters provoked anxiety and doubt in my own ability to keep my engine maintained (and keep my guests safe), but also the satisfaction of being able to fix the problem and get out of difficult situations. Alasdair had a similar relation to a troubled gearbox which was a constant source of frustration and worry, but then intense satisfaction when he finally fixed it.

Engines were heard with the ears and felt by the body, and gauges were watched but also tapped for reassurance and to check that the information they showed was up to date. Gauges showed oil pressure, engine revolutions per minute (rpm), and the internal temperature of the engine; they monitored the metabolism of the engine as its machinery transformed diesel fuel into steady forward propulsion. These were all important things to know, as I learned one afternoon. The skipper woke up from his nap, ambled into the wheelhouse, checked the engine temperature and rpm gauge, and started cursing. 'You have not been paying attention to the gauges', he said, accusingly. The engine was working too hard for the speed at which the boat was moving. It was under too much pressure, it was going too fast, it was too hot. This meant that something must be wrong with the gear, the net flipped upside down, or twisted, or filled with debris or a boulder that would have pulverised any prawns we had caught. The whole afternoon could be wasted, his nap a mistake, his trust in me to steer the boat while he slept a misjudgement. I turned red. He started the winch to pull in the 100 metres of wire between us and the net. 'You need to watch those gauges', he said, still annoyed. I had been careless: I apologised and tried my best to be helpful. Everything had seemed fine. But the gauges that monitored the health and metabolism of the engine told a different story. Winding in the wires and net, he emphasised 'The temperature should not go above 80 ... If you were watching it you would have seen it go up. We tow at about 1000rpms'. He continued, 'If you have to use more power than that to go 2.3 knots then something's not right'. The gauges did not just monitor the metabolism of the engine, but through them you could also read the health of the whole system: from the engine through the boat, and down to the fishing gear on the seafloor. The gauges spoke of the tension in the wires and the friction between the net and the seafloor, and the work required to drag a boat and a net through the sea. The gauges were a reminder that the machine must always be attended to and never taken for granted.

The state of the engine was critically important to the operation of the boat, but it also emotionally affected its operators and their subjectivities, and it played a role in social relations. It was a communication device, its constant rhythmic rumble a signal that everything was fine, its unexpected absence a signal that it was not. I spent a day with Graeme and his crew James travelling down the coast. James and I were chatting casually on deck when the engine suddenly stopped. James instantly dropped everything and ran into the wheelhouse. Graeme, who had been steering the boat, was already down in the engine room, and James jumped down after him, scrabbling through tools to hand them over to use. Almost no speech was necessary: the stopping of the engine followed by their own urgent movements provided the main communication. This crew were experienced in dealing with a boat in a poor state of repair, and they reacted to its needs instantly.

Jackson argues that 'work is often experienced not as a relationship between an acting subject and an inert field, but as an intersubjective and reciprocal relationship' (2007: 69). The effective maintenance of a ship builds up such strong relationships with the humans that operate them that these ship-machines and the tools used to maintain them become comfortable companions, 'partners'. Tools were a comfort there to help you in difficulty, they required care themselves (particularly around salt water), and they were used to work effectively and develop peoples' aspirations and expand their capabilities.

Trawling one day, the net got stuck on the seafloor, hard. We used the winch to start pulling it up, but then the hose for the hydraulic system that powered the winch burst under the extra strain. 'Bastard!' exclaimed the skipper, who quickly grabbed tools, tightened fittings, and taped up the hose in a flurry of frustrated activity. The repair seemed to work and very gently the skipper nursed the winch and managed to haul up the wires far enough to get first one, and then both of the very heavy trawl doors on to the boat. The deck was covered in hydraulic oil. The net was a twisted mess, still trailing in the water. The skipper brought more tools out. He attached a rope with a hook to part of the net to take the strain, and with this shifting of tension the net started to untwist so that we could bring it on board. We attached another hook and line and let that take the strain again, un-twisting, un-hooking, and then gently, gently with the winch and finally the heavy rubber hoppers were on board. The skipper and I pulled the net on board amidst the detritus of the past hour's struggles. We were satisfied at having successfully gotten out of a tight spot without having to abandon our fishing gear on the seafloor, and without injury. With the exception of the net, everything was now out of place, strewn about the deck. We had a victorious cup of tea and then started to clean up. I was still learning my way around the boat, so I gathered up all the tools and held them up one by one to ask the skipper 'where does this go?' For each one, he explained to me that it 'lives' under the skipper's seat, or in the lower shelf in the wheelhouse, or down in the engine room.

Tools 'live' in times of need, when they had been worked with, when the task was achieved, and when they were returned to their 'home' so that they were ready for the next crisis. The importance of tools living in their proper homes was expressed to me by a man with a long history of work on cargo ships. 'Have you ever worked on a proper ship, a ship where everything had to be in its place, where you could find things in the dark without thinking about it?' he asked me, and then continued talking about his land-based kitchen staff with scorn: 'Well, these people don't understand that; they just pick things up and put them down *wherever*.' Being in place was part of the helpful and reciprocal relationship between tools and their human operators, part of the organisation of the ship around the needs of the person, and the training and adaptation of that person to the needs of the ship. It is a reflection of the necessity of finding these tools 'in the dark, without thinking about it', perhaps an engine stopped, or a pump failing, or a hatch come loose, every second wasted increasing the danger to the ship and its crew. A useless thing would never come alive in this way.

The active relations of care and maintenance of machines I have described challenge analysis by well known philosopher of technology Lucy Suchman. Suchman says that 'when action is proceeding smoothly it is essentially transparent to us' and in these cases 'equipment has a tendency to disappear' until it breaks down (2007: 73). She cites Martin Heidegger's distinction of 'ready-to-hand' and 'unready-to-hand' and the description by Hubert Dreyfus of a blind man using a cane, to argue that only broken-down 'unready-to-hand' equipment is the subject of goal-oriented action, whereas normal operation involves no such thing. Yet it is not only through breakdown that we attend to machines – the care and maintenance they require relies on reciprocal relationships that are developed through the process of ordinary use. Watching the gauges and the sounder, feeling the boat and the net and tinkering and adjusting the other machines requires an active and attentive engagement with them. It was in living on the boat and enjoying it that I discovered all the things that I would like to change about it, not because these parts suffered breakdowns, but because use made me aware of the arrangements for tying ropes that could be improved to work more smoothly, the lights which could be moved to better illuminate the living space as I used it, and the machines that would be easier to use if their installation was adjusted. It is in use that a blind man might realise that he would prefer a cane that was two inches longer, or that if the shape of the handle was modified slightly it would fit more lightly and sensitively in his hand. The attention and ongoing labour required to work effectively with and to maintain machines should not be made invisible in analysis of them.

Interspersed at regular intervals in my fieldnotes are the lists I made to remind myself of the work that needed to be done on the boat: 'whip ends of lines, check anchor windlass, top up batts and clean terminals, find battens, clean locker, shift autohelm, check nav lights, new bulbs'. These lists were generated through the constant process of using each of these tools and noticing what I would like to improve about them. I found that if I didn't immediately make a note of these tasks, I would forget them completely until the next time I had to use those tools. Ingold points out in passing the need for maintenance because 'machines, unlike living organisms ... are incapable of making up themselves for the effects of wear and tear' (2000: 308). Yet the work that humans perform on machines also develops out of the particular interests and subjectivity of the person who works with the machine, their desire to improve that relationship so they could work better together, and the reward of extending their own abilities to make the immediate limits of their world recede. Commenting on a draft of this chapter, fishing skipper Alasdair described the relationship between a boat and its owner as a 'partnership'.

Like environments, machines have affordances that people can develop and enhance. In turn, developing the affordances of a machine can assist in developing the affordances of an environment. Over time, the effects of this work can be transformational. Figure 24 shows the changes made to one fishing boat over approximately 45 years. The boat had been worked by at least five different owners, targeting herring, prawns and other species, using different gear, under different

Figure 24  Four pictures of the same boat over 50 years. The oldest picture is on the bottom left, followed by the top left and top right (all taken in the 1960s). The picture on the bottom right was taken in 2007 when the boat was 46 years old. The 1960s pictures were supplied to me by the boat's current owner (photographer unknown).

Figure 24 (Continued).

regulatory regimes, and working out of many ports between Shetland and the Isle of Man. The boat's current owner supplied me with a closely written page of the changes he had made to the boat:

> 22" off stern. Virtually all above water line. Bulwarks replaced and doubled in height. Wheelhouse renewed, decision to put it forward was not finalised until after the 'new' wheelhouse arrived. This allowed for the removal of the old engine room hatch (aft of w'house).
>
> Winch was necessarily repositioned (again) and hold/engine room hatch adjusted. None of this is really major plastic surgery, more of a 'makeover'.
>
> Foc'sle/Cabin had already been enlarged early 90s (Honest it used to be smaller).
>
> Re-conditioned engine and gearbox plus new tanks (fuel) installed Nov 2004. This not at all visible but is a much more meaningful change than the cosmetic. Major heart surgery.
>
> Jan-Feb '09 Shelter replaced with (at a glance) identical one. Plywood (rotten, past its sell-by date,) to GRP.[8] Bum also clad in GRP and steel rubbing irons to curtail any more abrasion by wires/doors. 40 years wear and tear fixed by a barrel of plastic!

A close 'partnership' could develop between a skipper and their boat as they shaped and modified each other to work better together over time. Thus, experienced skippers who owned their own boat were usually identified by their boat's name: Ruaridh 'the *Accord*', James 'the *Iris*' and, famously, Angus 'the *Fairy Queen*'. Through their long history of working together, the boat became incorporated into the identity of the skipper. These relations were not always positive. Upside down and stuck on the seafloor, the net was a 'bastard!' So was the winch when it burst and squirted hydraulic oil all over the deck. These machines acted out, and it is an essential part of the skill of seamanship to diagnose these problems quickly and to bring these machines back in line, or better yet, to anticipate such problems before they occur.

Jackson describes how labour-action extends the body into new places and 'simultaneously transforms both the object worked on and the worker himself' (2007: 71). Close attention is required by those who used these techniques of extension at sea, where a minor breakdown could easily become catastrophic. This attention must be an active and intervening attention that anticipates problems and 'looks after people and things before they need it'. Boat owners attended to their seagoing machines with a purposive and transformational intensity that was not just mechanical but extended their hopes, dreams and aspirations as they changed their own capabilities and the affordances of their environments. Each transformation demonstrated new possibilities and facilitated the imagining of new transformations. Through this working process, boat owners developed subjectivities as effective persons able to maintain themselves and change their own place in the world.

## Losing control: machines and social relations

As boat owners, Teo, Calum, Alasdair, James and I had the immensely rewarding ability to tinker with and maintain our boats to fit our own needs and aspirations. Yet in 2008 I estimate that over 90 per cent of boats relied on young men hired as crew, and 60 per cent of fishing boat skippers and crews had no ownership or family ownership stake in the boat (Chapter 5). Their experience on working on the same fishing boats was often significantly different to the boat owners. Hired crew, especially on trawlers, would usually work for short stints on one boat or another, frequently quitting or getting fired (see Chapter 5). In the pub between jobs they would trade stories and make up unflattering nicknames for the boats they worked on, like 'the Steaming Pile' and 'the Virus'.

Graeme was a young but experienced fisherman who had spent several years as a hired skipper of boats other people owned. Unlike the owner-skippers, he generally referred to the boat as a 'shit-bucket'[9] or a 'piece of shit'. I spent a day underway with him and his crew, and after the unexpected engine stoppage described earlier, we tied up to a pier and met a more experienced skipper. Together, he and Graeme spent a few hours checking the boat to see if it was safe for the longer passage Graeme was about to begin. As they examined the engine, gearbox and electrical systems, Graeme vented his frustration about the boat owner, who refused to pay for any maintenance unless the boat had completely broken down. It was already unsafe: another skipper had told me the boat was missing a masthead light to identify it to other boats at night and a deck light so the crew could see what they were doing in the dark. Graeme explained:

> When I started working for the owner, I would collect receipts and submit them, and then the guy said well, why didn't he just give him £100 a month for expenses, and that didn't quite cover it but that was alright. And then it went down to £50, and then it just vanished. And now I haven't been paid for food, stores, and fuel for a month. And he hasn't paid wages to the relief crew that took the boat when I was on holiday.
>
> I have put so much money into this boat over the past few years! If I hadn't spent that money, if it would have come out of the boat's share[10] like it was supposed to – I would have been able to pay off my debts, I would be way ahead of where I am now. And now that bastard has it all!
>
> He can't be skint.[11] He must be making money! He is just tight and greedy.

Graeme's anger and frustration at the situation were palpable. He felt trapped; in order to make an income, he needed to work on the boat and catch prawns. Yet the boat was becoming increasingly dangerous, and as the owner refused to fix it, he was obliged to spend his own money, which prevented him from saving to get his own boat. The relationship of care and partnership with the boat I described earlier was completely transformed to one of alienation and resentment because any maintenance Graeme performed on the boat only damaged his own aspirations. In these circumstances, the boat became a 'shit-bucket', reflecting Jackson's point that 'the process of working on an object comes to be experienced as an inherent property of the object itself' (2007: 74). The subjective experience of working with a particular machine is framed by the social relations through which this work is conducted, in this case, the control and ownership of the machine. Graeme's experience reinforces the importance of political economy and class to the development and practice of techniques and technologies (Part II).

Ingold, Lawson and Mauss all discuss the potentially liberating effect of techniques in extending 'the whole person', re-making our world, extending our limits and transforming 'what it is to be human'. But what are the subjective consequences of not being able to realise such extensions and transformations? One consequence was the fact that Graeme and the other disgruntled crew members seemed to go from working on one 'shit-bucket' to another – no matter how well these boats were maintained. 'I've worked on 22 different boats', one young crewman told me. 'You just have to keep moving until you find a good boat to stay on. I bounced around a lot trying to find a decent one to work on that wasn't ripping you off on wages.' On only three of the 22 boats did he feel he was treated with respect and that the traditional share system of payment was fairly applied. Having found one of these rare circumstances, he declared 'I'm stopping[12] here!' Attending to the 'whole person' engaged in carrying out techniques must also include such economic and social relations, as they meant that skippers and crew could have a completely different relationship to the same boats or tools. The social and class relations of ownership and exploitation between boat owner and crew played a critical part in shaping the crew's experience of and relationship to the boat itself, and affected how they applied techniques and attended to the ship (Chapter 4).

The potential for frustration and alienation from machines is therefore not limited to circumstances where 'we feel that machines have ceased to do our bidding or have started to behave incomprehensibly' (Jackson 2002: 338). For Alasdair, the winch could be a 'bastard!' but as a boat owner with a reasonable cash flow he was able to go and buy the parts necessary to return the winch to its normally helpful behaviour. Because Alasdair was able to attend to the winch and to maintain it as he saw fit, his relationship to it *was* dependent on the particular circumstances of the machine's operation. Yet Graeme and other hired skippers and crew were frequently permanently alienated from the 'shit-buckets' they worked on. They had to adapt themselves to the often dangerous operation of poorly maintained boats in sometimes frightening circumstances, with no capacity to adapt these boats or the tools on board to their own interests and needs, and only a limited sense that they were able to maintain their own livelihoods through this work.

The process of selling goods to a market could also produce alienated relationships between owners and their boats (Schacht 1970: 87; Chapters 1 and 6). Competition over prices on international markets could significantly reduce them and owners might be forced to switch gear or species against their will, or be unable to pay for crucial boat maintenance or to sustain their own livelihood. Owners could even contemplate sinking their boat for the insurance money, or be pressured into unsafe situations that contributed to the sinking of their boat, and even their own deaths, as they struggled to keep up (Chapter 6).

The extension of the body's abilities necessary to work at sea required constant care and maintenance for systems to keep working and people to stay alive. This process could involve a temporary animation of the tools involved and their incorporation into the identities of the people who owned and maintained them, or it could be fraught with frustration and alienation if people had to deal with dangerously extended work situations without the resources they needed to protect themselves and develop their own aspirations. People's relations with the boat-machines they worked with was dependent on their ability to exercise some control of it, which is in turn dependent on the social, class and market relationships in which both person and machine were enrolled.

## Conclusion

This chapter has examined the technologies used to work at sea, but it has done so from the perspective of Marcel Mauss' analysis of techniques. This human-cen-tred approach to understanding technologies seeks to understand *why* people do things and *how* they use different techniques and tools and over time to achieve their aims. On one hand, many analyses of work at sea and fishing focus only on the human–environment relationship, ignoring the boats and tools without which it would be impossible to work at sea. On the other hand, focussing only on these technologies is misleading as their use and development over time can only be properly understood in the context of the challenges people use them to solve and the social and economic relations they are embedded in. An understanding of techniques links people's relations to environments, political economy and social relations because it focuses on the practical work processes that necessarily incor-porate all of these factors. Ultimately, fishing boat owners had to turn a profit on regional or international seafood markets in order to keep afloat. This overriding need strongly affected the social relations between owner, skipper and crew, and the relations to the machines and tools they used (Part III).

I have illustrated that it is possible for humans to control and manipulate large, complex and potentially dangerous machines, and to use these machines to extend themselves and their worlds from the centre of their own perceptual environments, to satisfy their own intentions, and to transform their own experience of the world they inhabit. However, this control cannot be taken for granted. The possibility of exerting control rests upon the social relations among people who own, maintain and design machines, as well as the market relations that machines are embedded in. Ingold points to the complexity of the relationship between humans and their tools and machines when he points to the ongoing 'task-orientation' of industrial work-ers, in situations where they are frequently highly alienated and have little control of their work environment, which they must instead 'cope' with as it confronts them. Even in such situations, workers are to some extent 'task-oriented' and carry out:

> skilled handling of industrial machines in the process of coping. [Such activ-ity] is person-centred, it follows implicit 'rules of thumb' rather than explicitly codified procedures, its objectives are set within the current of activity among all those involved in the work rather than following directives laid down from above, it is continually responsive to the other activities that are going on around it, and – most importantly – it is constitutive of personal and social identity. (Ingold 2000: 332)

Ingold is rather optimistic here – most workers must follow 'directives laid down from above' – but control is not complete. The experience of work under capitalism can be both alienating and relational, in the same activity (Chapter 1). Ingold also indicates that modern machines and 'machinofacture' (2000: 308) correspond to 'subject-peripheral' devices (2000: 317) that inherently dominate humans, implying that the limitations to workers controlling their work environments lie in the design of the machines themselves. Yet the range of relations I have described here with industrial and high technology machines points to the overriding importance of social relations – especially of ownership and class – in shaping these experiences. The experience of skippers and owners in this chapter demonstrates that a subject-centred 'high' technology *is* possible, and can be used to develop perception and affordances to satisfy human intentions and aspirations. More than just 'coping' with industrial machines, there is the potential for them to be adapted and transformed around the needs of one's own body and according to one's desires and aspirations – if you are the boat owner or a skipper in the right circumstances. Unfortunately, the majority of Scotland's fishers do not work under such circumstances. When producing for an international market, objectives are not set 'within the current of activity', but by the priorities of the market to which fishermen must adapt in order to 'get a price' (Chapter 5). For crew, there is little sense that their work is 'person-centred': if they don't get out of bed when the skipper tells them to and follow their directions they would soon find themselves skint and unemployed on the pier. A hardworking and capable man at sea may find his work humiliatingly valueless when the bottom drops out of the market. A cocky and popular young man at school might find himself ill and overwhelmed when faced with the motion of the sea and the skipper's multiple demands. A skilled skipper under pressure from the bank could push his boat and crew too far and lose control, drowning everyone on board. And the same boat that a skipper might regard as a partner and companion might be described as a 'shit-bucket' by crew frustrated with their small share payment, as, under pressure from declining prices and increasing fuel costs, the owner reduced the crew's share by sneaking critical maintenance costs into the boat's 'expenses' in order to keep up with his bank payments.

In the next chapter I will continue the focus on techniques at sea. I will examine the techniques used to orient oneself at sea, how GPS chartplotters and other machines were incorporated into these techniques, and the social and market relations these machines were embedded in and reproduce.

## Notes

1 Adult men often refer to other adult men as 'the boy'.
2 A few had experience diving for scallops but this occurs on different grounds. One former diver told me that there was no overlap between the grounds he used to dive on and the grounds he now worked on a prawn creel boat.
3 In the 1970s the sounder display was a light that flashed at the number that corresponded to the depth, with two or more flashes indicating a denser bottom. Today most sounders have colour displays on an LCD screen where colour indicates the density of the seafloor (red is the most dense).

4  Commenting on a draft of this chapter, skipper Alasdair told me, unprompted, that he thought my description was 'spot on' and similar to experiences he remembered with both a sounder and the radar in the fog.

5  Before 1984 trawling was illegal less than three miles from shore, but a boat had to be caught in the act. By leaving their net on the seafloor, fishing boats could argue that they were just passing through the banned area and were not actually fishing there.

6  Teo was originally from Argentina. Some prominent local boat owners played an important role on the British side of the Falklands War against Argentina.

7  The net coming fast on the seabed can be a serious problem, and in extreme cases can cause the boat to sink.

8  GRP is glass-reinforced plastic, or fibreglass.

9  'Shit-bucket' was not just an expression – most small fishing boats did not have a toilet so the 'shit-bucket' was something that you actually shat on yourself.

10  Most Scottish fishing boats operate on a share system. First, operating expenses such as fuel and insurance and port fees are deducted from the boat's total income. Fifty per cent of the remaining income goes to the owner and 50 per cent is divided among the crew. Boat maintenance expenses were supposed to be deducted from the owner's share, but frequently were not (see Chapter 5).

11  Being skint means to have no money.

12  'Stopping' means staying.

# 4

# From 'where am I?' to 'where is that?'
## Rethinking navigation

In February, 6.30 a.m. is still very dark in the north of Scotland. Alex, the skipper of the boat we were tied up to, was dropped off on the Gairloch pier by his visiting fiancée. Muttering 'I hate getting started late!', he climbed down to his boat, quickly turned on lights, cast off docklines, started the engine and then loudly revved it to show his impatience with the other boats still tied up outside him. Five trawlers left the pier at the same time, lights blazing, headed out to the grounds (Figure 25).

The morning was grey and misty, the horizon barely visible, the sunrise hardly perceptible. Alex and my skipper were good friends, and after setting our nets we worked side-by-side along the same edge of The Burma fishing ground. Alex towed a hopper net with rubber disks at the front for going over harder ground (Figure 10) and worked higher on the bank, and we towed a 'grass net' and worked the softer ground lower on the bank. We were often no more than a hundred yards apart. After setting the net and engaging in some telephone banter with other skippers in the area, my skipper went below to sleep. 'Just follow the 80 fathom line, and turn back south before you get to that red hatching', he said, 'Wake me up in about two hours'.

The other trawlers soon turned away south, but we kept heading north to explore the small area of ground that remained blank and unmarked on the GPS chartplotter screen between our position and 'the red hatching'. Although we discussed it as if it was a thing, the red hatching appeared only on the screen of our GPS chartplotter, marking an area of hard and rocky ground. I steered the boat, drank my cup of tea, and carefully attended to the boat, net, engine, sounder and GPS chartplotter as I had been taught over the previous months.

As we approached the 'red hatching' the depth sounder showed the seafloor becoming thicker and redder (which I had been taught meant harder ground), and the sea gradually shallowed no matter which way I turned. Nervous about catching a 'fastener' on this hard ground I decided to turn the boat around and head back south. I followed the skipper's example by turning the boat away from the bank so the net would go downhill, which would hopefully prevent it from getting stuck. As the boat turned, I watched us draw a graceful arc on the screen and became fascinated that I was both steering the boat *and* drawing that movement

Figure 25  Leaving Gairloch harbour, 6.30 a.m. on a February morning.

at the same time. But with all the gear dragging behind it, the boat did not turn smoothly. It sped up rapidly as the angle between the boat and the gear became sharper, and slowed back dramatically as the heavy gear was forced around and its weight gradually fell behind the boat. I was nervous that my turn would end up with the gear in a tangled mess. I had already seen how the trawl door could dig into a bank, or the net could flip over entirely, wires crossed (Chapter 3). I took the turn in stages, regularly steadying the course to check that the wires had straightened and the tension on them was even. For a foolish moment I was disappointed that this meant that I left squiggles in the otherwise smooth track of our course on the chartplotter screen.

The turn went well. I woke the skipper with a cup of coffee at the agreed time and we hauled the net back. The catch was the biggest I had seen so far, 17 baskets[1] of good prawns wiggling, squeaking and squirming on the deck (Figure 26). The skipper was very pleased, and immediately called Alex to report our catch. He was keen to help the young skipper, who had been off work for six weeks waiting for repairs to the hull of his fishing boat, seriously damaged when it had smashed into an island early one morning. Alex was furious. He skippered a bigger boat, with a bigger engine, towing a bigger net, but we had caught more prawns than him. He quizzed Alasdair, who took great delight in claiming ignorance as he had been in his bunk for most of the tow, and referred all Alex's questions to me. After some

Figure 26  My biggest catch: 17 baskets of prawns.

confusing relayed messages, Alasdair handed me the phone. 'You don't happen to know where you got those prawns, do you?' Alex asked me, swallowing his pride. I was genuinely baffled about how to respond. Alex had been within a few hundred yards of us for most of the tow, and he had seen the direction in which we carried on. Plus, how was I to know exactly where these prawns had come from after almost four hours of trawling? 'Somewhere along a very thin line?' I replied in earnest bewilderment. Alex repeated this back to me, incredulous at my apparent evasiveness. Meanwhile, Alasdair was doubled over laughing, although he took the phone back upon seeing my obvious discomfort.

Sorting 17 baskets of prawns was a lot of work, and it took hours of standing, shovelling, sorting and tailing to clear the deck. I 'picked prawns' continuously, trying intently to train my hands to move more quickly, while Alasdair darted back and forth from the sorting table to the steering wheel, and still 'picked' twice as many prawns as I did. I agonised that I had been rude and evasive to Alex. Alasdair was hugely entertained, and thought that I had nothing to apologise for. When the telephone call was made to Alex later to tell him exactly how many stones of good prawns we had sorted out, I got on the phone as well to apologise and to describe as best I could the information he was looking for: the depth we were towing at, the name of the bank we continued towing on, the fact that I had turned as the bank had shallowed and the trace on the depth sounder had reddened. I even used the chartplotter to look up the latitude at which my track turned and headed south again (I hadn't noticed this at the time). Until then, I had not understood how fine the details were that mattered in locating productive prawn grounds: a few hundred yards and a ten metre difference in depth could make all the difference between Alasdair's delight and Alex's frustration. I did not understand that you could watch another boat for four hours and still need to ask the question 'where do you think you got those prawns?'

Despite the fact that both boats carried at least one GPS unit on board, linked to a digital chartplotter, the information about location that mattered was not in reference to the absolute grid of latitude and longitude. What mattered was our position relative to specific features on the seafloor, features that were important to us because of the specific activity we were engaged in: trawling. What mattered was what bank, or edge, we were working, and the precise depth at which our net was positioned (not always directly below the boat, as it usually slid slightly down-hill). Latitude and longitude were only looked up and referred to afterwards, to describe our position to someone else.

In Chapter 3, I discussed the techniques fishermen used to extend their sensory perception and range of effective work into the sea. In this chapter, I will use a similar labour-centred approach to challenge received views about Western navigation and its technologies, and to put forward an alternate analysis centred on people's skills, intentions and techniques. First, I will show how fishermen oriented themselves through movement in the land and seascape, and second, examine the development of techniques to find one's position relative to particular affordances or obstacles. GPS chartplotters are a recent technique for solving the 'old' problem of relative position that is particularly useful for prawn trawlers. Finally, I will examine the social relations implicated in the significant investments owners made in GPS chartplotters and the social relations these devices facilitated.

## Western/European navigation?

Comparing the seemingly very different techniques of European and Micronesian navigators has become a classic move in anthropology, particularly in environmental perception (Ingold 2000), cognitive science (Hutchins 1995; Suchman 2007) and science studies (Nader 1996). Ingold, for example, argues that 'quite unlike the European navigator, with his compass and charts, the Micronesian seafarer feels his way towards his destination by continually adjusting his movements in relation to the flow of waves, wind, current and stars' (2000: 239). European navigation practices are typically portrayed as highly planned and abstracted in contrast to the responsive and sensitive environmental perception of the Micronesians and others.

Both Suchman and Ingold suggest that actual Western navigational practices may be different from these broad characterisations (Ingold 2000: 430 n.6; Suchman 2007: 26), but little ethnography of European or Western navigators exists. Suchman and Ingold cite anthropologists Thomas Gladwin (1970) and Edwin Hutchins (1995). Gladwin's ethnography of Micronesian navigation refers to his own sailing experience and is not an ethnography of Western navigation (1970: 144, 232). Likewise, Thomas Widlok compares his own use of a GPS to the orientation skills of the Hai||om whom he worked with in Namibia (1997). Hutchins' *Cognition in the Wild* is an ethnography of navigation practices, but only on board large US Navy ships. Much more actual ethnography of Western navigators is needed to make proper comparisons or analysis.

The navigation practices Hutchins observed being used by a US Navy navigation team bear very little resemblance to the navigation practices I observed on fishing boats in Scotland. There, Navy officers were frequently the butt of jokes among fishermen.[2] The expression 'paper charts!' referred to navigation practices similar to Navy ones, and was usually said with a derisive snort; such practices were seen as unnecessarily procedural, probably inaccurate, and characteristic of people who regarded themselves as far superior to fishermen and who should therefore be studiously ignored. Hutchins' generalisations about Western navigation practices are like observing the walking practices of a US Army drill squad and using them to generalise about Western walking practices.

In Western navigation, Hutchins claims, the chart 'or some representation of the environment' (1995: 13) comes first, is experienced separately from our movements in the world, and is 'the most important piece of technology in the position-fixing task' (1995: 36). We can only make sense of our movements, he argues, by finding 'correspondences' between the world as it encountered and some representation of that environment. 'We feel we know where we are', Hutchins explains 'when we have achieved a reconciliation between the features we see in our world and a representation of that world' (1995: 13). Other navigation instruments assist in finding these correspondences.

Yet an alternate history of Western navigation can be written, one which focuses on the process of navigation as the techniques that people have used to orient themselves and to move through the world. Westerners were able to navigate without a Mercator projection chart – but the chart facilitated locating and claiming position from 'centres of calculation', and therefore, the expansion of European empires (Latour 1987: 215). There has been a long struggle between the use of orientation techniques centred on the perceptual skills of the navigator on the deck of the ship, and those navigation techniques which collected mapping information in the absolute grid of latitude and longitude for the centres of calculation, and in turn relied on them (Latour 1987: 224). It is significant that authorities in these centres spent hundreds of years cajoling navigators to adopt their charts, instruments and techniques (Howard 1998). Typical was Amsterdam instrument and chart-maker Willem Blaeu's introduction to *The Light of Navigation*. After explaining the use of the astrolabe, cross-staff and associated charts to find the latitude of particular countries, he comments:

> It may be that some will object and say, that there be many Pilots which do not well understand such things, and yet they are able to go directly unto diverse places, whither they desire to sayle: which I confess to be true: but tell me, how many times are they deceived? How many times are they in great doubt and fear? (Blaeu 1964: [1612] D2)

Blaeu acknowledges that seafarers were able to orient themselves and travel at sea without his navigation instruments. Many anthropologists assume the sextant is representative of 'traditional' Western navigation (for example, Aporta and Higgs 2005: 745), yet it was only used for approximately 250 out of over 2,000 years of long-distance seafaring. Joshua Slocum famously left his chronometer[3] at home when he sailed single-handed around the world in 1895, scornfully remarking that 'in our newfangled notions of navigation it is supposed that a mariner cannot find his way without one' (2001 [1900]: 17). Western seafarers have long been able to orient themselves and travel at sea without using the navigation instruments that many assume are essential.

Researchers have classically theorised that navigation tries to solve the absolute question 'where am I?' (Aporta and Higgs 2005: 743; Hutchins 1995: 12). In this chapter I demonstrate that it is more accurate to say that navigation seeks to solve the relative question 'where is that?' The ethnography of practical wayfinding and navigation techniques I present here also demonstrates the value of Mauss' approach to studying technologies in the context of the techniques they are used for. The seductive power of navigation instruments is such that researcher after researcher has taken a technology-first approach to understanding navigation, an approach that obscures the real problem that navigators have sought to solve, and why.

One of Hutchins' Navy navigators reflects on the real purpose of the profusion of computational procedures and logbooks that he was required to use when entering a harbour on board a large Navy ship:

> You *can* go into San Diego by eye. But legally, you can't. If you haven't matched all the things and something happens, not necessarily to you, it don't have to. One of those buoys can float loose in the goddamn bay and rub up alongside you. Boy, you better have everything covered here, because they are going to try to hang the captain. They will try to hang him. Unless he can prove with data that everything he did was right. (Hutchins 1995: 38, emphasis in original)

The elaborate navigation procedures Hutchins describes may be a greater reflection of the processes of accountability within the US Navy and between the US Navy and American society as a whole, than they are about finding position at sea.

## Orientation: through movement, to affordances

A woman with a long history of living along the west coast commented to me that I must be 'good at the navigation', and that in contrast she 'would be on the first rock'. Like many others, she imagined navigation to be the most challenging and dangerous aspect of travelling at sea, and saw it as a very specific and mysterious set of tools and procedures, used only at sea. Yet the fishermen I worked with did not rely on 'the navigation' to orient themselves at sea. They used their own perceptions and experience built up in the ordinary process of 'wayfinding' through their seagoing environment: where a person ' "feels his way" towards his goal, continually adjusting his movements in response to an ongoing perceptual monitoring of his surroundings' (Ingold 2000: 220). 'Being oriented' is neither subjective nor objective, but both, combined through the process of movement, 'to the extent of having moved from place to place, from vista to vista'. In contrast to Hutchins' understanding, 'one does not need a map with a circle on it labelled, "You are here"' (Gibson 1979: 200). The process of exploring to find affordances and returning to understand and develop those affordances at different tides, times and seasons oriented fishermen to their seascape.

It is critical to distinguish between two different aspects of navigation in order to properly understand what navigation is and why particular practices or tools are used. I use 'orientation' to describe the general and comfortable sense of one's position in the world. This is distinct from the challenge of finding 'relative position' to specific affordances or obstacles. While most analyses of navigation assume that its purpose is orientation ('where am I?'), I will demonstrate that virtually all navigation devices are used in techniques to solve the problem of relative position ('where is that?').

In no situation did I observe anyone using a chart or digital chartplotter to orient themselves in the conventional sense of being 'lost' and needing to discover one's position, as Hutchins' theory of 'correspondence' would suggest. It is only in the most bizarre and unexpected circumstances that one could imagine discovering oneself in a location with no memory or experience of getting there. Even if you had gone below to sleep and were trying to determine the boat's position after waking, it would be your fellow crew who would orient you, taking time to point out different landmarks, the route you had taken to get there, anything unexpected observed along the way, and what was known about the course ahead. The skippers I observed all had a precise idea of where they were located *before* they consulted a GPS chartplotter, and consequently the plotter was almost always used at such a zoomed-in scale that I found it almost useless for orienting myself. It was the process of journeying through an area that oriented you to it, that gave you a sense of the shapes of islands, points, lochs and the routes for travelling between them (see also Tyrrell 2006: 228). This was just as true for novice sailors as for experienced fishermen. When I asked one woman who had begun sailing a few months before why she enjoyed it, it was precisely this sense of orientation she appreciated:

> The views are amazing. It looks so different, all these places I've been going to for ages, and it is amazing to see them from the sea. I've always been confused about Isle Oronsay and Armadale and where they were in relation to each other, but now I understand and I'll never forget because I've *seen* them. *I've been from one place to another and I've seen where they are.*

Travelling at sea, in fine weather, the air clear, the mountains rise from the shoreline, islands slowly shift past each other, coastlines open into bays, ports appear behind headlands, and roads and houses come in and out of view along the shoreline. It is all there before you, in depth and in constant motion as you are in motion. The dimensionality of the land, the shape of it, is experienced by going around it, and seeing it constantly in different arrangements, in views and vistas possible only from specific places.

On the west coast of Scotland, the specific visual arrangements of land experienced from specific places at sea were called 'marks' and used to locate fishing grounds and other places at sea. George MacLeod sketches the views and arrangements of islands as they are seen from the marks used by Bernera fishing boats in the Western Isles and describes the routes that skippers used to find them (2005: 105). These 'marks' are similar to the *meyds* used at sea around the Shetland island of Whalsay (Cohen 1987: 121). The *meyds* Cohen describes are highly individual: fishermen often construct them differently, using different combinations of landmarks, and various groups on Whalsay had different names for them. The men who were familiar with these *meyds* found them almost impossible to describe from their living rooms, and as one explained 'If I was on the water I could go right to it. But thinking about it – that's different' (Cohen 1987: 123). Thus, Cohen's informants did not use a 'mental map' (Frake 1985: 254; Gell 1985: 271) to think about their *meyds*, but located them in the process of movement through the seascape in which they were located. Commenting on the marks he used for fishing grounds Alasdair said, 'many of these marks tend to be remembered as they come into line. I would hardly remember most just now but put me on the ground and they are so obvious'.

Figure 27 'The chimneys on the bishop's house in line with the Abbey Tower' (on the far right). A mark for fishing grounds off Iona.

Cohen uses *meyds* as an example of the '*cognitive* mastery of conditions' (1987: 123) found 'all in the head' (Frake 1985: 256) because finding them does not rely on any instruments. Cohen contrasts these 'cognitive' skills with what he dismisses as the '*mechanical* competence' of 'the modern navigator, who has only to look up the tide table or read off the data from the electronic sensor without having any basic understanding of or mastery of the phenomena thus described' (1987: 123). Here, Cohen betrays a misunderstanding of how tide tables are used. Tide tables give the approximate heights of tides at particular widely-spaced reference ports, but what is important to fishermen is the tidal current, or horizontal movement of water, at their own precise location, as it is affected by the eddies around islands, formations on the seafloor, and wind direction (Chapter 3). No tide table in use on the west of Scotland in 2009 had data precise enough to predict the speed of tidal currents at a particular place or time. Even if currents were mapped that accurately, they also change with the weather. A tide table provides a reference point, but a considerable understanding of how tidal currents move in a particular area is necessary to properly understand them.

Other researchers have made similar worried observations that: 'Computer technology ... has made locating fishing grounds less an art and more a technical skill' (Menzies 2002: 20), and that the GPS may result in 'deskilling ... accompanied by a diminished relationship with the land and one increasingly mediated by the GPS and other devices' (Aporta and Higgs 2005: 737). Cohen distinguished between traditional 'non-technological' navigation and the 'technological' navigation found in the commercial fishery (1987: 124). Although he says that one practice can inform the other, there is an assumption that the presence of a device like a depth sounder or tide tables makes for fundamentally different navigation practices and human–environment relations.

But can such a sharp distinction be drawn between 'cognitive mastery' and 'mechanical competence'? *Meyds* cannot be 'all in the head', otherwise the fishermen that Cohen interviewed would be able to describe them from their living rooms. While the Whalsay fishermen may not use a tool to remember or use their *meyds*, it seems clear from his description that they are remembered and situated in the environment they are used in and are very difficult to separate from it. Ingold has described skill as 'a property not of the individual human body as a biophysical entity, a thing-in-itself, but of the total field of relations constituted by the presence of the organism-person, indissolubly body and mind, in a richly structured environment' (2000: 353). *Meyds* are techniques developed as people move through and use the affordances of their environments. Other navigational devices are also incorporated into these techniques and *meyds* cannot be separated out from this context.

Cohen's distinction between cognitive or non-technological *mastery* and mechanical or technological *competence* repeats Mauss' 'fundamental mistake of thinking that there is technique only when there is an instrument' (2006 [1935]: 82). It reinforces the importance of Mauss' approach to understanding technologies in the context of the techniques they are used in (Part II). In the analysis I use here, both Cohen's 'non-technological' and 'technological' fishers worked in environments they were thoroughly oriented in and familiar with – although the 'technological' fisherman had tools and machines that extended their capacity further offshore and into greater depths of water. Yet each of these fishermen used different techniques for finding their position relative to their preferred fishing grounds: the 'non-techno-logical' relying on *meyds*, and the 'technological' also incorporating a depth sounder and Decca Navigator into their techniques. Continuity can exist between these tech-niques. For example, a radar can be used in exactly the same way as *meyds* are used, by adjusting one's position at sea until specific landmarks are aligned on the screen. Using a radar in addition to your eyes or binoculars means that different landmarks become remarkable and that their alignments can be observed even in the dark or in thick fog, extending the usefulness of the technique. A radar also requires money to purchase it, a boat large enough to install it on, and electricity. However, we should not assume that the presence of new technologies necessarily means that people's sense of orientation in their environment or their relationships to it are transformed. Such an approach mistakenly elevates the effects of particular instruments above social relations and all other factors. Changes in human–environmental relations have their origins in changing social relations, market relations, and expectations of what the environment can afford for whom. New instruments and machines are developed and incorporated into human practices as part of these changes, but they are not the primary cause of them.

Navigation is not only a process of 'getting somewhere geographically, but of getting somewhere socially, in that one attempts to meet a certain person, to col-lect a certain fruit, or do a certain job' (Widlok 1997: 324). People became oriented in their environments through the process of finding particular affordances. The abstract question 'where am I?' is one people rarely ask and is a poor model for navigation and orientation practices. Widlok has also questioned whether 'map reading should be treated as a model for all cognitive processes involving orienta-tion' (1997: 325), as Hutchins suggests. The ethnography presented here shows that it should not. The process of orientation through movement is primarily based on techniques for finding relative position, into which charts may be incorporated. But charts do not come first – the general movement and exploration involved in 'getting somewhere socially' does.

## Techniques for finding relative position: a history

There is a difference between the skill of being generally oriented in one's environ-ment, and the more specific techniques fishermen have developed over time to solve the problem of finding their position relative to specific affordances (mainly fishing grounds) or hazards (such as a shallow rock). These techniques have ranged from 'marks' and memorised compass courses to radar, radio and computerised satellite and sonar instruments. A vast array of new electronic instruments have been incor-porated into navigation practices over the past 50 years. A historical perspective on these devices shows both the differences that new technologies have made and the ongoing continuities in the techniques they are used in. The purpose the GPS chart-plotter is used for becomes much clearer when set in this context, rather than treated as an isolated puzzle. At least once each decade, if not more often, a new kind of instrument has become available. Entire technological systems have been invented and become obsolete within living memory. Fishermen are eager to find out about new technologies and regularly visit each other's wheelhouses to inspect new purchases and to discuss and speculate on their merits, as well as doing the rounds of booths displaying the latest electronic gadgetry at the annual Fishing Expo trade show in Glasgow. However, they are also sceptical about the claims made on behalf of new technologies, realistic about their limitations, and worried about the consequences of their use.

The earliest techniques for locating relative position were the 'marks' or *meyds* discussed earlier. Alasdair emphasised the lack of electronics and charts when he started fishing in the late 1960s: 'We had a compass and a watch! That was it! We used nothing other than that!' 'Did you use charts?' I asked. 'No', he replied, 'What did we need a chart for? We *knew* where we were.' Another man who started fishing in the 1960s told me 'When I started, if you looked at a chart, the old timers would start talking about you, start asking "Is there something wrong with him?" You were expected to know, you had to learn'.

Alasdair explained that with a compass and a watch, memorised courses could be followed in case the fog rolled in and the land became invisible:

> Davey's boat, 1970. On a tide ebbing: 55 minutes from the mooring just at the pier in Iona, 55 minutes at 12 degrees west of south [a compass course] to Torran Rock. Seven minutes more against the flood tide.
>     From there if you went to the West Reef it was 17 minutes exactly due west. You ended up with an encyclopaedic knowledge of these, so even if you got fog, or it was night time, well, no problem!

These memorised courses helped to find locations with known affordances: the West Reef and the safety of the mooring. When I asked how these times were determined, he admitted that it was a mix of experience and 'You would cheat as well, you would cheat and measure on the chart occasionally'. Referring to a chart was 'cheating', and used not for orientation but for making specific calculations used as a back-up to find one's position relative to an affordance when it became temporarily invisible due to darkness or fog. Despite occasionally measuring distances on a chart to approximate the time it would take to motor between places, the number of minutes the journey would take on a particular boat (Davey's), at a particular speed (using no mechanical or electronic speed indicator), and at a specific state of the tide and current could only be determined through the experience of making that journey many times over. Using such calculations also required a closely cultivated attention to the speed of the boat as observed through the passing water, and felt through the vibration and sound of the engine. Like using a tide table, measuring the distance on the chart still only offered skippers a rough approximation of the time it would take. In practice, devices like charts and tide tables require skilled attention and detailed knowledge gained through experience to be useful. Even if a chart was used to make a specific calculation, it was not used for orientation.

Techniques for sounding the sea incorporated depth sounders from the 1970s onwards (Chapter 3). Sounders gave fishermen new information about bottom density, and a much quicker way of determining depth and topography than using a 'lead line' rope and weight, or the fishing gear itself. Trawlermen could attentively watch the sounder for banks and muddy holes, and lobster fishermen for an echo that would indicate rock and harder ground. Sounders could also be cross-referenced with the memorised compass courses to help find position: once Alasdair and Davey got a sounder, it is likely that they watched it closely as they approached West Reef to get confirmation from the shallowing water that they had indeed arrived.

Depth sounders could give a boat's distance from the seafloor and tell you something about its density, and radars had a similar capacity in relation to land above the surface of the water. Radars were incorporated into techniques for finding position relative to landmarks, and became common on small fishing boats on the west coast of Scotland in the 1970s. On a modern radar screen, the boat is at the centre, and hard and reflective objects above the surface of the water are arrayed around it in monochrome blobs. The screen accurately displays the distance away from the blobs, although it is up to the radar user to guess what any particular blob might represent. The radar used microwaves and like the depth sounder, it was developed as a military technology during the Second World War. After the war, radars were primarily used for meteorology, and then a new range of compact devices was developed for use on board small boats. In the dark or in very poor visibility, the radar makes it possible to find boats or landmarks that are otherwise invisible.

When fishing, the radar could be used to measure the distance from a point of land to mark tows or hazards close to shore. In the 1970s fishermen developed an ingenious technique to locate grounds further from shore, which Alasdair described as follows:

> In the 1970s and 1980s we had rather Heath Robinson[4] ways of doing things. We would put radar reflectors on peaks, and work with distances off the reflectors on the radar. You would put down two or three reflectors, and look at the distance and the echo sounder. If it looked right on the echo sounder, if you saw a nice bump, it was right. But to get back there was a nightmare!

James also remembered: 'We used to work with radar marks. It was a nightmare! There were books all over the wheelhouse with the distances and the bearings! We would use landmarks as well, the hill in line with that bit, the lighthouse over the point. Now it's all down in the plotters, all stored.' In describing this radar-based triangulation method, Alasdair emphasised that the radar was used to 'get back there': to find particular known places, rather than to find oneself. Fishermen also combined these techniques with older marks like 'the lighthouse over the point', emphasising the continuity between using one's eye and the radar to locate position using landmarks.

By the 1980s, the Decca Navigator Mark 21 and Mark 30 'became standard kit' used on west coast fishing boats to determine their position relative to affordances and obstacles, allowing relative position to be determined more directly, and recorded more easily in order to 'get back there' later.[5] Alasdair described it as 'an incredible advance on working with dead reckoning,[6] on working with the radar'. The system had first been used during the British D-Day landing in France in 1944, although it was switched off again the following day to preserve its secrecy. The Decca used radio signals sent from stations on shore consisting of three hyperbolic (curved) lines labelled red, purple and green. The position of the boat could be determined by plotting the readings from any two hyperbolas. Fishing boats used the digital readouts from the Decca to plot their positions manually on graph paper, a convenient way of replacing the 'books all over the wheelhouse!' Although the Decca system was switched off in 2000, skipper Ruaridh 'the *Accord*' still kept his Decca charts mounted on the wall of his boat (Figure 28). 'A lot of work went into that', Alasdair emphasised. The drawings were made with pencil on a long spool of graph paper approximately eight inches wide, with charts of different areas drawn on the spool at regular intervals. But because the straight lines on the graph paper represented gently curved hyperbolic lines, north was not up, and the world was stretched and distorted. No land was marked on these maps, just a dense patchwork of tows, with dots or boxes for 'fasteners'. Although the map Ruaridh showed me was of the familiar Back of Kyle area (Figure 8, Figure 30 and Figure 31), I had a difficult time understanding how the tows on this map corresponded to the ones I was familiar with.

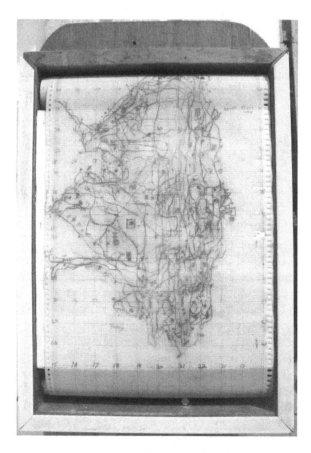

Figure 28  A map of 'Decca tows' made by Ruaridh for the 'Back of Kyle' area. The vertical lines run approximately north-east to south-west, corresponding to the Decca hyperbolic lines.

When Ruaridh started trawling he used radar techniques for about two years before he got his Decca Navigator. The first thing he did with his Decca was to mark in the fasteners and obstacles he already knew on the graph paper, sometimes in advance or sometimes at the same time as he followed his normal tows. He needed to know his relative position to these things. To map these 'Decca tows', he would read the numbers the Decca displayed while he was making the tow, and manually mark the intersection points with pencil on the graph paper grid. He did this at the same time as the normal work of skippering a trawler. The transition from and overlap with the radar system is clear, as there are notes on the 'Decca tows' showing the required distances off particularly bad fasteners which would have been determined by radar (for example 'Bever 0.85 off shore' in the top right of Figure 28, marking a wreck). Later, the Decca company produced the 350T model that was integrated with a bulky plotter which used a pen on paper that could be manually set down to start recording position, and lifted up to stop. Cohen's fieldwork in Shetland took place as skippers began to use Deccas and depth sounders.[7] Ruaridh's description of the painstaking work of mapping the ground is a far cry from Cohen's description of 'just read[ing] off the data from the electronic sensor' (1987: 123).

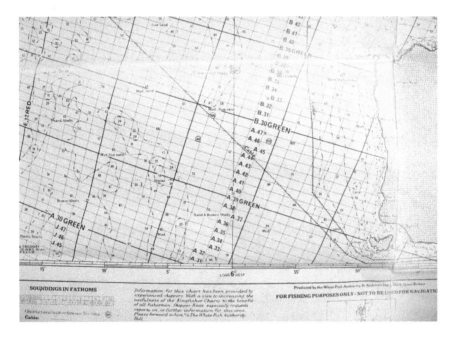

Figure 29  A section of a Decca chart near Gairloch. The diagonal lines represent the hyperbolic radio waves that the Decca used, corresponding to the numbers displayed on the Decca unit and marked on the edges of the graph paper shown in Figure 28. Skipper Ruaridh said he never used these charts: 'I got them at a Fishing show and then just stuck them in my attic.'

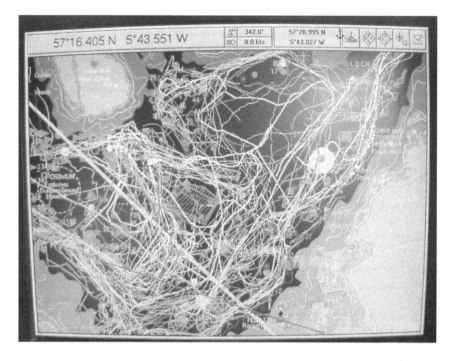

Figure 30 GPS chartplotter image for the Back of Kyle, the same area represented in Figure 8, Figure 28 and Figure 31.

Figure 31 The Back of Kyle from the north. A view from the south (and the other side of the bridge) is in Figure 5.

The increasing use of the Decca was directly related to fishermen shifting from ring-netting for herring to trawling for prawns. In 1975, the last ring-net for herring was shot in the Kyle of Lochalsh area. These quick-moving fish were caught in mobile schools in the water column and not on the seabed. John MacRae had worked on a ring-netter and explained that there 'was no need for the Decca with the ring-net – what you used for the ring-net was the sounder, to look for the fish on the sounder. You already knew what the bottom was like'. Moreover, herring were mostly caught at night and the Decca radio waves 'would go haywire at sunset'. The Decca 'was no use with the ring-net', but it 'came in with the trawler'.

The crash in the herring fishery and declining prices for prawns in the 1970s meant that there was a considerable expansion in the fleet of small trawlers on the west coast in the 1980s. Trawlers could catch prawns at a lower cost than creel boats. A few inshore trawlers started working out of Portree in 1972, and in 1980 Ruaridh was the first to convert to trawling in the Kyle area. According to Ruaridh, 'heaps' of inshore trawlers got started when the legal prohibition on inshore trawling was lifted in 1984. Many skippers were developing new affordances in familiar environments, affordances that were essential to the development of a new fishery. Technique and affordance were developed together, as Ruraidh explained: 'It was easier to open up new tows with the Decca than it was with the radar. It was harder to track the tow you had done with the radar to be able to do it again.' Ruaridh persevered in trawling with just the sounder and radar for two years before he got the Decca to systematically map his tows and the hazards he found along them. A few years after Ruaridh got his Decca, he got his first colour sounder. 'That made the biggest difference', he said, 'that was when a lot of tows were opened. With the black-and-white, you would see a steep bank and you wouldn't venture there. Then with the colour sounder you could see that it was more steep than hard. It was so much more efficient'. The process of opening up a new fishery meant that new affordances in new grounds were found and developed. New techniques for locating position relative to those grounds were directly related to the ability to find and record the productive prawn tows that were the affordances that this new fishery required.

The radio stations that broadcast the Decca signals were switched off in March 2000, but the Decca maps like the one Ruaridh made remained in circulation. It was a generous and appreciated gesture to give someone new to an area the local Decca tows, as James did to Alasdair in Chapter 1. These Decca tows formed the basis of the information entered into many GPS chartplotters. Although the conversion 'took some headscratching', it would help skippers avoid the obstacles that others had already mapped.

The Decca system was switched off because a new system took its place, the now-ubiquitous GPS, or Global Positioning System. Combined with the personal computer, the GPS is now mostly used in the form of a chartplotter, a digital form of the Decca maps that Ruaridh had labouriously made with pencil and paper. The first GPS devices provided a latitude and longitude read-out, which could then be manually plotted onto a Mercator projection chart. Later, GPS chartplotters were developed that showed the position of the user embedded into an electronic chart. Further developments allowed people to insert marks or draw onto the electronic chart for later reference. The chartplotter screens in Figures 11, 30, 34 and 39 are all photographs taken in 2006 and 2007 of the chartplotter of one fishing boat I worked on regularly.[8] I have already shown how chartplotters recorded places like Wullie's Peak (Chapter 2) and were closely attended to in the course of opening up and working grounds (Chapter 3). Chartplotters facilitated the same techniques earlier instruments were used for to find position relative to affordances and obstacles and to store one's history of work in order 'to get back there'. However, the chartplotter vastly increased the amount and precision of the information that could be stored, and the ease of collecting it.

Chartplotters consisted of a vibration-proof personal computer running a chart plotting software package (Olex and Trax were popular brands), with a digital Mercator projection nautical chart installed. The plotter was wired to a GPS unit, which triangulated the boat's position from satellite signals, and then computed the latitude and longitude. The position of the boat was displayed as a moving icon on the chart on the colour screen. On most trawlers the chart was displayed on a 12- to 18-inch flat-screen computer monitor, but many creel boats and yachts used smaller and less expensive units which integrated the GPS and the plotter functions into one box with a smaller black-and-white screen. The most commonly used function of the plotter was to 'track' the progress of the boat, leaving an accurate trail behind the boat on the screen, made in any number of colours, patterns and weights, and with information on date, time, boat speed and direction electronically stored. The user could also draw lines, boxes, circles or other marks directly on the screen, or write text, or insert an icon. As these inscriptions made by the user built up over time, they gradually superseded the importance of the pre-loaded digital navigational charts. New and far more detailed readings of depths were entered, inaccurate harbour entrances were re-drawn, but most importantly, the ground that was worked was inscribed over and over again with the tracks made and places marked while working it. Thus the Mercator projection of latitude and longitude provided a framework for positioning one's experience, and the GPS unit and associated satellites provided the tracking capability. But the real reference used on a day-to-day basis was to one's own working experience, as inscribed on the chartplotter over several years, a form of detailed, spatialised 'notes' about fishermen's own working experience.

More recently, companies developed programs to merge GPS information with readings from the depth sounder to reconstruct the shape of the seafloor in three dimensions (Figure 32). Only a few boats had these tools in 2006–7, and they were the subject of much head-scratching and wheelhouse visits as other owners and skippers debated if they were worth the investment. James 'the *Iris*' showed me his Olex three-dimensional plotter, explaining that: 'Using the Olex was surprising. There's a lot of guess-work; you had an idea there were a lot of gullies, but it showed you which way to work them. You can find your way up banks easier, where you couldn't before. You can find the gullies and things, and follow them up or down the bank.' Like the colour sounder, James felt the Olex expanded the affordances and grounds available to him.

Figure 32  Photograph of a three-dimensional chartplotter in use. The white, grey and red
blob is the boat and the dark blue line the direction the boat is heading.

The stylised reconstruction of the seafloor on a three-dimensional plotter appears as a kind of barren moonscape, the boat hovering mysteriously above the seafloor. There is no water in this image – it is a peculiar vision of what Helmreich describes as a '*sounded*scape' (2007: 625). It is not the same as seeing underwater. The seafloor is surveyed using the distance measured from the constantly mobile platform of the boat, so the boat's motion, the waves, and the action of the tide produce anomalous readings in the forms of spikes, which all need to be smoothed out to join the points together. The image in Figure 32 was produced only after many smoothings of the data collected.

Some skippers were sceptical of the usefulness of the three-dimensional plotter. A young skipper who preferred to work on rocky ground complained, 'It shows the bottom as so spiky it's frightening, you would never want to go in there!' Even salesmen for the units said that the three-dimensional plotting was a bit of a gimmick, and that most fishermen continued to rely on the two-dimensional chartplotter which showed their work and tows. While James thought that his three-dimensional map of the seafloor was useful, the information he relied on and which he didn't want others to see were the tows stored in his two-dimensional plotter.

Like the radar, sounder and the Decca, the GPS has a well-documented military history (Widlok 1997). Fishermen were well aware of this: out one day with Alasdair, the boat's position on the chartplotter inexplicably moved around and occasionally disappeared. 'Is there a war on? The GPS is awfully jumpy today', he inquired rhetorically. During the 1991 Gulf War, he said, the GPS signal in northern Scotland was particularly disrupted. For the first years of the GPS operation, the US military did not allow civilian units to reach the maximum precision, precision that fishermen wanted and needed in locating obstacles on the grounds.

Fishers are always already oriented to the environment they work in as they move through it. Over time they have also developed many techniques to meet the additional challenge of finding their position relative to the affordances or obstacles they needed to know about in order to fish successfully. These techniques have incorporated dead reckoning, sounders, radars, Deccas and GPS chartplotters. Despite the enormous difference between memorised 'marks' and GPS chartplotters, they were both used to solve the same basic problems: where is the West Reef? How far am I away from the Beaver Boat wreck? These devices by themselves have not fundamentally changed human–environment relations as some anthropologists have worried. The effects of technologies must be examined in the context of the transformation of sea creatures into valuable commodities with a variable price in faraway markets, and the alienation of fishing crew from any ownership relation with a boat and from the sea as the source of a reliable livelihood (Chapter 5). But the GPS chartplotter does mean that fishermen can store increasing volumes of information about their own working history, and therefore more effectively develop the affordances they have sought over time, expanding their grounds and extending their capabilities.

## GPS chartplotters: mapping affordances

After my clumsy conversation with Alex and after sorting through the 17 baskets of prawns, the weather started to deteriorate. It had been a sociable morning, but now the boats went their separate ways. We ended up on our own, working a complicated patch of hard ground that required careful attention and a lot of sharp turns. The seas became steep and lumpy, and the boat's motion quite unpleasant (Figure 33). I began to feel queasy. Every motion required more effort, and my body became much, much heavier. The increasing waves and strengthening wind made every necessary turn more difficult for the boat too. The boat looked as if it was only ten metres long, but with all the fishing gear stretched out behind it, Alasdair reminded me 'you have to remember you are steering a 1,300-foot long boat'.

There was tension and claustrophobia in working that piece of ground: the autopilot unable to steer the boat properly because of the force of the wind and waves and the gear stretched out at awkward angles, the wheel creaking and protesting as it was turned around and around and around, frequent exclamations of 'bastard!' from the skipper, the boat heeling over sharply, pulled over as we turned by the weight of the fishing gear stretching down to the seafloor. Me, trying to catch the loose objects sliding across and crashing down while hanging on, and

Figure 33 Trawling in lumpy waves and strengthening wind. The morning's bumper catch is in the fish boxes in the centre of the boat and on the deck.

both of us anxiously checking the trawl wires stretched behind the boat for any warning that the net had become caught on the ground, which was 90 fathoms (540 feet) below. The skipper used all of his skills and concentration to try to feel the ground before the net became caught and to precisely manipulate the net so that it would come close to, but avoid, the hazards around us.

On the chartplotter in Figure 34, boxes of red and yellow hatching marked the hard and rocky ground around us. The discovery of this ground was still visible in the red and green tracks of earlier tows which ended abruptly as the skipper tested and re-mapped the extent of the rocky ground to the north. It was more than likely that these tows ended with the net caught hard on the ground below, or worse, on the 'stones' relief skipper 'Buckie' John had marked on the northernmost bank. 'Stones' was a euphemism for the enormous boulders which could become caught inside the net and cause no end of headaches and damage: such 'stones' were only discovered through bitter experience.

The photograph in Figure 34 shows Skye visible a few miles away through the drizzle, but to the west and north the sea stretched for miles, a few other boats barely visible on the horizon. The horizon was open, the sky was open, but we were crashing and banging and manoeuvring tightly around obstacles that were far below us and which we could not see. The contrast was dizzying. It was the

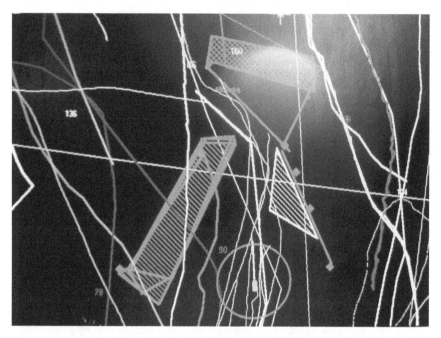

Figure 34 Above is the view of the chartplotter in use, with the boat near the bottom with a circle around it and a line extending forwards to show the direction of movement. The hazardous patches of hard ground and 'stones' are marked around it with hatching in rectangular and triangular shapes. The skipper was attempting to follow the solid white line beside the boat, which marks a safe route through the ground. The photograph below is taken a few minutes after the one above.

chartplotter, not the view around us, which gave some explanation for the difficulty of working this ground. The dashed (instead of solid) tow lines[9] indicated that the ground was hard enough to require a hopper net (Figure 10). The red hatched areas showed large areas of ground too hard to tow on and indicated that it would likely be challenging to work between them. On a calm day, this would be the kind of ground that was rough enough that you could feel it vibrating in the wheelhouse window or through the soles of your shoes.

'An affordance', said Gibson, 'is neither an objective property nor a subjective property; or it is both if you like ... It is equally a fact of the environment and a fact of behaviour' (1979: 129). What makes the chartplotter so useful is that it offers the possibility of mapping both the objective and subjective qualities of such affordances. It is not a map of the environment, but of the experience of seeking particular affordances in an environment. The chartplotter dispenses with the strict distinction between 'mapmaking' and 'map-using' that is built into Mercator projection charts and other conventional maps (see Ingold 2000: 231). In contrast, 'mapping' using the chartplotter brings these two processes together so that 'the forms or patterns that arise from the mapping process' are maintained in the ongoing process of mapping, use and re-mapping (Ingold 2000: 231). Chartplotter maps are made up of 'condensed histories' (Ingold 2000: 220), and they continuously 'grow, line by line with every additional gesture' (Ingold 2000: 231) – like my slightly squiggly curve or the line extending behind the boat in Figure 34. Fishermen used the GPS infrastructure produced by a centre of calculation and the US military, along with digitalised forms of Mercator projection charts, to make a very different kind of map that overlaid and superseded the original, a map that reflected their own experience of seeking particular affordances, and an indispensable and constantly updated tool in developing those affordances.

The affordances recorded on the chartplotter changed and developed over time, but there was a consistency to the experience of the same skipper returning to the area to carry out the same kind of activity with the same kind of fishing gear and a similar level of attentiveness. Chartplotter maps are specific to the person making them, their boat and their gear. 'What is that!' another skipper exclaimed when he saw my photographs of the chartplotter in Figure 11, Figure 30 and Figure 34, appearing genuinely baffled at the profusion of tracks and markings, 'my plotter does not look anything like that!' Yet these two skippers were good friends and often worked the same grounds. Chartplotter mapping involved a 'spatialization of memory' (Gordillo 2004: 7), and the maps produced were highly individual.

In the process of mapping and re-mapping the chartplotter display itself becomes part of the environment that is closely attended to. The view the chartplotter presents has the user suspended and moving forward in a map of their own making, with most of their working history immediately visible and accessible on the screen around them. The chartplotter reflects the experience of 'ordinary wayfinding' where 'the world is apprehended from within. One makes one's way *through* it, not over or across it' (Ingold 2000: 241). One's history of work in a place is made real and – almost – concrete. Boat crew talked about marks that existed only on their chartplotter like the 'red hatching' or 'the purple star' as if they were geographical landmarks.

The incorporation of significant subjective elements into chartplotter mapping runs counter to most anthropological writing about the GPS. For example, Ingold laments that 'the making of maps came to be divorced from the experience of bodily movement in the world', a divorce 'taken one step further' with the development of GPS (2000: 234, 430 n.4). Widlok observed that 'both a map and a GPS depend on a history of human-environment interactions (observations, measurements, triangulations) from which the experiential aspects of the humans involved have been systematically eliminated to leave nothing but formalized, de-personalized procedures' (1997: 326). Yet it was precisely the possibilities for informal and personalised mapping that made the GPS chartplotter so useful, and was such a significant development from the first GPS devices which simply gave one's position in latitude and longitude.

GPS chartplotter maps made working history material and demonstrable in case of conflicts. 'I'll show anyone my chartplotter. They can see where I have been working. I can show them exactly where my gear has been', 'Buckie' John would say when simmering tensions flared up and accusations were made. Claims to the historic use of a particular piece of ground could be demonstrated. 'We were getting a good fishing at the Wall of Death', John complained, 'but I can't get in there now! It's all polluted, plastered with creels. Look! [he points to the chartplotter and uses the mouse to click on different tracks] 9 April, 10 April, 12 April, 25 July – I was in there, at 40 to 50 fathoms'. However, the process of mapping and sharing experience could also fall victim to the competitive pressures of commercial fishing. One skipper told me that if he got a particularly good catch, he would get on the radio and tell other skippers he caught a boulder so they would mark it on their plotters and keep away from the area. 'Readings just get passed on until no one is quite sure where they came from', said another skipper.

Most skippers closely guarded the contents of their GPS chartplotters.[10] The plotter was almost always set up with the skipper's chair located between it and the wheelhouse door so that they could shield it from any visitor. One boat owner told me about reporting the theft of information from a chartplotter to the police – although I never heard how they dealt with his complaint. When a local boat was sold to some Irish fishermen, it was only after the new buyers arrived that the local skippers realised in some panic that information about local tows remained on its chartplotter. The skippers cooperated in an elaborate ruse of distraction in an effort to remove the information without the new Irish owners noticing. 'Imagine if those Irish twin-riggers[11] got into Loch Hourn!' they shuddered.

The extraordinary usefulness of a chartplotter in mapping affordances did have limits. Ultimately, what mattered was not the past recorded in the plotter but the present: the weather, tidal and light conditions, now, the location of prawns, now, the gear you were towing, now, the effort you wanted to put into fishing, now, and the manoeuvrability of your boat and gear in current sea conditions. Chartplotter mapping could only inform the skipper's constant monitoring of current sea conditions and affordances. 'I'm getting so that I could tow along here with no chartplotter', said skipper John, speaking of a familiar tow he had worked every now and again over the course of a few years. 'It is good to know in case it [the chartplotter] packs up. I could just use the sounder and the landmarks.' It was the sounder that was essential in providing constant feedback about the ground being fished, not the chartplotter. Another fisherman, 'Yogi', explained: 'The chartplotter just tells you where you've been. It doesn't tell you where the crabs are. It is just a diary.'

Alasdair did worry that 'the skill is going out of the job. The knowledge base built and passed on from father to son is a bit irrelevant, and has been supplanted by a memory stick'. The unparalleled usefulness of the chartplotter often meant that when it 'packed up' – software crashing, electricity supply malfunctioning, or the mouse refusing to respond after too much manipulation by wet and salty hands – a fishing boat would usually give up fishing for the day and head back into port. I pressed Alasdair further, looking for an example of where people had lost the ability to orient themselves because of new technology, or where technology really had taken away skill. He could not think of one. 'OK, you have spotted a crack', he said. 'Technology is great but it needs to be complemented. Some people have the attitude that you can throw money at the problem, that you can put a £10,000 bit of kit in the wheelhouse and that will solve your problem. But it won't.' A GPS chartplotter could not replace a skilled skipper.

A chartplotter did not record the light conditions, the swell, or the state of the tide in which a tow took place, and the effect of all these conditions combined with season and time of day on the affordances of the ground. Only an experienced skipper would understand how these factors might combine, how the tide ran through a set of islands, of the kind of swell that a particular wind direction would produce and what areas were sheltered from it, and what grounds produced good quality prawns in February, but tiny 'beetles' in the summer. A multi-dimensional sense of orientation to the detailed and dynamic affordances of the environment over time was required in order to be a successful skipper – not just a chartplotter.

Even if a chartplotter could be invented to incorporate and monitor, in real time, all the objective environmental conditions I have described above, there is still one insurmountable problem. As affordances are both objective and subjective, there will always be a limit to what the chartplotter can record about the unique subjective circumstances in which each tow takes place: was the skipper intent on catching after a long break or exhausted after working too many days? Was the crew daydreaming, or hung-over, or trying earnestly to learn? Were the net and doors recently balanced and repaired, or were they stretched out and damaged? Had the skipper just fallen out with the rest of the local fleet making it difficult for him to get information, or was he developing new friendships and opportunities for cooperation?

Just as much anthropological writing about the GPS has underestimated its subjective aspects, it has also overestimated the power of GPS devices. For example, Aporta and Higgs' study of hand-held GPS devices by Inuit in the Canadian Arctic argues 'we should be concerned about the effects of GPS technology' because of 'the power of devices to separate people, in this case Inuit hunters, from engagement with focal experiences' with their environment and others (2005: 745). They argue that the 'concealed mechanism' of the GPS unit makes finding location a 'commodity' rather than a skill (Aporta and Higgs 2005: 743). Yet I have demonstrated that skilled fishermen almost never used the GPS to find their location, but instead to position themselves precisely in relation to affordances and obstacles they already knew about or were in the process of exploring.

Aporta and Higgs conflate two distinct processes: of being oriented, and finding one's position relative to a particular location. In the opening paragraph of their article, they describe a young man searching for, but unable to find, a broken-down snowmobile in 'unforgiving' conditions, and use this an example of being 'lost or being unable to find one's way' (Aporta and Higgs 2005: 728). Yet it is likely that the young man was well-oriented himself (otherwise the story might have ended in tragedy), but simply unable to find his position relative to the snowmobile, which had been abandoned by someone else. The GPS which was later used to find the snowmobile *had* been at the scene of the breakdown and marked the location, and thus could be used to find the position of the snowmobile relative to the searcher. This is a good example of the significant difference between being oriented in one's environment and finding one's position relative to objects and affordances in it. It illustrates the importance of the technique-oriented analysis that I have made, which does not start with objects themselves but instead with an attempt to understand 'the purpose they serve' (Mauss 2006 [1935/1947]: 114). Understanding the purpose a device is used for helps us understand why a device is used and the techniques it is integrated into.

The implication of Aporta and Higgs' analysis is that it is the functioning of the device or instrument itself which causes disengagement from the environment and from the skill of navigation and orientation. Yet engagement with the environment is both possible and necessary when using a GPS. A much broader view of social relations among persons and how these relate to the machines people work with is required to understand the reasons for disengagement and alienation. If 'technology' is seen as the main source of disengagement and alienation, other and possibly deeper causes of alienation can be overlooked. It also reinforces a narrow view of technology that sharply divides primitive 'tools' from modern 'technology', which is betrayed by statements like 'technology has already become the setting in which much of our daily lives take place' (Aporta and Higgs 2005: 746). As I argue in Part II, the entire course of human history has been marked and facilitated by the development of technologies, tools and techniques.

I have described the timings of bearings and distances, the dropping of radar buoys and the recording of the distances off them in a profusion of books scattered all over the wheelhouse, the painstakingly created Decca charts, and the digitally dazzling chartplotters. The primary purpose of these navigation techniques and instruments is not orientation, but finding one's position relative to affordances and obstacles. These techniques were also used as a backup to more ordinary forms of orientation when visibility became very poor, and thus they extended working time and conditions. They allowed boats to more finely 'work the limits of the weather', to push those limits, and to cope with unexpected changes. These techniques do not create an abstract map of an environment but are a fascinating attempt to map affordances and each skipper's intentions as they find and develop affordances in their environments over time. Yet their very goal is what makes them always inadequate and incomplete: the subjective element of affordances means they can never be fully mapped and they are remade with each interaction. In the process of finding and mapping affordances, fishermen develop a fine-tuned sense of orientation to the affordances of their environment in a deep and integrated way that was both extended by and exceeded the capabilities of the tools and machines they used in the process.

## The GPS chartplotter and social relations

While many anthropologists have worried that digital navigation instruments may affect human–environment and social relations, few have examined the class and social relations they embody. These were raised with me in the pub one evening by 'Irish' Sean, a 40-something man with long experience of working as crew of prawn trawlers and scallop dredgers up and down the west coast. He asked me about how I coped with the scanty toilet facilities on board small fishing boats (often just a bucket). Aware that my ability to cope on a fishing boat was a constant source of speculation I shrugged off the question, replying that I had become fond of the sea-view and the fresh air. He snorted derisively, like I had exposed myself as a mere dilettante, and the conversation unexpectedly turned to digital navigational equipment: 'All these fancy electronics on the boat, thousands of pounds worth, and they can't buy a fucking toilet! And there I am, out on the deck at night, going for a piss, and thinking, what if I go over the side just now? Would anyone miss me? Nope, they would just keep right on going!'

'Going for a piss' and determining the character of the seafloor are both activities which must take place on most fishing boats. Yet thousands of pounds were invested in navigation equipment, while usually no money was invested in toilet facilities – 'shit-buckets' were regularly available for free, caught in the cod-end of a trawl net (Chapter 3). Why is it that only particular aspects of activity on a fishing boat are invested in with elaborate and expensive instruments? The process of production under capitalism has two aspects: a labour process and a valorisation process, 'a process of adding value … whereby inputs of a certain value give rise to products of a greater value' (MacKenzie 1996: 29). In his analysis of technology, Donald MacKenzie draws on Marx to argue that the 'social form' of how production is organised, in this case valorisation, has the greatest influence on the design and development of machines. Therefore, in his how-to handbook for inshore fishermen, entrepreneur and fisherman Robert Leakey[12] baldly explains that in commercial fisheries 'you don't go to sea to catch fish. You fish to earn money' (1974: 77), with the goal being 'to convert fish into money'. Leakey gives detailed advice on what kind of gear to spend money on in order to get the greatest return, effectively, the valorisation process that MacKenzie and Marx describe. Many fishing boat owners believe that 'a £10,000 bit of kit in the wheelhouse' like a chartplotter will bring a greater return, or at least allow them to maintain the same return in the context of other pressures (Chapter 5). Whether this equipment will actually fulfil these expectations is another question. But one thing that skippers can be quite sure about is that spending £10,000 on a toilet will not increase profits. Thus 'Irish' Sean will continue to piss over the side of the boat in the black dark and wonder if anyone will miss him if he stumbles over the side, and the owners of the boats that Irish Sean works on will continue to buy the latest sounders, sonars, two-dimensional and three-dimensional chartplotters, in the hope that these devices will improve, or at least maintain, their profits. Aporta and Higgs argue that a process of commodi- fying location arises from the GPS (2005: 743). However it is the transformation of prawns themselves into commodities and the reorganisation of fishing into a process of producing value for a market that has shaped prawn fisheries, navigation instruments and fishing gear today (Chapter 5).

Marx famously explained that 'capital is not a thing, but a social relation between persons which is mediated through things' (1976 [1890]: 932). For many crew, the shit-bucket and the chartplotter embodied their social relations with boat owners. The shit-bucket was what they got to use, how they experienced their time on board, and it was how many of them described the boats they worked on (see Chapter 3). They not only experienced the shit-bucket as degrading, but as a potential threat to their survival. If the shit-bucket represented a lack of concern for crew's living conditions, the GPS chart plotter represented the opposite: the owner's obsession with catching prawns to convert into money, and subordinating everything else to this goal.

Not everyone had the same attentive relation to the dazzling chartplotter dis- plays I have described, and not everyone's experience was recorded there. Some crew chose not to attend to these representations. One skipper complained: 'I drew [a young crew] a double yellow line on the chartplotter, and I couldn't even get him to follow that!' This double yellow line cuts diagonally across the chartplotter in Figure 30, an enduring reminder to the skipper of what he saw as the incom- petence of that particular crew member. Like many of the young men described in Chapter 3, the crew occasionally worked on fishing boats but did not see it as a career he wanted to pursue. He was not the least bit interested in the representa- tion of fishing grounds on the chartplotter, and he certainly was not asked to con- tribute to the mapping process. Instead, he looked at magazines, he daydreamed and, after a relatively short period of time, he was fired.

Engagement in the process of orientation and finding relative position is not determined by the navigation device people used, but the attentiveness of the per- son using that device. Some people attended to their chartplotter and sounder obsessively, and some did not. Social relations of ownership and class made the difference, not the presence or absence of a GPS. In Chapter 3, Jackson pointed out that how we experience relations with persons and machines 'will depend upon the degree to which we feel in control of these relationships', as well as 'the degree to which these relationships are felt to augment rather than diminish our own sense of well-being' (2002: 336). Owners and skippers who felt some control of these devices and the financial benefit they could produce engaged with them attentively, crew who felt alienated from and even threatened by them did not.

Social and class relations affected the relationship between people and machines, and these machines also facilitated particular social relations. Earlier in this chapter, skippers voiced their anxiety that the GPS chartplotter reduced the skills of their peers. More precisely, the chartplotter reduced the skills required of crew. Although the crew member cited above did not follow the double yellow lines down the middle of the chartplotter screen, the existence of such lines are significant. They meant that I, as a competent sailor but novice fisher with no experience working in the area, could follow the instructions of the skipper and the lines he drew on the chartplotter, and still be reasonably successful in catching prawns and avoiding obstacles while he slept. While the employment of increasingly international crews even on very small Scottish fishing boats has its origin in global market forces, the chartplotter makes it possible for people trained on boats fishing on other oceans to very quickly function as effective crew members on Scottish fishing boats (Chapter 5).

The equipment carried on board commercial fishing boats and the priority given to particular investments is directly related to the valorisation process – will this device help the boat earn more money? Crew were well aware that this meant that the boats they worked and lived on were shaped by priorities that had little to do with them, and they frequently felt alienated from the boat, its electronics, and the whole fishing industry as a result. It was these class relations that led to 'deskilling' and 'diminished' relationships with their work and their environment – not the GPS, as Aporta and Higgs worried (2005: 737). Class relations structured the relations that people had with machines (Part III). While machines could facilitate new social relations, they did not create or determine them. It was not the GPS that determined how skippers and crew related to each other or to their environment, it was relations of ownership and political economy.

## Conclusion

In this chapter I have examined orientation and techniques for finding relative position historically, ethnographically and from a labour-centred perspective, always trying to keep the focus on how people used these techniques to develop affordances and satisfy their intentions. I have argued that despite the often rapid changes in the devices used, there is continuity in the basic problem that these techniques try to solve: that of recording the experience of locating oneself relative to specific affordances or obstacles, and providing backup when conditions deteriorate. I have tried to show that particular tools are adopted, developed and discarded as new tools become available and the affordances that people seek change.

The emergence of the GPS chartplotter in the process of position-finding shows the perpetual importance of the subjective and experiential aspects of human orientation in a digital age. The GPS chartplotter is valuable precisely because it allows people to inscribe the personal and the experiential literally on top of the formalised and de-personalised: a kind of digital wayfinding. The GPS chartplotter is an attempt to map affordances – an incredibly useful attempt that will never quite succeed precisely because both the subjective and objective aspects of affordances are always changing.

Tools and techniques are always developed and used within particular social and market relations. As Widlok observes, the GPS involves 'not a higher degree of artificiality but a different degree of dependency (above all on the US military and on manufacturers) than when being trained by elders, and ultimately a shift in the distribution of power' (2005: 750). The shift in power I identified with a GPS is an increased centralisation of knowledge and power from the crew as a whole to the skipper as an individual, supported by an array of electronic instruments. This is a change that is happening in parallel with increased competitive pressures on fisheries from declining prices and global markets, and it facilitates a shift in the crewing of fishing boats from kin or locality-based, where crew would become familiar with working in a particular area over time, to fishing boats as employers of a global workforce in a race to secure the lowest possible labour costs. It is these pressures and to the changing circumstances of fishing boat crew that I turn to in the next chapter.

## Notes

1 'Baskets' are a standard size orange plastic basket the crew shovel the catch into before they sort it (Figure 15).
2 For example, a well-known west of Scotland joke lists useless things on a boat such as a wheelbarrow, a snooker table, a spirit level and a Navy officer.
3 A chronometer is an accurate clock used in combination with a sextant to find longitude.
4 Heath Robinson was a British cartoonist and illustrator who was known for drawing elaborate and imaginative machines, or 'anything cobbled together with knotted string and equal quantities of hope and science' (Beare 1987: 9).
5 The earlier Mark 21 Decca Navigator was introduced in 1969 (Blanchard 2010) so larger trawlers probably started to use it in the 1970s.
6 'Dead reckoning' is the formal term for the calculation of speed, time, distance and bearing Alasdair described using to get from Iona to the West Reef.
7 Cohen's field work in Shetland took place in 1973–1978, 1974–1975 and 1985–1986 (1987: ix). The large Shetland trawlers are likely to have had cutting-edge equipment for the time.
8 All the photographs of plotters I have included are from one boat, so they look relatively similar. However the GPS chartplotters of each other skipper I saw looked quite different.
9 The lines don't appear dashed in this photo, only when the chartplotter is more zoomed in, which is the way it is usually used.
10 The skipper of the boat I worked on board was happy for me to take and use pictures of his chartplotter, which are now quite out of date. I did see other chartplotters, but sensed that it would be unreasonable of me to ask to photograph them.
11 A twin-rigger tows two nets, and has a much increased catching power.
12 In addition to writing *Modern Fishing Gear: A Guide for Beginners and Experts*, Leakey made and sold fishing gear and helped to establish the prawn creel fishery in the Inner Sound in the early 1960s.

# Part III

# Capitalism and class

The grounds, skills and techniques I have described emerged through strong relationships developed between people, their environments and their tools in the process of their work to make fishing grounds productive. In these intimate and collective processes, places were made, boats and their gear were customised to the bodies of their skippers, and detailed digital maps were developed of the affordances people relied on. But these relationships could also be fraught with tensions and contradictions. I contrasted the rewarding relationships of maintenance that many skippers had with their fishing boats to the frustration of hired crew and skippers like Graeme, who described the boats that they worked on as 'shit-buckets' (Chapter 3). Skippers attended closely to their GPS chartplotters and guarded their contents carefully, but many crew expressed their resentment of these devices, or simply ignored them (Chapter 4). I emphasised the multiple skills and sensitivities involved in successfully fishing with the aid of the GPS chartplotter, but also how the consequent centralisation of knowledge about affordances reduced the need for crew to have local fishing experience, allowing the employment of migrant workers as skilled crew (Chapter 4). In each case, there were significant differences in the relationships that different groups of people (hired skippers, skipper-owners, owners ashore, and hired crew) had to the daily work process and tools of fishing. The divergent experiences of these groups lead to these differences: the frustration of hired crew and skippers about the lack of control over and reward for their work contrasted with the ability of most skipper-owners to feel in control of their work, practise their skills, shape their working environment around their needs, bodies and interests, and gain as much reward as possible from this process. In this section and the following chapters, I will examine the social relations of political economy that gave rise to these divergent experiences and in turn have generated distinctive classes of people with particular relations to the processes of production in the fishing industry.

Marx has pointed out that what requires explanation 'is not the *unity* of living and active humanity with the natural, inorganic conditions of their metabolic exchange with nature ... but rather the *separation*' (1973: 489). This book has mainly explored the unity of people with their tools and environments, but now I focus on the separation, alienation, exploitation, ruptures and violence they experienced. Chapter 5 offers a historical political economy analysis of how class relations have developed and continue to develop in west of Scotland fisheries, and Chapter 6 explores the violent consequences of these changes. I will outline some 'tools to think with' (Bernstein 2010: 10) in analysing the role played by political economy in social relations. I support the view of Chris Hann and Keith Hart that anthropology can benefit from a greater engagement with political economy, and with the broader contexts and histories this entails (2011).

Four key questions of political economy that 'concern the social relations of production and reproduction' are outlined by Henry Bernstein:

> Who owns what?
> Who does what?
> Who gets what?
> What do they do with it? (2010: 22)

These questions are applicable in a wide range of economies and can be investigated ethnographically. Anthropology would benefit from the emphasis on distribution and ownership that these questions address, which have not usually been its focus (Hann and Hart 2011: 167–172). While previous chapters in this book have addressed 'who does what', in the next chapter I will examine 'who owns what' and 'who gets what': how boat ownership and the distribution of fishing surplus have changed over time with significant effects on social and class relations and how fishing itself is carried out. Developments in the traditional 'share' system of distributing the fishing catch are ultimately related to the ownership of the fishing boat and gear, and social relationships in this 'traditional' system have changed significantly over time (Chapter 5). These relationships are dynamic, and will continue to change into the future. Changes that took place in the fishing share system over a century that shifted it from a form of shared ownership and reward to a form of payment for casual labour were in turn leading to a further change in the early 2000s: the employment of migrant workers as waged fishing boat crew. These transitions have taken place in the context of intensifying capitalist relations – the 'commodification of subsistence' (Bernstein 2010: 34) for crofters who lost access to land and were in increasing need of cash to pay for the necessities of life. Capitalism as an economic system is characterized by commodity production of everything, traded on a market for accumulation, and even, most uniquely, the commodification of people's own labour. These features have emerged unevenly over time in different economies and parts of the world (Bernstein 2010: 25–7) – and quite recently in west of Scotland fisheries.

Chapter 5 examines the historical development of the fishing share system that was usually described as a fixed and enduring 'tradition'. The changes within the share system offer a view into the emergence of new classes within fisheries. Class structures are 'continuously constituted and reworked' (Patterson 2009: 137) because they arise from the attempts by one group to appropriate surpluses created by the labour of another group. In order to successfully institute and maintain this appropriation, labour processes are reorganised, which in turn can facilitate greater appropriation of surplus, and potentially more differentiation in the activities undertaken by different groups and the rewards they accrue from this process (Patterson 2009: 155). This emergence of class structures is a dynamic and contested process, occurring in constantly changing circumstances.

Foundational to this analysis is a relational understanding of class, brilliantly articulated by G.E.M. de Ste Croix:

> *Class* (essentially a relationship) is the collective social expression of the fact of exploitation, the way which exploitation is embodied in a social structure. By *exploitation* I mean the appropriation of part of the product of the labour of others ...
>
> A *class* (a particular class) is a group of persons in a community identified by their position in the whole system of social production, defined above all according to their relationship (primarily in terms of the degree of ownership or control) to the conditions of production (that is to say, to the means and labour of production) and to other classes. (1981: 43)

This analysis is 'relational, processual, and specific' (Sider 2003: 64). As anthropologist Gavin Smith emphasises, 'classes *are* relationships before they are groups to be identified through sociological statistics' (1999: 92). Key aspects of this understanding is its emphasis on 'the whole system of social production' and the relationships of ownership or control within this system. Ste Croix goes on to criticise accounts of class that 'are not dynamic in character but merely lie side to side, so to speak, like numbers in a row'. Callinicos elaborates that the value of a class analysis lies less in describing 'social gradations', and more in understanding '*social change*' (G.E.M. de Ste Croix quoted in Callinicos 2004 [1987]: 53). People's subjective experience of these processes is linked to their ability to control 'their own' labour and tools, not labour power in the abstract (Elster quoted in Callinicos 2004 [1987]: 51). The division 'between the capacities of the whole person, inseparably mind and body, and the agency that puts those capacities to work' is a key aspect of capitalism, and it must be recognised that 'to say that a man works from his own *knowledge* is not the same as saying that he works of his own *volition*' (Ingold 2000: 300). Marx's claim that 'It is always the direct relationship of the owners[1] of the conditions of production to the direct producers ... which reveals the innermost secret, the hidden basis of the entire social structure' (1971: 791) can be read as both a class analysis and an ethnographic manifesto.

The definition I have outlined is in sharp contrast to how class is frequently discussed: as a static structure into which people are born, as equivalent to inequality, or as a sliding scale of relative wealth. Such understandings have led to the stultifying 'class maps that we have inherited' (Kasmir and Carbonella 2008: 6), which many have come to identify with the concept of class itself. The consequences are that by the 1990s, in academic literature ' "working class" came to be read as by definition white, male, racist, and sexist' (Russo and Linkon 2005: 3). People's understanding of 'labour' became tied to particular forms of work (especially factory work) and when those forms of work changed, some dismissed labour as a useful term of analysis. Anthropologist Gavin Smith argues 'these views are in stark contrast to those of Marx, who believed that "labour" was synonymous with social life' with very different historically-specific forms (Smith 1999: 172; see also Chapter 1). These obstacles to a serious class analysis reflect broader shifts in academia to post-modernism and post-structuralism, and a generally triumphant period of neo-liberal capitalism. How much academic fashions will change as a result of the economic crisis that began in 2006 and which has resulted in depression in many parts of the world remains to be seen. Class remains an unfashionable concept in anthropology, but there have been several recent calls for a renewal of interest and work in this area (Barber *et al.* 2012; Carrier and Kalb 2015; Kasmir and Carbonella 2008).

In the chapters that follow I will show how the dynamic tensions of capitalism are felt every day on the decks of fishing boats, how they are tearing and re-forming social and class relations and how they are incorporated into people's subjectivities. Class relations are not a code for poverty and wealth, or one of many possible forms of domination, but are a description of the kind of social relations that govern whether, and to what extent, people are able to maintain control of their bodies at work, the way they exercise their skills, control their conditions of work, how the products and surplus their work generates is distributed. This process must be examined in its full historic dynamism, ethnographic detail and geographic connections.

The kind of class analysis I present here is usually not applied to the Highlands of Scotland. Instead, the marginality, rurality and isolation of this region is emphasised, giving the impression that it is beyond or outside of capitalism. Here it is worth recalling the brief historical sketch given in the Introduction about the ways in which the origins of the Scottish fishing industry and the life histories of those living on the west coast are bound up with the development of capitalism, and continue to be enmeshed in global commodity and labour markets.

In the chapters that follow, I will examine the historical processes of change in the relations of production and distribution of surplus in the form of the share system (Chapter 5), and the structural violence of market pressures and class-divided relations of production (Chapter 6). Chapter 6 also includes some experiences of people working in the offshore oil and gas industry and cargo shipping, particularly the 'supply boats' that made deliveries to oil platforms from Aberdeen. Thousands of people from all over Scotland, including from Skye and Lochalsh, worked in the North Sea oil industry. Most people I spoke to regarded 'the oil' as the main alternate employment to fishing and many people had worked in both industries. Seafarers on offshore supply boats worked in a strictly wage labour situation with sharply differentiated roles and relations to production on board. Their relation to their own skills, to the ships they worked on, and even to their bodies was substantially different from the fishing boat owner-skippers they also worked and socialised with. I examine how people experienced the contradictions of these relations and the multiple subjectivities that were generated in this process, subjectivities that were called upon as people were drawn into new relations with each other and as they chose how to act and react to them.

Exploitation, tension, alienation, violence, dynamism, transformation, and new tensions and new forms of exploitation and class relations have long been a feature of Scottish rural life, especially on the coast. An understanding of the political economy and class relations that human–environment and human–technology relations are embedded in is essential to a full understanding of these relations.

## Note

1 Here, ownership means 'effective control' and is not a legal definition. See discussion in Callinicos (2004: 47).

# 5

# 'You just can't get a price'
# The difference political economy makes

As I made dinner, typed up notes and did bits of boat maintenance on board in the evenings, I would often leave the VHF radio on. Fishing skippers monitored VHF channel 13 and expected others to do the same, using it to call each other, listen in, and to broadcast information to the fleet. A conversation one evening between the skippers of two scallop draggers illustrated the strong and potentially devastating effects that fluctuating commodity prices have on fishers:

> Donnie: Did you hear? Clams [scallops] are £37 a bag now.
> Billy: Fuck's sake! How are you supposed to make a living on that?
> Donnie: That is £9.50 a kilo. The Americans are putting it on the market at £11 a kilo. They say they will have to pay boats here £8.50 a kilo to compete! That's another one [a fishery] fairly fucked, like. They say that American factory ships are processing the stuff on board, that's how they can sell it so low. Doesn't take a big drop to stop making it viable.
> Billy: Aye, remember when the pursers[1] went to the wall a few years ago when the price of mackerel dropped? After all the Soviet countries broke up and the Klondykers[2] stopped buying?
> Donnie: And did you see that new clam boat [scallop dragger] just coming out of the yard in the *Fishing News*? If I was that boy in MacDuff [the new boat owner at the boatbuilding yard] I would be fucking crapping myself just now! His new boat was supposed to be £2 million, and they say it is on the wrong side of that.
> Billy: That is a lot of clams at £37 a bag! It would cost more in insurance! I wouldn't be surprised if he goes around the pier head with the seacocks pulled [to sink the boat].
> Donnie: Yeah, or a major fire.

A fishery in Scotland could become 'fairly fucked' because fishing boats on another continent found a cheaper way of processing their catch. Highly efficient multi-million dollar purse-seiners could go 'to the wall' when the price of mackerel dropped. Declining prices might cause people to contemplate destroying a brand-new state-of-the-art scallop dragger. 'Market relations may have a strong organisational component to them', anthropologist Gavin Smith has pointed out (1999: 185), and in this chapter I explore these organising effects: how sea creatures like crabs and prawns were made into tradeable commodities, and how commodity relations affected ownership of boats and gear and the distribution of the fishing surplus among owners and crew. Commodity relations extended to the commodification of fishermen's own labour, and permeated and structured social relations between fishermen, generating new forms of class relations. In the next chapter I will examine the violence of these commodity and class relations and how this violence was obscured. Through both chapters, I will demonstrate the understanding that political economy can bring to anthropological and fishing studies, and also in understanding 'why things are this way' (Desjarlais 1997: 25, Introduction).

## Making seafood commodities

Fisheries are frequently described as if their existence was a natural fact that simply reflects the presence of fish. However, commercial fisheries are created through risky and painstaking effort and experimentation with boats, gear, transportation and markets. It is difficult to make a sea creature into a valuable tradeable commodity with an ongoing viable market, usually located at a considerable distance from the fishery itself. Each commercial fishery has its own history of how this commodification has been achieved and what the unfolding consequences are. When commercial fishermen described their own history, stories about establishing markets and consequent price fluctuations were critically important to them. Fishermen explained their choices about what fishing gear to use and what species to try to catch in relation to the emergence and disappearance of such markets and changes in prices.

Despite the £77 million value of the Scottish prawn fishery in 2009 (first-sale value only, Scottish Government Statistician Group 2010), Nephrops prawns were historically neither caught for food nor sold as a commodity (Johnson and Johnson 2013: xiii). Within living memory, prawns have been transformed from an obscure deep water sea creature to a valuable exported commodity whose sale supported over 1,800 fishing boats and their crew (Scottish Government Statistician Group 2010).

Most prawns live in deep water, well beyond the range of the fishing gear used before the invention of technologies such as strong and light plastic (nylon) ropes and compact motor-driven winches. They were sometimes caught as by-catch on herring ring-net boats and whitefish trawlers as nets swept across the seafloor. Occasionally fishermen ate them at sea or at home – but only as a novelty. Crew on herring ring-netters recalled that 'They were just a nuisance! We used to shovel prawns over the side, or keep them for ourselves'. Large whitefish trawlers from Fleetwood in northern England used heavy mechanical winches and fished in deeper water off the west coast of Scotland in the 1950s and 1960s, and caught a lot of prawns as by-catch. 'The boats didn't sell prawns then, there was no market. Same thing with the monkfish, they were no use until the chippies got a hold of them, and then the Spanish', explained prawn trawler skipper James Corrigal, whose father and uncle had helped establish the prawn fishery. Confronted with these prawns in significant volumes, James described how the whitefish trawler crew experimented: 'the Fleetwood skippers didn't mind people doing a wee cash job on the side, the crew would pickle the prawns and take them home for personal use, or sell them on the side to the wee shops in Fleetwood'. Just catching prawns did not make a commercial fishery – a market had to be developed so that prawns could become commodities with exchange values that made it worthwhile to target them. Before this market was established, James explained, 'They had a job getting rid of the prawns, getting a market for the beasties!'

In 1954 the first systematic attempt to develop a commercial prawn fishery in Scotland was made, using a trawler on the east coast. Charles Eckersley, a seafood buyer who owned Moray Seafoods in Buckie on the east coast, developed markets for Scottish prawns in Europe (Mason 1987: 89–91). Eckersley paid fishermen around the coast £5 for a stone (6.35kg) of prawn tails with their heads removed, encouraging many to start to fish for this new market.

In the early 1960s, some of the ring-net herring boats based in Kyleakin experimented with prawn trawling, but they lacked the expensive higher powered engines and winches necessary to tow a prawn trawl net across the seafloor – ring nets were lighter nets used near the surface of the water. Instead of using a trawl net, west coast fishermen started catching prawns in lobster creels redesigned to have smaller entrances to entrap the narrower bodies of prawns. In 1962 Billy Finlayson and his brother Sandy began to try to export large live prawns to Paris, working with Ruaridh Hillary, the son of a Skye landlord who owned a business that was already exporting lobster and game to Paris. Margaret Finlayson laughed as she remembered her first confusing experience of their attempts to catch and sell prawns. Her husband Sandy left a quarter cran[3] herring basket full of prawn tails in the kitchen, and 'I put them all into potato sacks and took them around all the neighbours to get rid of them' – according to the usual practice at that time of sharing fish around the village. 'I didn't realise that he was trying to sell them!' she exclaimed, amused at how much had changed since.

After some experimentation with the methods used for exporting live lobster, Billy and Ruaridh found that if the prawns were caught in creels and carefully packed in sawdust, put on the train to Inverness, and then flown to Paris, they would arrive alive at the Paris Halles market, and could be sold for a premium price. Ruaridh Hillary paid fishermen a much higher price of £8 for a stone of whole prawns, and said that 'everyone followed Billy's example, because he was getting a much better price', including Portree fishermen like Tommy and Alfie Corrigal. However, Ruaridh's prawn export business went bankrupt in about 1966 after a dispute with his Parisian buyer.

After the end of this first attempt to sell whole live prawns, west coast fishermen went back to tailing all the prawns they caught, and selling them to seafood buyers like Eckersley for the lower price of approximately £5 for a stone of tails. The prawn fishery continued to expand through the 1970s. But with no difference in the markets that trawlers and creel boats sold to, trawlers were able to catch higher volumes of prawns at a lower cost than creel boats. Trawlers from the east coast would use the Caledonian canal to transit to the west coast and fish the waters around Skye, and at first local fishermen using creels 'would put old engines and stuff on the seabed' to keep them out. But soon, the men who had established the prawn creel fishery like the Corrigals found 'you couldn't make a living from the creels then, it was all tails, there was no price, and people *had* to switch to the trawl'. When they switched to trawling, Dan Corrigal explained the increased volume and efficiency 'made a big difference to the earnings'.

Skippers often had to experiment with different techniques and markets to find what would pay. Prawn trawler skipper Ruaridh bought his present boat in 1978: 'It was set up for scallop dredging when I got it, but the scallops got poor. The Japanese were flooding the market with farmed scallops, and the price went from £24 to £10 a bag in a matter of weeks. We packed it up and went back to the [prawn] creels, we still had the gear.' But by 1980 Ruaridh had switched from prawn creels to prawn trawling as well.

Through the 1970s and 1980s trawlers selling relatively low-value tails domi-nated the prawn fishery. But in the late 1980s, a man from Uist invented and patented the plastic prawn 'tube', which kept captive prawns alive for several days and could be floated in a tank on a boat or in a sea loch (Figure 35).

Figure 35 Three sizes of prawn 'tubes' sitting in tanks of seawater and ready to be filled on board a creel boat. Creels are stacked in the stern of the boat. Similar tubes were are also used occasionally on some trawlers.

Prawns could be exported in a tank of seawater in the back of a truck driving overnight to Spain, or repacked into boxes before being loaded on a plane so they would still be alive when they reached the market in Spain. Skye creel fishing boat owner 'Yogi' described working through the practicalities of using the 'tubes' with two men sent by a Spanish seafood company to find a source for whole live prawns. Their export business became very successful and they started buying prawns from ten regional harbours and exporting 500–600 5kg boxes of live prawns per day to Spain. 'The other Spaniards were jealous,' he said. 'They didn't have these prawns! They are desperately competitive. They got on their bikes and tried to set up other companies. They would speak to [other fishermen] and offer them twice the price just to cause problems.' These developments allowed Scottish prawn creel fishermen to sell to higher value live prawn markets in Europe and export volumes climbed steadily (KPMG and Sea Fish Industry Authority 2004).

'The tubes made a big difference to the price, a big, big difference' explained James Corrigal. It was very significant for fishermen in the 1980s that 'when the tubes started you would get almost double the price, £10 a kilo!' I asked creel fisherman 'Yogi' what the consequences would be if there was no live prawn market buying prawns at such premium prices. He replied, 'Well, there wouldn't be as many creel boats for one thing. The price we get would not be as good, it would not be as viable'. The development of the live whole prawn market with 'a better price' was crucial to the revival of the prawn creel fishery, a more labour-intensive method of fishing which could not otherwise compete with the trawlers on price. With fisheries and fishermen frequently labelled as 'ethical' or 'unethical', this is a critical point to understand.

Seafood buyers also developed an intermediate 'fresh' (whole but not live) market which got a higher price than prawn tails. Most of the small prawn trawlers in the Inner Sound in 2005–2007 sold to this market and only tailed the very smallest prawns. A few small trawlers set themselves up to sell prawns in tubes when prices were high or quota was restricted. Some Skye and Lochalsh trawlers sold to large east coast processors, and some to the local west coast processors set up by Spanish companies. Local creel boats often sold directly to Spain, loading their tubes into tanks in the backs of trucks that would drive there directly. The development of prawns into a commodity and the variations in the price that fishermen were able to get for them in different markets had a structuring impact on what fishermen caught and why, and is crucial to understanding the development and present composition of Scotland's prawn fishery.

## The pressures of commodity markets

The development of new prawn markets was an opportunity which encouraged the development of the prawn fleet. Some did well: the Corrigal family owned three trawlers, a creel boat, a fish and chip shop, a restaurant, and two tour boats. Yogi, who had no previous family history of fishing, but had helped develop both the crab creel fishery (Chapter 1) and live prawn exports, owned two creel boats (one fished by his son), drove a BMW, and lived in a spacious and beautiful home overlooking the water.

But not everyone was able to take advantage of the opportunities provided by new prawn markets. Overall, prices have fallen. If prices had stayed the same, one stone of live prawns worth £8 to creel fishermen in 1965 would be worth £115.94 in 2008, or £18.25 per kilo (according to changes in the Retail Price Index).[4] Yet in 2006–2007, most creel fishermen received £10–15 per kilo for relatively large live langoustines, and the trawlers selling generally smaller prawns to the 'fresh' (whole but not live) market received an average of £3–5 per kilo. To make the same relative income as in 1965, a fishing skipper now needs to catch almost twice as many prawns in the same period of time, before accounting for fuel and the extra distance travelled and the latest fishing gear and electronics now required to catch the increased volume needed to keep up with other fishermen. One trawler skipper explained that since the 1970s: 'The money is still good, but you have to work longer hours for it. The prices are about steady, but the cost of living is up. We used to work four out of seven days, now we work 10 out of 14.' Or as another skipper exclaimed: 'the prawns are fine, but you just can't get a price!'

Commercial fishing is not just about the act of catching fish: it encompasses both the labour process of fishing *and* a valorisation process that transforms sea creatures into valuable commodities that produce surplus value for the boat owner (MacKenzie 1996: 29). This profit is then re-invested to keep up with competitors and make more profit in an endless cycle of accumulation (Bernstein 2010: 25). In this system, the boat owner needs to sell what the crew are able to catch for a higher price than the combined expenses of the boat and payments for the crew, and use the difference to buy the latest chartplotters and fishing gear. Fish exporters need to be able to buy the catch and transport it at a lower price than they sell it for. Boat owners and the buyers are all manoeuvring and competing with each other in a global market as they try to increase the surplus value that they get by decreasing the time and expense necessary to produce the same quantity of prawns. But while they may be able to get an advantage for a period, the overall effect is that the surplus value they are able to make decreases over time. Fishers are in a vulnerable position: if they can't sell their catch right away, it becomes worthless. New technologies and efficiencies created competitive pressures on other fishers to reduce costs and make the same investment to keep up. Living expenses were a constant but as anthropologist Gerald Sider has pointed out in Newfoundland fisheries 'output' (in the form of fish catches) and 'remuneration' (in the forms of price) could vary considerably (2003: 99). This means that 'rural domestic commodity producers are characteristically forced into situations where they must sell their commodities at exchange rates that are somewhat below the full social costs of producing these commodities' (Sider 2003: 313). Under pressure from the markets they sell to, seafood buyers are constantly testing to see how low a price they can pay fishers, and how long they can get away without paying the fisherman for their catch. The development of new fishing techniques and new markets can raise profits for a time, but eventually the same process takes over and the prices begin a long overall decline. These processes link the fate of people in no direct contact with each other across the world: changes which reduce the cost of scallop production in America or Japan could cause scallop fishermen in Scotland to 'fucking crap' themselves as they scrambled to match that cost reduction. Sider pointed to the tension 'between the autonomy of work processes and the imposed constraints to produce' to maintain a livelihood (2003: 99). Fishermen tried to resolve this tension by catching more prawns, working longer hours and changing labour arrangements in order to maintain their income.

The pressure on fishermen increased significantly between 2006, when I began my fieldwork, and 2008. Figure 36 shows the significant fluctuation in profit from year to year, even aggregated across the many boats in each sector of the fleet, the general decline across this period, and low rates of profit on smaller, less capital-intensive vessels. It also shows the low average crew share per person: less than £20,000 annually on single-rig trawlers, and around £20,000 annually on twin-rig trawlers.

Understanding the economic pressures on commercial fishers is not the same as saying that fishers behave as 'rational economic man', a premise that anthropologists and geographers have criticised (Nightingale 2011; Orlove 2002; St Martin 2007). Rather, it is to recognise that these pressures are real and cannot be ignored, either by fishermen or by those who seek to understand their lives. They are not abstract concepts, but are experienced every day on the pier, on the phone with the buyer, as the catch is sorted and landed, and are constantly discussed up and down the coast. For commercial fishers, the pressures of dealing with a capitalist marketplace to remain 'viable' are as everyday and essential as those of negotiating the weather and the sea.

How skippers and owners chose to deal with these pressures was an integral part of their fishing strategy and affected their relations with their crew. In making these choices, they were also significantly constrained by the regulation of quota, closed areas, days-at-sea limits, the regulation of fishing gear, and what the market would buy. The general pattern was that reduction of labour costs and competition generated constantly declining prices, pressuring more capital investment to try to increase the efficiency of prawn-catching. But the investment loans required put fishermen in increasingly precarious and potentially catastrophic situations (like Donald and Charlie in the Introduction). In the next sections, I will examine how these pressures articulate with the underlying relations of ownership and distribution, and how they are reflected on board the fishing boat in the distribution of surplus and the relations between owners, skippers and crew.

## Who owns what? Boat ownership

'Who owns what?' is a key question of political economy (Part III; Bernstein 2010: 22). Access to boat and gear ownership is an under-examined aspect of access to fisheries, with fisheries literature usually focussed on access only in terms of legal rights to fish (Campling et al. 2012). However, no one can fish without fishing gear and (usually) a boat, and this often required significant capital investment.[5] In

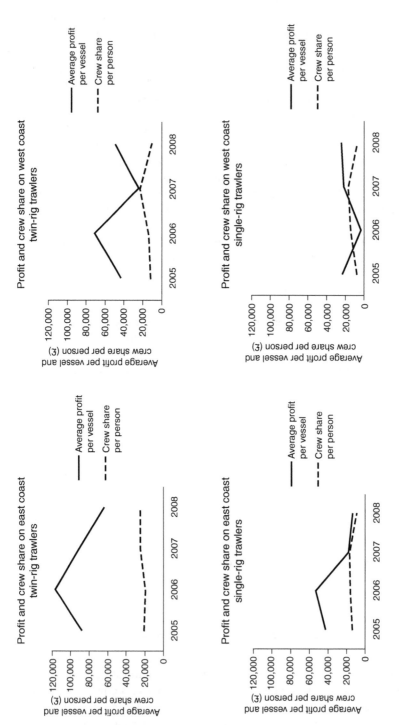

Figure 36 Average profits per vessel compared to average crew share per person (in £) in four segments of the Scottish prawn trawler fleet. Profit is shown after expenses but before depreciation, interest and tax. Sources: 2005–2007 data Curtis *et al.* (2009: 30–33, 61–64) and 2008 data Curtis *et al.* (2010: 41–46, 92–97). The 2008 data on crew share per person was extrapolated from the report by dividing the total crew share by the average number of crew reported for that fleet segment. Note that Seafish financial data for fishing fleets before 2005 is not comparable with later years. Another change in boat categorisation took place in 2009 which also makes comparison with previous years difficult.

this section, I will discuss how market pressures in the fishing industry articulate with changes in boat ownership and in the share system that distributes fishing income between owner, skipper and crew.

Fishermen in Scotland have historically been paid in proportion to the value of the catch their boat lands. This remains the case for crew from Scotland today, and this is how I was paid. However, within this system the crew's degree of ownership of the vessels they work on (and their fishing gear) has changed significantly. In the Introduction I outlined how east coast landlords once supplied boats, with the fishermen who worked them keeping a share in proportion to the catch. Later in the nineteenth century, both east and west coast fishermen were able to pool their resources and buy their own boats, using a share system to distribute the fishing surplus among the crew that also reflected their ownership of the boat and gear.

Many west coast crofters worked seasonally for wages on the large east coast fishing boats, and fished for subsistence and sometimes the market at home in quite different circumstances. Shared ownership could help with the cost as people pooled their wages. A man who volunteered at a west coast local history centre described his family's experience of shared fishing boat ownership in the 1870s and onwards: 'My grandfather was at the groundnets for whitefish in the winter, and at the driftnets for herring in the summer. He was part owner of a boat, with his neighbour. This was quite common, to have two families in it together and to operate as partners.' Lachie Gillis, a retired fishermen who was also widely regarded as a local Skye historian, described the share system used by his father, a crofter-fisherman who participated in the winter lobster fishery in the 1920s and 1930s:

> Now, they would have, in this area especially, say from October onwards, it would be lobster fishing they would be on, they would have four of a crew, each would have a couple of dozen of lobster pots, everybody provided his own gear you see, there would be, say, eight dozen pots worked. Now, that would be carried on right throughout the winter, that kind of fishing, lobster fishing.
> *And the boat would be shared by a few people?*
> Well, the boat, the boat would probably be one owner, or it could be also, people well, say now, some boats would have two shares in it, two owners, or three but the maximum would be four.

The people fishing from the boat were also part owners of it: Lachie insisted that only four people could share ownership of a four-person boat, and each of them needed to provide their own fishing gear. Neighbours and kin pooled their resources and their labour in order to provide food for themselves and their neighbours and to sell the surplus, if one was produced. In contrast to the larger east coast boats, most west coast fishers used small open rowboats up about 25 feet long, like those built by Alastair MacKenzie south of Portree in a workshop on the water behind the family house. There were also a few commercial ground net, herring ring-net and lobster boats based in Applecross, Kyleakin and Portree from the early twentieth century onwards. West coast boat ownership did expand from the 1960s onwards due to investment from the Highland and Islands Development Board.

The link between vessel and gear ownership and the distribution of vessel income through shares persisted until the early 1970s. As a young man in 1968, Ruaridh remembers being asked by the owner of a creel boat visiting from Tiree if he wanted a share in his creel boat. 'But I had no money', he explained. 'So I got a gear share and put half the gear on the boat. I made the creels – I bought the frames and then covered them.' Alasdair MacPhail remembers that crew who supplied fishing gear for the lobster creel boat he worked on in 1970 in Iona would also split a separate 'gear share' (see Table 1). Thus crew were also part-owners of fishing boats and/or fishing gear, significantly blurring the boundaries between boat owners and crew, which were further blurred by the prevalence of family crewing of fishing vessels. The strong sense of egalitarianism in Scottish fishing villages was identified with kin-based ownership and crewing (Cohen 1987; Nadel-Klein 2003), and reflected in many people's beliefs about the share system. 'The fishing share system is one of the fairest ways of paying people', one skipper who used the system told me. Yet it is important to recognise that in Scotland, the roots of a share distribution of surplus lie not only in an egalitarian *ethic*, but in the actual shared *ownership* of fishing boats.

Patterns of boat ownership on the west coast have changed significantly. Although a share system of payment is still used to compensate the crew, it no longer bears any relation to the ownership of the boat. In 2006–2007 I saw no evidence of crew members (apart from skipper-owners and their sons) sharing ownership of a boat or its fishing gear, in any sector. On the fishing boats based around Skye and Kyle of Lochalsh[6] in 2008 (a mix of prawn trawlers and creel boats, with a few creel boats targeting crab and lobster) only six out of 34 boats (18 per cent) had kin-based ownership, skippering or shore-support: most skippers I met had no family history of fishing, were not related to their crew, and many were hired.[7] Apart from the skipper, 94 per cent of boats relied on hired crew, and I estimate that 63 per cent of local crew and skippers at any one time were hired with no ownership stake in the boat.[8] A 2009 industry survey of fishing skippers across Scotland found that only 9 per cent of skipper-owners had a son in the industry to carry on their business (Brown 2009).

Over the twentieth century, the way in which Scottish fishing boat owners use the share system has changed substantially: from a system of shared contribution and ownership directly related to shared surpluses, to a system for calculating the share-based pay of usually casually hired crew. In 2006–2007, share owners did not work on the boat and they were almost always investors with money to spend (sometimes they were also family members). Ownership of the boat has become increasingly separated from the crew actually working on board. Divorced from its links to shared ownership, the egalitarian appearance of the share system could also obscure significant exploitation, which I will explore in the next sections.

## Who gets what? Owners

Menzies described the family-based fishers in the Bigoudennie as 'perched on an economic precipice', with the consequence that 'the relations between skipper and crew at sea become a key site of struggle in defining the survival of petty capitalists who are struggling to hold onto their boats in the swirl of a world system of production and distribution' (Menzies 2002: 20). In Scotland, the pressures of commodity production have also had a significant effect on the relations between owners, skippers and crew, changes that have profound consequences for the future of the fishing industry and which have become some of its most politically sensitive and hotly debated issues. As owners have made greater capital investments in boats, Scottish crew have become casual labourers with variable pay that protects owners' investments and profit. Many trawlers now employ highly exploited migrant wage labourers working in legally marginal circumstances. Changes in the structure of the share system are critical to understanding how this has happened.

In the Scottish fishing share system, the boat owner subtracts the boat's regular expenses, primarily fuel, from the total value of the seafood landings made during a trip to arrive at what I describe as the 'fishing surplus':[9] effectively, the difference between the cost of operating a commercial fishing boat and the money that the owner gets for the catch (see detailed analysis in Howard 2012b). Shares to crew and owners were calculated only *after* this deduction was made: as it was explained to me, half was allocated to the boat owner (who also paid for capital investments and maintenance), and the other half was divided equally among the crew. In practice, adjustments were made: a hired skipper or more skilled crew could get a larger share, and as we shall see, the average division of surplus between owners and crew across the fleet was not actually 50/50. Fishermen simply described the share system as 'traditional', and did not refer to regional variations, which would have been noted because many boats and crew worked on both coasts of Scotland. The system was enforced only by custom and expectation and implemented according to the practices of individual owners, and what was accepted by hired skippers and crew. No mention was ever made of any legal mechanisms for enforcing the share system, only the potential disapproval of peers and avoidance of that boat by Scotland-based crew. The Scottish share system is largely administered by specialised fishing industry accountants contracted by boat owners, although it was not uncommon for skippers to give their crew a cash advance of their wages shortly after the catch was sold. The system is very similar to what the ILO describes as 'the traditional system of remuneration in the fishing industry' around the world (2003: 13) and the New England 'broken lay' share system (St Martin 2007).

Both fishers and the industry body Seafish described the split of the vessel profits between boat owner and crew as 'historically' or 'traditionally' 50/50, but Table 1 shows that, at least on the west coast, owners used to receive a much smaller portion of the catch. The 50/50 split actually represents an increase in the proportion of fishing income going to the boat owner and the financial institutions that supported them, and a reduction of the proportion of vessel earnings going to crew. As recently as the 1960s and 1970s, only 25–40 per cent of vessel profits went to owners. An older example from the Clyde gave the owner an even smaller 23–25 per cent of vessel earnings. One reason for this change was the pressure for greater capital investment and economic expansion, supported by the Highlands and Islands Development Board (HIDB) and financial institutions. The HIDB offered loans and grants to new entrants to fisheries in the 1970s. But as retired fisherman John explained, 'When the HIDB started giving grants and loans, they required the boat to keep 50 per cent of the profit. They wanted to make sure they got their money back!'

The trend of increasing fishing surplus going to owners continues. In 2007, Seafish described the 50/50 split as 'historic' (Anderson *et al.* 2007: 16). A 2008 report explained that the 50/50 split only applied on 'small boats', and that on larger ones the split was actually 45/55 in favour of the owner (Metz and Curtis 2008: 7). The next year, Seafish simply noted that that the crew share was 'declining', but did not give a percentage (Brown 2009: 11–12).

Over time, fishing revenue has become increasingly concentrated with vessel owners and their capital investments in fishing boats, with a smaller and smaller proportion of it going to the crew actually working on the boats. Over 80 years, owners have more than doubled the percentage of the boat's profits that they keep. The increasing share of owners and declining share of crew mirrored each other, binding them together in a relation of 'intimacy and antagonism' (Sider 2003: 294). Class structures mean that 'resources of different kinds – material, cultural, organisational … are available to agents because of their position within production relations'. Such structures are not 'inert limits, restricting the alternatives to agents. They are also enabling and are present in the actions actually pursued by individuals and groups' (Callinicos 2004 [1987]: 275, 96). As divisions between owners and crew sharpened, resources of different kinds became available to them, enabling owners to act in new ways. The exclusion of crew from vessel ownership gave owners more power to appropriate a larger share of the catch and to make more investments in their boats – but at the expense of their crew. Is it possible that centralisation of revenue to boat owners was necessary for the success and profitability of the prawn fishery as it presently exists? Certainly, prawn trawlers required much larger engines, heavier gear and the development of specialised digital navigation instruments (Chapters 3 and 4). Perhaps this increased capital investment was required to sustain this fishery and for it to remain competitive with other fisheries in the global seafood marketplace. But ultimately capital is a social relation, and for boat owners to successfully appropriate more of the value of the catch (Marx 1976 [1890]: 932) for capital investment also meant changing the social relations between skipper, owner and crew. The rate of exploitation of crew was increased and ultimately owners could choose to spend thousands of pounds on navigational equipment and not provide a toilet for their crew (Chapter 4).

There is no point in vilifying individual boat owners for being 'greedy'. They were responding to the logic of a market which they relied on, which they needed to compete in, and over which they had no control. The pressures to reduce labour costs and to increase capital investment in fishing boats and equipment are competitive and international, and enforced by government agencies. For the individual owner-operator, these pressures could be very difficult to negotiate. They were squeezed, individually, each day, and to an ever-increasing extent, by the bank, by the competitive pressures of the international seafood market, and by

Table 1 *Seven crew share systems on west coast fishing boats from the 1930s to 2008*

| Vessel | Shares used to calculate allocation of fishing surplus | | | | Crew portion of fishing surplus | Owner portion of fishing surplus |
|---|---|---|---|---|---|---|
| | Boat owner shares | Fishing gear shares | Crew shares | Total shares per boat | | |
| **2008 east coast prawn trawler (>10m)** | 11 | – | 9 (divided amongst the crew) | 20 | 45% | 55% |
| **2007 west coast prawn trawler (<10m)** | 2 | – | 2 (1 per full crew) | 4 | 50% | 50% |
| **1970 Iona lobster creel boat** (crew contribute gear) | 1 | 1 | 3 (1 per full crew) | 5 | 80% | 20% |
| **1970 Iona lobster creel boat B** (crew do not contribute gear) | 1 | 1 | 3 (1 per full crew) | 5 | 60% | 40% |
| **1960s west coast herring ring-netter A** | 3 | – | 6 (1 per full crew) | 9 | 67% | 33% |
| **1960s west coast herring ring-netter B** | 2 | – | 6 (1 per full crew) | 8 | 75% | 25% |
| **1930s west coast herring ring-netter** with no cook | 0.5 | 1 | 4.5 (1 per full crew, 0.5 for cook) | 6 | 75% | 25% |
| **1930s west coast herring ring-netter**, cook on board | 0.5 | 1 | 5 (1 per full crew) | 6.5 | 77% | 23% |

*Source:* The examples from the 1960s and 1970s are from my ethnographic research, those from the 1930s are from Martin (1981: 214). The 2008 example is from Metz and Curtis (2008: 7). Two examples are given for 1960s west coast herring ring-netters as 'everyone did their shares a bit differently'.

the fluctuations of a complex ecological system. Instead of sharing ownership, responsibility, and reward with a group of people they worked with everyday, the owner-operator became isolated. The consequences were real and social. As James put it, skippers don't speak to each other anymore because 'everyone's worried that someone will get a prawn or two more than them' (Chapter 2).

The additional revenue that owners were able to accumulate was not just invested into their own boats and equipment, or into their own personal income, it was frequently used to buy another fishing boat. Of the 34 fishing boats around Skye and Lochalsh I surveyed in 2008, 17 had only six owners (in one case a family had shared ownership of four fishing boats). The remaining 17 boats had one owner each, some working on board full-time, part-time, or not at all. In many cases, these multi-boat owners had started as owner-operators, done well, and had invested their profits in a new boat. In other cases, they had owned a white-fish trawler which had been decommissioned as part of a government scheme to reduce capacity in the whitefish fleet. The money the owner received as compensation for decommissioning their boat was not to be re-invested in the whitefish fleet, so many invested in the prawn fleet instead. Patterns of ownership could be more concentrated. For example, a number of local hired skippers had previously worked for the Kenning family in Mallaig, who owned 20 boats at their height, and John MacAlister (who was also chair of the Mallaig and North-West Fishermen's Association) owned approximately nine scallop dredgers and prawn trawlers based in Oban.

Multi-boat ownership has sharpened relations between owners and their hired skippers and crew. These groups have developed into relatively distinct classes of people with quite different daily lives and relations to fisheries production processes, and different resources available to them. That is not to say that capitalist employment relations in the fishing industry are the same as (for example) a large factory – the fishing industry has its own distinctive relations and dynamics which must be examined in their own right. There is a diversity of ways in which exploitation and accumulation can be carried out under capitalism.

Fundamentally it is the commodity relations which commercial fishermen are drawn into which puts owners under pressure to invest increasing amounts of capital in their boats, and to reduce costs and change share arrangements to appropriate more of the boat's surplus which otherwise would have gone to the crew. These relations and actions in turn create owners as a distinct class of people and present them with new opportunities for accumulation and expansion – and lead to greater exploitation and alienation of crew.

## Who gets what? Crew

The fact that the share system is no longer linked to ownership has profoundly changed the nature of the system, even though it superficially appears to be very similar. Fundamentally, the share system has shifted from a method to pool resources and share income, to a method for calculating a casual and variable payment to crew, which has many similarities with more conventional alienated wage systems in which people's labour becomes a commodity to be bought and sold (Howard 2012b). As a result crew were employed as casual labourers who rarely had a long-term relationship with any one fishing boat. Ownership of the boat and authority over the crew was increasingly centralised. Significantly different relations to production have developed as owners who may not work on the boat at all have appropriated a greater and greater proportion of the profits from the labour of crew, under the cover of an ostensibly egalitarian share system. The result was not just financial, it affected people's control over and subjective experience of the work process, and was even embodied in devices like the GPS chartplotter, a capital-intensive piece of equipment that centralised knowledge about fishing affordances (Chapter 4). This shift in reward and control was part of the common experience of skippers, owners and crew, making it possible to make some generalisations about their experiences as classes of people with distinctive relations to production.

As competition and commodity relations have changed, the balance of power, risk and reward between owners, skippers and crew has also changed, shifting the ways in which exploitation is embodied in the social structure of fisheries. Careful analysis of the share system shows that the crew share has actually become more like a wage (Howard 2012b). First, the labour of the crew is clearly sold by the crew and bought by the boat owner, or their representative, the skipper. Second, the crew do not contribute any capital, in the form of money or equipment, to the boat, only their labour. They have no ownership share. Third, crew have no alternate ways of providing for their own livelihoods other than selling their labour to other employers – generally in a fish farm or in the offshore oil industry. Fourth, crew are paid only in the form of money and are certainly not free to 'borrow' the boat or to take a portion of the catch to sell themselves – the boat and the catch are the exclusive property of the owner. Fifth, crew paid through a share system frequently described their pay as 'wages', much like they would any other job. Finally, Figure 36 shows owners appropriating large profits while crew wages remain more or less steady. Profits for the three largest sectors increased substantially between 2005 and 2006, but crew share remained flat. A similar pattern happened again in some sectors between 2007 and 2008. Thus profits were not 'shared'.

One important attribute of the share system for boat owners was that the boat's operating expenses (food, fuel, landing dues, pier dues and other regular items) were paid first. Only *after* this deduction was made were the shares for crew calculated. No matter how much work the crew puts in, the owners only need to pay them if the boat is profitable. Although crew have no ownership or control over the vessel, they are expected to shoulder an equal (or greater) share of the risks to body and livelihood involved in working in the commercial fishery. The share system does ostensibly mean that crew have the opportunity to share in the reward when the vessel is particularly profitable. However, in particularly profitable years, there are indications that owners used the increased crew share to hire more crew instead of sharing profits with existing crew (Howard 2012b).

The change in the underlying structure of the share system had a significant effect on how crew experienced the job, on their relations with owners and skippers, and on the industry as a whole. As the relationship between owners and crew attenuated, some owners became much wealthier, especially those owning multiple boats. In contrast, the crew's situation became worse, as Seafish summarised:

> Average crew share per man in 18 out of 24 fleet segments was considerably lower than the average earnings of UK males in 2005, and three segments paid wages lower on average than the minimum wage for a full time worker in 2005 ... around half the vessels surveyed have altered their crew share allocation system (historically a 50/50 split between vessel and crew) in favour of the vessel to remain profitable ...
>
> Most skippers reported that potential young crew members are discouraged from entering the industry, as they are able to find alternative employment opportunities elsewhere that provide safe, better-paid and more sociable working conditions than going to sea. (Anderson *et al.* 2007: 16)[10]

One despondent young trawler crew explained what being paid according to the share system meant for him: 'There are no regular deposits into your bank account. How can you get a mortgage or a loan or anything? You get paid shit, you never know what is going to happen. Try telling a bank manager, "Well the weather has been poor, the engine broke down, I took the arse out of the net." Not likely. But what else is there up here? Fish farms? They pay £200–£250 a week, I can't live on that!' Like this young man, most crew lived from one uncertain pay cheque to another. The situation was better for creel boat crew whose owners sold into premium markets, but this was a small minority of vessels.

Shocked and exhausted novice trawler crew described the experience as like being a 'construction labourer during an earthquake, but you had to live on the job site too! ... it seems like a hell of a hard way to earn a living'. Experienced crew told stories about being out fishing for 21 days and 'by the time I paid for my tobacco I only made 28p!' Gavin was a crew member in his mid-20s who was regarded by local skippers as one of the 'grafters',[11] 'a serious young man, one of the few', and 'the best of that generation'. It is an illustration of the problems facing fishing crew and their difficulty in finding stable, enjoyable and decently paid work that despite how well-regarded he was and his current stable job on a boat he enjoyed working on, he had previously worked on 22 different fishing boats:

> I worked on a 75' boat out of Fraserburgh that was terrible for expenses. They needed £6,500 a week just to stay even! One trip we made £23,000 in 10 days, and I only got paid £1,100. I didn't like that. The other crew thought it was normal, but he was a drunk and it was the only place that he could keep a job.
>
> It is a problem in a lot of bigger ports, boats not paying you. You just have to keep moving until you find a good boat to stay on. I had to leave a lot of boats because we weren't getting paid right. I bounced around trying to find a decent boat to work on that wasn't ripping you off on wages.

Other skippers explained to me how the 'expenses' could be, and often were, 'fiddled' as Gavin describes, with vessel maintenance and capital expenses reducing crew pay and guaranteeing owners that these costs would always be covered.

Pay and condition for most young crew were much worse relative to other available jobs. I was told, 'in Mallaig all the young guys are off to work offshore [in oil and gas]. With starting salaries at £25,000, it is hard to guarantee that in fishing these days'. Many of the most promising young fishing crew on Skye boats ended up making the same decision to leave the fishing and to work offshore. This is in sharp contrast to Ruaridh's description of switching from work as a builder's apprentice to working on a small creel boat in 1968. After finishing his apprenticeship, Ruriadh said that he would have made £16 a week as a builder. But in his first full week at the prawns he made £40, and in the herring ring-net fishery he said that £100 weeks were not uncommon - although some weeks they made only the £12 per week subsidy the government paid to herring fishermen at the time. After 18 months Ruaridh had saved up enough money to buy a second-hand boat, a feat that would be very unlikely today. In contrast to Ruaridh's rapid advancement in the 1960s, one novice crew gave me his initial impressions of the situation in 2007: 'Unless you are the captain, the only thing you are doing is pushing around a wheelbarrow. There is no clear path to advancement, on any realistic time scale. If you are crew, you are doing it because you have to. Money was always the main motivator discussed, not advancement, or improving your skills.' The problems in the variability in pay were compounded by unsociable working hours, the poor living conditions on board some boats, and the difficulty, monotony and scrutiny of the crew's job. Nadel-Klein reports asking a young fisherman what sort of young men became fishing crew nowadays. 'The stupid ones', he replied (2003: 146).

The casual employment of crew has greatly changed the balance of power on a fishing boat, and the control that skippers have over the boat and the crew. I asked one skipper about his criteria for good crew. 'Reliability is number 1, 2 and 3', he explained. After watching the interactions of many skippers and crew, what this appeared to mean was the willingness of the crew to put themselves at the disposal of the skipper, at any time. I saw crews summoned for work with only hours of notice, or left on the pier when the skipper decided to leave earlier than arranged in the morning. Some boats had regular work schedules, but many didn't, so crew often had no idea when they might be working. If they slept in or were ill, they could be fired on the spot. Skippers may have had their own very good reasons for taking these actions, but it did nothing to encourage crew in the job. The general shortage of crew did mean that good crew could easily leave vessels they were unhappy with, and be assured of quickly finding new employment. They had the leverage to negotiate time off for concerts, football games and other pursuits, something which skippers grumbled about as it was often difficult to find replacements for them.

It was a hard job. My most difficult crewing experience was an unusually successful and arduous ten-day trawler trip one February. We worked sorting prawns almost continuously from one tow to the next and landed an average of 30 stones (191 kilos) of prawns each 18-hour day. These prawns weighed 191 kilos *after* they have been sorted, cleaned, and the small ones tailed, and all this was done by two people who between them were also steering the boat, handling the net, cooking and eating, gathering information from other skippers, monitoring the weather, negotiating with the buyer, taking fieldnotes and photographs, and finding some time to sleep. My arms and back ached from shovelling prawns into baskets, lifting and dumping them onto the table, sorting and sorting, rinsing each basket, lifting them into the tank to store, and then, at the end of a very long day, heaving the boxes far up onto the pier and into the buyer's van. I wrote the following account:

> Dumped out on the table, and it is all about speed, how quickly can you sort through this basket and get to the next and the next and the next and the next and the next? I learn to pick them up at their hard carapace, to hold bundles of them loosely in my hand, the satisfying sound they make tossed into a basket on top of other prawns, meaning, money in the bank.
>
> I have to concentrate, hard, to keep myself going as fast as possible, and at this point I can't even claim to be fast, perhaps just not quite as slow as when I started.
>
> For the smallest ones: pick up the ones that lie the same way on the table, right hand to the head, left hand grasping them just below where the tail joins the body and twist the tail off cleanly. Try not to get the guts, the legs attached, you just want the clean translucent flesh bulging out slightly. Sometimes the prawn's claw will grab onto your glove and stay attached even after the prawn has lost the other half of their body, sometimes their legs squirm slightly below the head as it lies on the table. Gently roll your fingers and thumb together slightly to scooch the tail down into your palm, and again, and again, and again until your hand is full and you drop them into the big basket of other tails by my feet.
>
> I feel the hard crunch as I step on one accidentally, and look down, hoping that it is not a big one that I have ruined; that's money. Someone puts a prawn tail in my tea as a prank; it cooks perfectly before I find it and almost choke. I find prawn legs stuck to my jacket, in my mug, in my pockets, on the cabin sole. I spend the evening trying to dig out a broken-off head spike from my index finger, the tip of my finger painfully red and inflamed by this tiny act of vengeance.
>
> Hours go by I'm still not done yet. Shovelling more baskets, dumping them on the table, trying my best to concentrate, concentrate, so that I can just finish and sit down, and still there are more baskets stacked behind me. I almost wish the skipper would stop catching them, but it all means money, and I could sure use some of that.

In his oral history of fishing in south-west Scotland, Angus Martin makes the following comments about the experience of trawling for prawns:

> An air of tedium and drudgery hangs about the legacy of prawn-trawling. The skipper in his wheelhouse, chatting interminably to other skippers by radio and perhaps chain-smoking to ease the relentless boredom, and the crew on deck, gathered around a heaped board, screwing the heads off tens of thousands of small crustaceans, hour upon hour, are the average fishermen's abiding memories of the job.
>
> A notable Tarbert ring-net skipper, forced for the first time to prawn-trawling, was reputed to have shovelled a catch overboard while on passage back to port. When the crew re-appeared after a cup of tea, they found him hosing down an empty deck. 'I winna tail them masel, so A'm no gonny ask you tae tail them', he explained. (Martin 2004: 48)

I met only one man who seemed to enjoy the task of sorting and tailing prawns, and he was widely regarded as being crazy for doing so. But although it was difficult and monotonous, sorting and tailing prawns was also seen as crucial to the value of the catch as significantly different prices were paid for different sizes of prawns. The result was that many skippers constantly scrutinised the 'picking' process, worried that inattentive crew might be reducing the value of the catch. Rumours circulated that on some larger boats CCTV cameras were installed above the sorting table so the skipper could continuously watch and growl down the intercom at crew who they felt were not sorting quickly or accurately enough.

As the share system developed to concentrate power and profits with boat owners while relying on a highly casualised, alienated and poorly paid pool of crew, owners faced a growing problem of discipline, or 'reliability', of these crew. With very few exceptions (like Gavin), and arguably because of these circumstances, most trawler crew did not see fishing as a serious career option, but more as an occasional and convenient source of cash. Skippers complained that crew 'can't get up in the morning', 'they don't want to learn', they had drug problems, they couldn't stay out of the pub, they turned up for work drunk, when you needed them most, you couldn't get them out of their bunks. They weren't interested in learning about the job. 'Young guys from this country don't want to go fishing!' grumbled Arthur, a trawler skipper-owner, on the pier one day. 'Or if they do, it is only when the fishing is good, and as soon as it gets poor they are away!' Our conversation wrapped up. Arthur said he had to go, he needed to get ready for four new Filipino crew he had arriving that evening. His young Scottish crew was still on board, cooking a fry-up. He explained excitedly that he was off to join his uncle who worked as a crane driver on an offshore oil platform and made £70,000 a year.

### Migrant crew: 'two men for half the price of one'

With the combination of unpredictable and generally low pay, unsocial hours, the need to live on the boat for days at a time and endure a high level of scrutiny, it was not surprising that young Scottish men might choose to work elsewhere if they had the option. At the same time, owners found that crew could be found from other countries who were 'well qualified and worked their socks off'. I was told about a boat owner 'who got sick of the young guys on their mobile phones, not turning up and wanting to be off for football matches. So she says "tie the boat up for a week, I'll call an agency and get this sorted"'. In 2008, a survey found 57 per cent of Scottish fishing vessels employed foreign crew (Metz and Curtis 2008: 13). In 2008, six of the eight deaths on UK fishing boats were of people from South-East Asia or Eastern Europe (Figure 37). A 2008 report produced by the International Transport Workers Federation (ITF) estimated that 1,000 men from the Philippines worked in the Scottish fishing industry. Until 2010 these men were employed on 'transit visas', normally issued to crew joining a ship that was about to leave UK waters – except that most of these crew never worked more than a few miles from shore. Their visas also required that they live on board the ship, which gave boat owners far more control over their working (and leisure) time. The report describes considerable abuses of these men by their employers, including practices that 'contain elements akin to forced or compulsory labour' (ITF 2008: 2). If there were 1,000 Filipino fishers working in Scotland in 2008–2009,

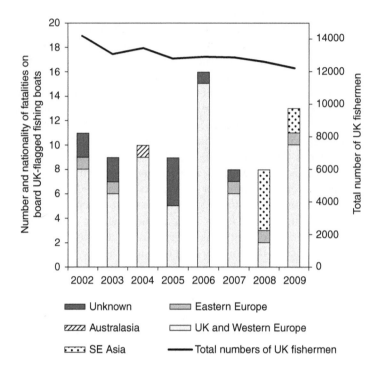

Figure 37 Total number of fatalities and their regional origin on board UK-flagged fishing vessels (left hand side, bars), and the total population of fishermen (right hand side, line). Data on fatalities was provided by the Marine Accident Investigation Branch (MAIB). Total population of UK fishermen is from Marine Management Organisation (2010).

they had a fatality rate over three times higher than the already very high fatality rate for UK fishers.[12]

Most of the Filipino crew working on Scottish fishing boats are concentrated in the larger ports of Peterhead, Fraserburgh and Mallaig, where there is more centralised and corporate ownership of fishing boats. However, this is changing. In 2006, only one boat based on the Inner Sound employed Filipino crew. By 2009 that had increased to five, all small boats with only two or three crew (including the skipper), and including owner-operated vessels. I met two of these Filipino men on the pier one afternoon. They told me that they had previously worked on large Japanese tuna boats, with 18 to 23 crew, which would stay at sea for months. It was very hard work. One man had also worked on squid boats that worked all over the Pacific: Hawaii, the Solomon Islands and Fiji. The Scottish owner of the boat had found them through a Filipino employment agency, and they had 12-month contracts. The men told me how they wanted to get a job in Europe, and this was the first thing that came up. One day, they said, they would like to go to America. I asked them how they liked Scotland. 'The Scottish people have been very warm. They are very nice', one man said. But they worked long hours, the longest was in the spring time when they worked 30 days straight without one day off. They recently came back from the east coast, where they worked both day and night due to different fishing conditions. But it was getting better now, he added. Poorer autumn weather meant the boat had to take more days off, so now they got more rest. Other skippers had explained to me that this boat had two skippers who alternated shifts while the crew worked continuously.

I told these crew that I also worked on a fishing trawler, and much like Scottish crew they asked me lots of questions: 'You are the only trawler-women we have met!' Finally, one man asked, 'How much did you get paid for working on the boat?' I explained to him how the share system worked for Scottish crew, and said that in February I worked for ten days and made £900. They looked at each other, gasped, laughed nervously, and shook their heads. I wondered if I should ask them the same question, and then I did. Nervously, they explained that they were paid USD$500 each month, about £250. Embarrassed, they assured me that the owner paid for their airfare and employment agency fees, and they got to keep all of the monthly USD$500 payment. I was shocked, as the lowest estimate for the pay of international crew that anyone else had given me was £120 a week. 'You should know that the skipper is making a lot of money from the work that you are doing', I said. 'Yes', they said, 'yes'. 'Do you at least have lots of food to eat?' I asked, remembering the saying that was bandied about when I worked on boats: 'The more you eat the more you get paid!' They looked at each other. 'No', they said, again laughing nervously.

In addition to the greater control that owners had over these crew members and the much longer hours they worked, their lower wages also made employing these men an attractive proposition for owners in the context of increasing fuel expenses and declining profits for the prawn fleet (Figure 36). In a 2008 survey of the Scottish fishing fleet skippers estimated that they would spend 30–50 per cent less on crew wages than the previous year (Metz and Curtis 2008).[13]

The employment of low-waged migrant labourers is by no means unique to the fishing industry. Skye and Lochalsh was integrated with national and global movements of labour: most hotel and bar staff, and increasing numbers of construction, fish farm and fish processing workers were from Eastern Europe and outside the EU. Over 600,000 Poles travelled to work in the UK between 2004 and 2008 (UK Border Agency 2008), and over one-third of the seafarers in the global shipping industry are agency workers from the Philippines (Glen 2008). Thus, although the employment of foreign crew is a new development in the Scottish fishing fleet, it is not surprising. At first, crew were employed from Poland, and then Russia, Latvia, Lithuania and Romania, and now the majority are from the Philippines. The shift to a wage system among the most profitable sectors of the prawn fleet is demonstrated in Figure 36 with wages on these vessels remaining almost flat when profits increased. Large portions of that fleet have effectively moved from a share system to a conventional wage system for paying crew, and owners have profited significantly from this transition.

On one hand, the shift from a share system employing Scottish crew to the employment of very low-waged migrant workers appears to be radical. It certainly represented a step-change in the already-increasing rate of exploitation of crew. However, the difference in the systems of payment that owners use for casualised Scottish fishing crew and for Filipino men on agency contracts is more of a formal difference in how their payment is calculated rather than a radical change in relations to production – the change in employment relations that laid the groundwork for the transition to fully waged labour took place when crew stopped having ownership shares in boats (Howard 2012b). In large sections of the Scottish fishing industry, share-paid or not, labour is clearly bought and sold in the process of producing commodities for a profit. Despite these continuities, owners' use of low-waged migrant labour has new implications.

Gavin, the young 'grafter' who nevertheless had to 'bounce around' from boat to boat and port to port looking for an owner who wasn't 'ripping you off' told me about working alongside Romanian crew on a large boat based on the west coast:

> When I arrived at the boat, the first thing the skipper told me was not to tell the two other crew what I was making. It was two Romanian guys I was working with. So the first thing I did when I met them was to tell them.
>
> They were not very happy. One guy had spent three years up there, he was a qualified engineer. They were getting £200 a week, which maybe is good for them, but for the job it is pathetic. With those two foreign staff, the skipper was raking it in!
>
> There are a few rich owners in [that port]. It is pretty unfair. They get two men for half the price of one.

I asked Gavin why he had defied his skipper in favour of the Romanians. In his mid-20s, he and his girlfriend were eager to move out of the town they grew up in and were trying to earn enough money to make that happen. The skippers he defied were men he knew, who may have known his family, who he might have gone to school with. It was then that he told me about the 22 different fishing boats he had worked on and the owners that were always 'ripping you off on wages'. Although he and the Romanians hardly knew each other, spoke different languages and ate different food, as crew, they had similar experiences with 'unfair' owners because of their similar relations to production. They were all frustrated and deeply disturbed that owners could get 'two men for half the price of one' and pocket the difference. Through his work, Gavin had come to the conclusion that his anger with the owners and common interests with other crew, class interests as I have defined them, were more important to him than the ties of nationality or local loyalty. Through their work, these Romanian men also became (at least temporarily) part of the working class of Scotland, and their future and Gavin's future were was bound together in ways that neither of them had chosen.

For Scottish crew, a sense of their own exploitation, of anger that owners can get 'two men for half the price of one', and of not being tied to a particular boat has meant that they are beginning to identify themselves more generically as crew, rather than as part of a *particular* boat's crew (Howard 2012a). Whether Scottish or Filipino, and no matter how their payment was calculated, they are a part of the massive, differentiated and increasingly internationalized and exploited class of landless (and boatless) proletarianised rural workers (Bernstein 2010: 110).

Gavin's cosmopolitan identification with these foreign crew was not universal. While the skills and hard work of the Filipino men was very much admired, some skippers referred to these crew purely instrumentally: as 'flip-flops' who arrived 'fresh out of the package'. Simmering beneath the relationship between owners and crew is the reality that paying ultra-low wages might give the owner the opportunity to pay off a loan, or do some maintenance on the boat, or to buy a new car. Thinking through their own justifications for this situation, owners would come up with 'it's a lot of money where they come from', and of potentially cramped living conditions 'it's luxury compared to what they are used to', and of the lack of time off 'they just want to work their socks off', and of the sometimes inequitable distribution of special treats and food in general 'they just don't like our food'.[14] This situation and these justifications can translate into the scene I was told about in a pub one evening: a skipper, drunk and rambling at the bar at the end of a successful fishing trip, buying steaks and rounds of beer for the Scottish crew and desperately asking anyone who would listen 'I left the Filipinos on the boat, does that make me a bad person?' Global inequality is made local, significantly increasing exploitation, class divisions and the potential profits of owners. The production and maintenance of these vast gulfs on a small boat in a small village is jarring, and I could see people struggling to create new ideological justifications for this state of affairs. As one hired skipper told me, 'my dog has an easier life than those poor guys'. Taken together, these incidents are evidence, unsettling for many in the fishing industry, that their self-image of egalitarianism (Nadel-Klein 2003) is increasingly becoming a delusion.

The crewing of fishing boats became one of the most sharply debated and controversial issues in the fishing industry over the course of my fieldwork. After two high-profile incidents in Fraserburgh in 2008 in which three Filipino and one Latvian fishermen working on Scottish fishing boats were killed,[15] in early 2009, the UK government announced that non-EU fishing crew were working illegally and would be deported within the next few months (Brooks 2009; Crighton 2008b). The ITF trade union inspector for international seafarers became involved (Money 2008). Fishing industry leaders claimed that the industry would collapse without being able to employ Filipino workers, and convinced the UK government to create a special temporary visa for non-EU fishing boat crew, tied to improvements in their working hours, pay and living conditions, including the provision of accommodation on shore. The employment of non-EU crew remained a very sensitive subject – so sensitive that in June 2009 the secretary of a fishing boat owners' association successfully demanded that I be removed from a three-month research post with Seafish because I had been quoted criticising employment practices in the industry in two newspaper articles ten months previously.[16]

In August 2010, the UK government warned fishing boat owners that only 44 of the new visas had been issued for non-EU fishing boat crew and that boat owners found to be employing crew illegally would face stiff penalties (UK Border Agency 2010). My fieldwork was over by this time so I could not verify either these numbers or whether the promised improvements in conditions had taken place. Anecdotal evidence indicates that in that year there were far more than 44 non-EU crew working on Scottish fishing vessels. The temporary visas were originally scheduled to end in September 2011, but were extended. It seems that most owners did not send their low-waged crew back home once fuel prices declined from their 2008 highs and alleviated the cost crisis that purportedly drove owners to hire migrant workers. The practice became normalised and spread even to small owner-operated vessels as a way of maintaining profitability while coping with the other pressures. One owners' association, the Scottish Fishermen's Organisation, even set up its own Filipino crewing agency and advertised it on their website (Scottish Fishermen's Organisation 2011).

Nadel-Klein notes a 'growing class division between the successful and the not-so-successful' in fishing communities (2003: 143). At the same time, there are indications that increasing links of solidarity between crew on different fishing boats, rather than among the crew of one boat, are developing. This may challenge the 'segmental' separations that have been described in other parts of rural Scotland (Cohen 1987), and lead to the development of more horizontal social divisions. This has not just been an internal process. This example of the 'ways in which different cohorts of the working class were brought into the process of capitalist accumulation' (Wolf 1997: 379) involves Romanian, Scottish and Filipino men engaged in the uncomfortable process of discovering their unexpectedly converging class interests as they stood for hours tailing prawns on the decks of small fishing boats in the North Atlantic and struggled to understand how the owners could get away with it. What does this mean for the fishing industry? One new development was the involvement of the ITF trade union inspector Norrie McVicar (Bynorth 2008; Money 2008). Likely familiar with the assistance that ITF inspectors could provide from previous work in cargo shipping, Filipino crew in Peterhead called him for assistance. This was possibly the first trade union activity in the Scottish fishing industry since 1937 (Martin 1981: 214). In the context of a competitive market-oriented fishery, it is worth considering whether the employment of a significant number of workers on very low wages will mean that fishing boats who *want* to continue operating a genuine share system will be able to remain viable. These issues may profoundly affect the Scottish fishing industry and the communities it supports.

Constant competition between fleets, boats, seafood buyers and markets and efforts to cut costs drove seafood prices down and meant that boats had to land more and more prawns just to stay even. Declining profits and pressure for increasing capital investment meant that boat owners appropriated more and more of the value of the catch, centralising their authority, increasing inequality, and creating new kinds of relations among crew as they produced fish for the market. A system of shared ownership was transformed into a system for casual payment, and the associated deteriorating pay and working conditions led to increasing problems for owners in maintaining a disciplined and reliable crew. The change in production relations that took place under the auspices of the share system increasingly differentiated between skippers, owners and crew. In combination with global and local increases in migrant labour and the willingness of the government to look the other way, these changing relations enabled, and even encouraged, owners to take the step of hiring low-waged migrant workers to crew their boats. One pattern of relations led to another, which in turn led to yet another, producing classes of people with very different relations to their own labour and to their bodies through the processes of production they participated in. The 'harnessable vulnerability' of some groups functioned 'as a subsidy to capital' (Sider 2003: 317) through the vastly lower expense of the labour of these workers, which functioned to discipline other groups of workers and further increase the resources available to owners. The costs to the workers in question were not just financial: their precarious position made them over three times more likely to be killed doing the same job.

## Conclusion: commodities and ecologies

In this chapter I have stepped back from a close phenomenological examination of grounds, places, techniques and orientation to look at the key questions of political economy that have shaped 'why things are this way' (Desjarlais 1997: 25). Examining 'who owns what', 'who gets what' and 'what do they do with it', in a historical context, has allowed a significantly deeper understanding of a whole number of contemporary issues: the alienation of crew and the social separation I observed between them and fishing skippers, the conflicted relations people had with the tools and machines they worked with, the obsessive discussion of buyers and prices, why I was able to get a job on a fishing trawler so easily when there have historically been firm prohibitions against this, how the prawn fishery came into being, its links to Spain, the relationship between east and west coast fishers, and the growing numbers of Filipino fishermen in tiny Scottish villages. Asking these structural questions deepens our anthropological understanding of people's relationship to their environment, tools, and to each other.

Asking about political economy also gives a much better understanding of fisheries ecologies, and crisis. Critical research that attempts to synthesise ecological, social and economic aspects of fisheries is in short supply. Too much fisheries research depicts 'the individual producer as an autonomous isolate engaged in the technical act of catching fish' (Pálsson 1991: 21), or, focuses exclusively on either fisheries ecology or management systems, with no economic context (Campling et al. 2012). Fisheries anthropologist Charles Menzies argues that an understanding of the pressures of capitalist commodity production, and the social relations it requires, are important to understanding fisheries. When researchers overemphasise the 'uniqueness' of fishers from broader social and economic systems, important avenues for comparison, understanding and analysis are lost (Menzies 2002: 23).

The changing crew dynamics that I have documented in this chapter and the different structural resources available to skippers and crew also had ecological consequences. Constant competition to cut costs between fleets, boats and buyers selling to markets around the world drove seafood prices down and meant that boats had to catch more and more 'bulk' in order to make bank payments, buy fuel, maintain the boat and pay crew. This in turn affected the grounds that skippers would work: 'going for bulk' involved working smooth 'clean' ground, which meant lower fuel and gear costs, but also hours of unpleasant and labour-intensive tailing for the crew. Crew who felt confident about their position would resist the efforts of skippers to 'go for bulk'. In the pub one evening, John, a successful boat-owner, reminisced about time he spent working as crew in the 1980s: 'I remember once we were tailing shite [very small prawns] for no money down by Canna. I told the skipper, "if you are going back to catch that shite, then you can drop me on the dock because it is not worth it". The other guy I was working with told the skipper the same thing.' John and his fellow crew were able to use their skipper's reliance on them to force him to avoid working on the most unpleasant and labour-intensive grounds. The unpleasantness of the task of tailing and sorting the smallest prawns is reflected in the way they were referred to: as 'shite' or 'lice' or 'beetles',[17] reinforcing Jackson's point that 'the process of working on an object comes to be experienced as an inherent property of the object itself' (2007: 74). As crew, when this kind of haul came on board your heart sank. Boats whose skippers regularly targeted these kinds of grounds were known as 'beetle busters', and any sensible crew would avoid them. But the increasingly unequal relations on board, and in particular the employment of isolated Filipino crew on agency contracts, have enabled skippers and owners to undertake the strategy of 'going for bulk' (instead of 'going for quality') if they choose, and left crew with fewer resources to resist these choices. The skippers and owners of boats employing marginalised crew on agency contracts had a much greater ability to target whatever size of prawns on whatever grounds they felt like, as they did not have to negotiate fishing strategies with their crew. For owners, the problem of disciplining crew to undertake and complete the most unpleasant tasks on board was solved.

When a boat 'goes for bulk', they must catch many times more tiny prawns in order to make the same income, and these tiny prawns are much more labour-intensive to sort and process. Such a strategy is likely to have a much greater ecological impact on prawn populations. It is possible that catching and processing vast quantities of tiny prawns would not be economically viable without the very low wages that were paid to Filipino crew for doing so.[18]

Looking at the key questions of political economy is also important for understanding contemporary political debates in fishing. In 2009 skippers organised across Scotland to sign an open letter, which noted the substantial reduction in price over the past year and crew wages at 'unacceptable' levels. It called for vessels to be limited to 200 days at sea per year, and for those days at sea to be 'non-transferable' between boats, and therefore not be able to accumulate a value. They argued that a combination of market conditions and market-based fishery regulations meant that 'the once lucrative, quality nephrops sector' had been turned into:

> nothing more than an industrial fishery, which we consider to be a misuse of a valuable resource. Presently, those who catch the most – at the lowest price and quality – will be best off! We want to reverse this trend before it becomes accepted practise, to the ultimate detriment of the nephrops industry and its fishermen. (*Fishing News* 2009b: 3)

The letter was featured in the *Fishing News*, with an editorial that characterised 'the general thrust of fisheries management philosophy in the EU' as 'allowing market forces to operate to balance fleets with available quotas. This of course leads precisely to the "survival of the fittest" that the prawn skippers are trying to avoid' (*Fishing News* 2009c: 2). The centre-spread of the *Fishing News* featured the launch of new high-tech million-pound fishing boats almost every week. Yet the launch of these expensive new boats relied on consolidated quota and licences purchased from smaller boats that were being squeezed out through the process the skippers described. The 'fittest' were those who could work the most days and catch large quantities of small, low-value prawns: precisely the strategy that was enabled by hiring migrant workers. As Alasdair and I discussed this state of affairs, he exclaimed in frustration: 'The Filipino guys working on these new twin-riggers are relying on charity just to get their winter work clothes!' By the following week, *Fishing News* reported that 114 skippers had signed the letter (2009c: 2).

Alasdair also blamed this 'survival of the fittest' approach for the death of his good friend Findus, who was lost at sea while trying to keep up. A labour-centred understanding of human–environment relations offers us a way of tying together these strands: the creation of grounds and the experience of working them, how this experience is shaped by political economy, and the human and environmental consequences of these interactions. The next chapter will explore some of the devastating human consequences.

## Notes

1  Purse-seine fishing boats targeting pelagic species such as mackerel and herring.
2  'Klondykers' were fish-processing ships from Russia and Eastern Europe that bought fish from Scottish trawlers and then processed it on board for export.
3  A cran is equivalent to 170.5 litres.
4  According to the recommended method for showing changes in commodity values over time, at www.measuringworth.com/ukcompare.
5  A licence was required to fish and vessels over 10m in length usually needed to purchase quota. However, the cost of the boat was much greater.
6  This survey did not include places further north on the mainland such as Plockton, Applecross or Loch Torridon, where most of the vessels are owner-operated prawn creel boats.
7  Two creel boats were crewed by a father-skipper-owner and son-crew, the son of one creel boat owner-skipper skippered the second family-owned boat, and three trawlers were skippered by sons who had inherited the boat from their father, who provided shore support to their son and his hired crew.
8  Most of the 34 creel and trawl boats surveyed had two crew, with some employing three and a few operating single-handed. I estimate 70 crew and skippers worked on these boats at any one time (due to the high turnover of crew, the potential pool of fishing boat crew is larger). With a generous estimate of 23 owner-skippers and three owner-skipper-sons, at any one time approximately 44/70 crew and skippers were hired.
9  A significant quantum of the surplus value generated from fishing will be contained in what I describe as the 'fishing surplus'. Of the proportion of the fishing surplus going to

the crew via shares, much will be payment for necessary labour and crew's livelihood, and will not be surplus value. Of the proportion going to the boat owner, a significant amount will be surplus value and will take the form of profit. The total surplus value from fishing will be contained, in part, in that profit; and will be distributed, in part, in the form of rent (fishing access, harbour dues, etc.) and interest (bank loans for boats) and taxes; *and* will also be 'captured' downstream the commodity chain by trading companies and processors. Thanks to Liam Campling and an anonymous reviewer of a journal article for this insight.

10  As the situation for crew has worsened, Seafish has reduced their reporting of it. Each annual report subsequent to the one quoted had less to say on the subject. The 2010 report did not even include the data on crew share per person, I had to extrapolate it from other figures provided in the report (Curtis *et al.* 2010).

11  A 'grafter' is a hard worker.

12  Five deaths in an estimated 1,000 Filipino fishing crew in 2008 gives a fatality rate of 500 per 100,000. In 2009, there were two more deaths, giving a rate of 200 per 100,000, assuming 1,000 Filipino crew (data on fatalities supplied by Marine Accident Investigation Branch). Averaged across the two years the rate is 350 per 100,000, compared to the average rate of 102 per 100,000 among all fishermen 1996–2005 (Roberts and Williams 2007).

13  Reduced crew wages could also be due to higher fuel prices. On boats that still pay their crew by share, the cost of the fuel is deducted before the share is calculated.

14  Food is incredibly important on board fishing boats. Stories about an unfair distribution of food on board were the most common examples that fishermen gave me about the poor treatment that some Filipino crew received.

15  The prawn trawler *Vision II* caught fire on 1 August 2008 in Fraserburgh harbour, killing crew Benjamin Potot and Remitito Calipayan, both Filipino, and Rimants Venkus from Latvia. On 14 August 2008 Filipino crew Reynaldo Benitez fell overboard from the Fraserburgh-registered prawn trawler *New Dawn* while at sea off northern Scotland (Crighton 2008a).

16  The articles are Money (2008) and Bynorth (2008).

17  Martin (2004: 46) also records 'immature' prawns being referred to as 'lice'.

18  This raises an interesting question about whether instituting a minimum landing size for prawns could reduce the incentive for highly exploitative labour practices. Alasdair also pointed out that such a rule could help smaller boats that tend to 'go for quality'.

# 6

## Structural violence in ecological systems

During the time I knew Alasdair and worked on his small fishing trawler, he told me Findus' story again and again. The first time was after a month of patiently tolerating my questions about environmental relations and fishing practices. Alasdair gently pointed out that I had never asked him about losing friends at sea, and then he told me about Findus and the wreck of his fishing boat, which still lay on the seafloor six miles west of the rugged coast of Skye. Almost four years later, Alasdair brought up Findus again as fishers were signing a protest letter about fisheries management systems. 'It is decommissioning by bankruptcy!' Alasdair told me, his voice shaking with anger and tears rising in his eyes, 'and look what that did to Findus!'

I began the research this book is based on in 2006, only a few weeks after the *Brothers* was wrecked, and Neil (skipper) and Davey (crew) were lost (Figure 38). Findus and his Australian crew Lance had been lost two years before. Over the time of my research, several local fishing boats smashed into familiar rocks and islands in the area – some boats sinking, some repaired (Howard 2016). All crew survived these local wrecks, but in other parts of Scotland they were not so lucky. I received a few texts like this one from Alasdair:

> If you heard on news that unity a fife boat sank, 2 crew safe skipper missing, yes
> we were both good friends of his, john bowman. A real good egg. Another one.

These wrecks were produced and people were killed when the enormous physical challenge of catching creatures you cannot see in places you have never been collided with the inexorable pressure of market competition and the struggle to stay afloat economically. They were produced by a particular trawl door caught in a particular seabank and by a whole grinding economic system; fishers caught between the skill of catching fish and the skill of making money, between hope and fear, between what they must do and what they must not do, what they knew and what they tried not to know. What it meant to be a safe mariner and what it meant to be a good fisherman were frequently in conflict with each other. Fishermen were 115 times more likely to be killed at work than the average UK worker. The violence they experienced was obscured by an underlying 'ideology of nature' that naturalised the sea as an inevitably dangerous wilderness, and an official

Figure 38  Oil rising to the surface from the wreck of the *Brothers* fishing boat just north of Skye. Both crew, David Davidson and Neil Sutherland, drowned (MAIB 2007: 11).

ideology of 'accidents' that blamed fishermen for being irresponsibly responsible for their own injuries and deaths. Fishermen themselves rejected these ideologies but coped by not keeping track of the deaths of other fishermen. Fishermen and seafarers who did confront the constant danger posed by the impossible contradictions they had to cope with usually left the industry – or carried on in a jittery traumatised state.

### Kathryn Jane

For Alasdair, the *Kathryn Jane* 'just went off the face of the earth'. He told me about the many scrapes that Findus got into, the poor condition of his boat, and then trawling next to Findus on 28 July 2004. Alasdair remembers heading into port that day as the wind increased and the weather deteriorated: 'I thought it strange when Findus didn't appear behind us in Portnalong', he said, but 'there could be a perfectly satisfactory explanation'. A week later, Findus' wife called, a child's birthday had been missed and he wouldn't have forgotten. More phone calls were made, and Findus was reported missing. Harbours were searched and phone records were procured and examined. For four days the Coastguard broadcast a message over hundreds of miles of coastline, requesting anyone who had sighted the *Kathryn Jane* to contact them, and for four days the crackly ominous message echoed out of hundreds of radios up and down the coast. And then:

It was Lachie Clark that found it. His net stuck on something that shouldn't be there. Stuck. [And, as if we, too, were on the boat, and Alasdair himself was the skipper] 'Shouldn't be sticking here!'

Hauled up. It was a wire and a trawl door. Findus' gear, he'd been trawling when the boat went down.

It was the next week that Findus himself was found on the shore of Lochmaddy across the Minch in the Western Isles. Lance's body was never found. He is assumed to be dead as his mobile phone and bank transactions ceased on the same day as the wreck (MAIB 2005).

With great affection, Alasdair spoke of Findus: 'He was a one-off. Rubbed a lot of folk up the wrong way. I had a lot of time for him. He did his own thing. That's not a crime. God rest him, that was Findus.'

*Kathryn Jane* sank while trawling. The boat and its net and heavy doors still lie streamed out across the fishing grounds as a constant obstacle for fishermen to negotiate. Figure 39 is an image from Alasdair's digital GPS chartplotter (Chapter 4). The area around the boat and net are marked as a hazard with red hatching, but it is surrounded by activity: each solid and dashed line represents a tow made by Alasdair's boat. The tows made through the wreck area were probably made while the *Kathryn Jane* was still afloat.

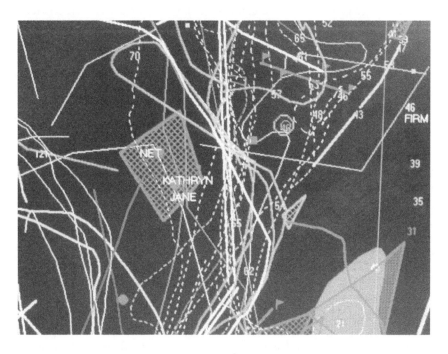

Figure 39  Image from a GPS chartplotter showing the wreck of the *Kathryn Jane* as a hazard to avoid among the solid and dashed lines recording trawling routes.

Out of sight on the seafloor yet made present through the chartplotter, the wreck of the *Kathryn Jane* was a grim reminder of the thin line between success and the sudden and total catastrophe that was the potential consequence of the efforts by fishermen to extend and over-extend the capacities of their small boats and fragile bodies as they struggled to catch enough prawns to remain 'viable'. Despite the isolated mystery of how the *Kathryn Jane* sank, the haunting inconclusiveness of death at sea made the sinking a public event with a wide and ongoing impact over hundreds of miles of coastline.

## Seamanship, and being a safe mariner

A year later, Alasdair speculated about what had happened to the *Kathryn Jane*:

> Nobody knows for certain what happened to it, but a fair bet? From where he was and where his gear was, he stuck and he was turning. He has had a hell of a strain coming on to his [Alasdair paused to mime the action of the boat with his body, situating it in the familiar underwater topography] – turning starboard off the ground – his port wire [running from the boat to the net] and the weak corner of his deck, back of the deck hatch where it was rotten with rust, has just, whhhst, opened up like a bean can.
>
> The boat would have gone down in seconds if that had happened. It was a shitty kind of day.

When a net caught on the seafloor, the forces involved were immense. The relationship between the boat and the net was illustrated in the official accident investigation report (Figure 40). Findus' steel boat may have 'opened up like a bean can' while the tension from the net, engine and wind pulled the boat over and the waves filled it in the twilight. 'Coming fast' is not uncommon, but the weakened steel of Findus' poorly maintained boat made it much more dangerous.

In Chapter 3 I discussed the almost-always over-extended working practices that trawling required, the constant maintenance of fishing gear and close attention to the boat and to 'feeling the ground' necessary to avoid a catastrophe. The gear could get caught on a bank or a boulder or a wreck, the net could flip over, the winch hydraulics could blow out, the engine could shut down from a cooling hose jiggling loose or blocked fuel filters. Skipper and crew could find themselves in a frightening and precarious situation that they had to fix, alone. I have described Alasdair's disconcerting habit of putting the kettle on and having a cup of instant coffee and a cigarette in moments like this, of keeping calm, and thinking carefully and methodically about the problem. He had the experience and the physical and temporal resources to be able to slowly and methodically use the weight of the net and the force of the winch to fix the situation, rather than becoming over-extended, and overcome. Seamanship was the 'ability to catch a kettle before it falls and to look after people and things before they need it' (Nicolson 2004: 180). Ships needed to be carefully maintained, to have the right tools on hand and enough time available to avoid such problems. Skippers needed to decide when the weather became too 'shitty' to be able to deal with such problems, and leave themselves enough time to make it home safely. Crew also needed to be 'maintained' with

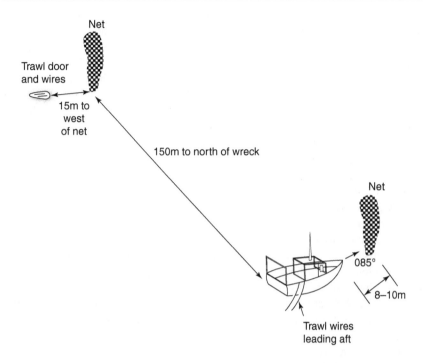

Figure 40  The *Kathryn Jane* and her net, as they were found on the seafloor (MAIB 2005: 12).

enough sleep and food to ensure that they could stay awake through the hours of steaming through the 'black dark' and could make the right decision when it was needed.

Taking this time and care I will call the logic of seamanship – of being a safe mariner. Crew learned these skills at sea, from their skippers and fellow crew, and often through bitter experience. But the time and space to practise these skills was usually under constant pressure from the logic of the market that fishermen sold to and which determined their ability to stay afloat, economically.

## The logic of the market, and being a 'good fisherman'

In the same conversation as Alasdair described the likely 'hell of a strain' coming on to *Kathryn Jane*'s net, he explained the broader situation Findus was caught in. Empathy mixed with sadness as he recounted:

> Findus. Knew his boat was a bloody death trap but yet he persevered.
>     He got into a state, the boat got into a state where he needed a pretty heavy injection of money to bring it up to anything like a reasonable standard. And he just – the boat wasn't capable of catching, or working steadily enough and catching at a rate that that was ever going to happen.

With the *Kathryn Jane* in poor condition, it was much more vulnerable to the strain of bad weather and nets. Alasdair had been in this situation himself. 'I was going ahead', he said. 'Another winter, another year's work and I would have had the boat in good enough nick to get her surveyed, insured, and if I hadn't lost her then, I would have replaced her.' In other words, Alasdair and his boat were in bad enough shape that he could not pay for repairs to fix it to a standard that would allow him to get insurance for it. Despite the poor condition of the boat, he had to keep working to keep 'going ahead'. Then the boat was wrecked. Luckily Alasdair survived, but without insurance, he still had to make payments to the bank for a boat he no longer had.

In commercial fisheries, people depend on selling their catch for more than it costs to catch it, and using the slender difference to maintain themselves, their family, their boat, their crew, their bank loan and their house. These economic pressures form a critical but often neglected aspect of the analysis of commercial fisheries, which are often treated as if they structured simply by the relationship between fishermen and their environment (Campling *et al.* 2012). Sider described how Newfoundland fishers often sell their catch at prices below what it cost to produce them (2003: 313). In Louisiana, Brian Marks documents the 'cost-price squeeze' that that has strained relationships in shrimping families and meant 'the boat eats first from the family table' (2012: 244). Menzies describes the difficult choices for fishers in France between 'becoming more fully capitalist' or 'risk losing their boat and other family property' (2002: 23). In the west of Scotland, regional and global competition forced down the prices paid to fishers for their catch. This pressured them to cut costs, and make more capital investment in expensive equipment to try to catch more prawns at a lower cost (Chapter 5). But the loans required to buy new boats and new equipment put fishermen in increasingly precarious and potentially catastrophic situations.

Commercial fishermen had a direct, individual and often unmediated experience of the global seafood market. The pressure of 'getting a price' was incorporated into fishers' language, their daily discussions, and the satisfaction they got from their jobs. Most skippers could mentally add weights, estimate prices (which varied considerably according to the size of prawn), and multiply these into totals and subtract expenses with lightning speed, whether they were estimating the results of their own catch or information gleaned about the catches of others. Almost everyone kept a calculator in their wheelhouse.

Who was selling to what buyer and at what price was a constant source of intrigue. With three buyers based in Skye and Lochalsh, another in Torridon and still others that sent trucks over from Buckie, Peterhead, Eyemouth, Fort William, the Clyde and Spain, there was plenty to speculate about. Rumours would fly about what price each buyer was paying and whether it was rising or falling. Boats would sometimes switch buyers several times in the course of a year, or supply more than one buyer at the same time. Guarded conversations about even the identity of buyers began 'I shouldn't be telling you this but …'. A niche buyer paying a high price, or even a well-known one raising prices, was a secret to be shared only with one's closest friends, and maybe not even with them. As the normally very expansive crew for a skipper who prided himself on always getting the highest price told me: 'You don't need to know where he [the buyer] ships them to, and I don't want to know in case I tell you!'

The value of the catch had a strong effect on the overall outlook of fishermen, often making the difference between a good day and a 'waste'. Catching a net full of squat lobsters or jellyfish or kelp was 'no use' on a commercial fishing boat, as there was no market for them. 'A lack of prawns' would put any skipper in a foul mood. A day or two of poor catches was tolerable but would inspire frantic comparison with others. But before long, paranoia, self-doubt and depression would creep in. Most respondents to a 2009 survey of Scottish fishing skippers characterised the mood of the fleet as 'poor' or 'very poor', a drastic decline from 2007 when it had been mostly been characterised as 'good'. The overwhelming reason skippers gave was the substantial decline in price (Brown 2009: 3). It was the price fishermen got for their catch that made their work valuable, that gave them a livelihood, and that made the difference between fishing being 'viable' or a 'nightmare'.

Some skippers constantly monitored the price at the market, and would receive a daily phone call from Spain telling them to hold back prawns if the price was low or to send everything if it was high. Many had an antagonistic relationship with the seafood buyers they also relied on. Complaints about particular buyers would be aired publicly on the radio: 'I'm not going to put up with [a seafood buyer] anymore! They are paying bottom prices and ripping us off on weights!' 'Good' buyers weighed and recorded prawns as they were landed, but a surprising number refused to. Fishermen could only trust that they were paid for the full weight of their catch, and I witnessed many disputes over weights (including ones that affected my own pay). A number of boats purchased small digital scales so that they could log their own precise measurements of weight in case there was a dispute. While such strategies could increase the price that fishermen received for their catches, in the longer term they also reinforced the precarious livelihood of fishermen and their dependence on a market they had no control over. Fishers were 'chronically insecure', and saw themselves 'as persistent veterans of a more extended or chronic kind of crisis … each cohort has learned from its elders never to take its livelihood for granted' (Nadel-Klein 2003: 134).

The alienating effect of relying on market selling to survive has been explored by social theorist Richard Schacht. In such situations, a fisher is required to 'produce[s] large quantities of the same item, which he [sic] cannot use' for a fluctuating market that is not 'subject to his control, and has no regard for his welfare' (Schacht 1970: 87). The result is that producers feel themselves to be subjected to an 'inhuman power' which 'rules over everything' (Marx quoted in Schacht 1970: 87). The product 'is "alien" to its producer in that it reflects the profile of the market rather than of his own personality. And it is "hostile" to him in that it strengthens the "inhuman power" which operates to his detriment, and satisfies the demands of the market only at the cost of the sacrifice of this physical wellbeing and personal self-realization' (Schacht 1970: 88). Market conditions can also cause producers to feel alienated from their 'own purpose' through the demands of earning an adequate income. Schacht cites the example of 'an independent farmer or shop owner who is only able to sustain himself through the total expenditure of his time and energy, and is therefore never able to do the things he really wants to do' (1970: 92).

As markets became more interconnected, this 'inhuman power' became increasingly pervasive and difficult to predict. Reductions in the cost of scallop production in America and Japan could cause scallop fishermen in Scotland to 'fucking crap' themselves. When fishing for crab, it was prudent to keep 'an eye on the weather in the south of England. If it is poor or the tides are strong, the price will go up'. The global recession which started in 2008 meant that 'Easter never came in Spain', and Scottish fishermen didn't receive the usual holiday price rise. There was high demand for prawns leading up to Christmas, which increased prices and the pressure to work when days were the shortest and dangerous weather was common. The post-Christmas slump meant that 'if it is good weather in Scotland it is a nightmare', because there might be an oversupply of prawns lowering prices. Buyers might even refuse to purchase your catch: 'I have had some weeks I fished and I never got paid. I went to land my catch and was told that there was no market for it' explained Iain, another experienced fisherman. He had studied agricultural economics and told me that there was 'so much subsidy' for farmers in the EU, but fishers were 'just abandoned to the free market. Minimum prices would be a start'.

As a result, the skills of a 'good fisherman' included negotiating the capitalist marketplace to remain 'viable', and were demonstrated by the value of their catch. Legendary catches were described not by volume, but by value, as in: 'Graeme has the record for an under-10: £10,000 in a week!' One skipper told me a long story about 'my best day ever, a £2,300 day!' Nadel-Klein quotes a retired skipper who told her 'at the end of the day, fishing is cash' (2003: 159). A novice crew described learning about prices from an older crewman who had fished all his life: the experienced man made a special point of teaching him what price each type of fish would fetch, particularly the most valuable. ' "That's a Dover sole, it would cost you £40 in a restaurant" he would say, and then chuck it over the side!' (the boat only had a licence to catch prawns). Prizes for 'top fishing skippers' were determined by the gross value of their catch (*Stornoway Gazette* 2007).

The same person who told me that that hired skipper Graeme had the record for an under-10 explained that he was 'a really good fishermen, he often gets half as much again as a lot of guys. He is a lot braver in where he is going'. 'The boat makes money', his crew told me, with considered respect. Another local skipper was described to me as a 'good fisherman, I'll give him that, but he's also a bastard. He does well for himself'. Being a 'good fishermen' meant maximising the value of your catch, even if you were 'a bastard'.

## Multiple subjectivities

The subjectivities of fishermen were shaped by the logic of the capitalist market they relied on to survive – and the fact that this logic frequently conflicted with what fishermen knew to be good seamanship. Fishermen had to constantly reconcile these pressures. They needed to leave themselves enough space and time to cope with the inevitable crises that would arise, and to get the situation back under control – to avoid panic, to have a cup of tea or coffee, and to calmly assess what needed to be done. Yet at the same time they needed to maximise the value of their catch in order to keep 'going ahead' and to be able to support their families, make bank payments, keep the boat maintained and avoid 'going under' financially. When 'good fisherman' were described as 'braver', this frequently meant taking the chance of ignoring good seamanship, and seeing if you could get away with it, and survive.

The anthropological literature on 'subjectivity' traces the connections between peoples' dispositions and the economic and social relations that shape their life-experience. 'Our affect', say Kleinman and Fitz-Henry, 'is always both internal and external to us – located as much within the contours of our bodies as within the shifting parameters of our socio-political worlds' (2007: 64). Fishermen were subjected to (at a minimum) two contradictory logics, so they did not have a single subjectivity. Social theorist Göran Therborn argues that 'in the course of a single human life a large number of subjectivities are in fact acted out' (1980: 78), as people respond to calls made upon them through different ideologies. For example, Therborn describes how in a strike a worker may be addressed as:

> a member of the working class, as a union member, as a mate of his fellow work-ers, as the long-faithful employee of a good employer, as a father or mother, as an honest worker, as a good citizen, as a Communist or anti-Communist, as a Catholic and so on. The kind of address accepted – 'Yes, that's how I am, that's me!' – has important implications for how one acts in response to the strike call. (1980: 78)

Each one of these calls is based in a specific ideology and social formation the worker is a part of and implies a particular course of action in the situation of a strike – some of which may be entirely contradictory. Like Therborn, Gramsci argued that workers may have 'two theoretical consciousnesses (or one contradictory con-sciousness)' (1971: 333). Gramsci is clear that this is not a result of 'self-deception' (or 'false consciousness'), but is based on people's actual, and contradictory, experi-ences of the world, and is 'the expression of profounder contrasts of a social histori-cal order' – like the contradictory logics fishermen had to reconcile every day at sea (1971: 326; for a discussion see Crehan 2002). The result is what Ingold describes as a 'painful process of negotiation' between our task-oriented socially situated expe-rience (such as fishermen's skills of seamanship) and 'a commodity-based institu-tional and ideological framework that seeks at every turn to deny the reality' of that experience – their subjection to the market (2000: 338).

New fishermen learned the essential skills of feeling and extension described in earlier chapters in the context of this competitive, pressurised market logic. Fishermen challenged themselves and each other to 'open up new ground', 'go higher on the bank', 'work an edge' and to be prepared to mend 'damage' to nets and gear. Fishermen also pushed to 'work the limits of the weather', and of day-light, to try to extend their fishing time as long as possible. As the 'good fisherman' Graeme told me: 'I take risks, I don't know if it is because I try harder, or because

I am stupid or crazy, but I like to take a risk to get results.' He described more cautious fishermen as 'lazy' and 'unmotivated'.

The constant pressure and competition encouraged poor vessel maintenance, boats staying out in bad weather, crew pushing past the limits of fatigue, and owners regularly increasing the size of their fishing gear and the power of their engines. 'New boat engines now have so much torque that if the net gets caught then the whole boat is dragged under', Alasdair told me. 'A new one went recently like that, they had second-hand lifejackets. A Polish guy died.' Long working hours led to crew exhaustion and falling asleep at the wheel. It was not uncommon for boats to smash headlong into completely familiar rocks, cliffs and islands. These wrecks had nothing to do with navigation problems or being 'lost' – these boats would have passed these hazards hundreds of times before and known exactly where they were. The *Brothers* collided with Eilean Trodday in such circumstances (MAIB 2007), as did three other local boats during my fieldwork. One of these boats was run into a cliff in the early morning darkness. The skipper managed to reverse it off the rocks and limp into port for repairs. The boat must have been very strongly built and the cliff very sheer, said Alasdair, 'because nine times out of ten when you do that the boat will ride right up on to the rocks … and then get smashed to bits by the swell'. The frequency of such events was further emphasised the following year when the same boat ran into a different island and sank. This skipper was known and continued to be known as a 'good fisherman' because he pushed himself and his crew to consistently make good catches. Afterwards, he told me that he could no longer sleep when the boat was underway. At least one of the crew was prescribed medication for post-traumatic stress.

The contradictions between the logics of the market and of seamanship was most vividly illustrated in how it affected fishermen's judgement of the weather. Donald had been a successful fishing skipper and boat owner, but had sold everything and left the fishing industry about seven years before I met him, and sometime after his bank manager had committed suicide and he had repaid the bank the required £40,000 (Introduction). Donald explained that if a fisherman was not able to keep up with the finance payments on their boat, the only way out was to get together with someone else and buy a bigger boat. Donald had owned a 50-foot trawler. 'Where do you go from there?' he asked rhetorically, 'A Campbeltown 87, a £3 million boat!' He shook his head:

> I had a friend who wanted to do it, we looked into it, but I decided no, I didn't want to get into that. You never get out, it is a vicious cycle.
>     My friend went on to do it anyway, and the boat was lost with all hands up north of Orkney. Seven guys. They had to work in all weather. They couldn't take a day off or they would not be able to make payments. And it killed them. No, I'm not interested in that.

Part of the skill of seamanship is the judgement of weather conditions, which in this circumstance was trumped, with deadly consequences, by the pressure of making a livelihood on the market and being individually responsible to the bank. As one crew described in Chapter 5: 'Try telling a bank manager, "Well the weather has been poor, the engine broke down, I took the arse out of the net." Not likely.' Market dynamics increased the incentive to fish in the most dangerous weather. For example, the title of a *Fishing News* article proclaimed 'Weather lifts prices' and the article's opening sentence breathlessly reported 'just one turbot weighing 9.52kg made over £170'. Poor weather meant that the two boats that 'battled the weather ... got very, very good prices' because supply was so short (Lockley 2009: 5). Alasdair explained it was expected that 'top-notch skippers' would 'work in weather that nobody else will risk'.

At the same time as the market encouraged and rewarded risky behaviour by pushing fishermen to their limits and beyond, it also pushed out those like Findus who couldn't keep up. The *Fishing News* described a de facto EU fisheries policy of ratcheting up the pressure on fishermen by 'allowing market forces to operate to balance fleets with available quotas, leading to the "survival of the fittest" ' (*Fishing News* 2009c: 2). This was the situation that Alasdair described with sadness and anger as 'decommissioning by bankruptcy' – which he strongly felt had deadly consequences. 'Decommissioning' referred to earlier schemes to buy fishermen out of the industry – except this time there was no buy-out: fishermen were simply pushed to the edge and then over.

While the call to be 'a good fisherman' was constant and unrelenting, no one ever called on fishermen to be safe – except in the context of berating them for not wearing a lifejacket, or for not being sufficiently environmentally conscious. Many fishermen felt themselves to be living in 'a state of siege' (Taussig 1992: 10). Many skippers were on 'happy pills'. Their young crews worked sorting prawns with a factory-line intensity, and they bounced from trawler to trawler, describing each one as a 'shit bucket' no matter how well it was maintained (Chapters 3 and 5). There were many other pressures too: 'the greens coming at you from every angle', and fishermen furiously rejected the proposal to create a Coastal and Marine National Park in the waters around Scotland. 'Tossers in suits' were responsible for the management of fisheries, and the tension between them and fishermen was palpable at every consultation meeting I attended (see Nightingale 2011). The representatives of fishermen's organisations often tried to play a mediating role, but it was sometimes difficult to distinguish them from the civil servants, both usually equipped with expensive suits, cufflinks and BlackBerries; many fishermen believed that they were 'at it' too.[1] 'If you are a trawlerman', I was told, 'you think everyone is out to get you'. These pressures mixed with a long history of 'stigma, stereotype and marginality' of fishers and their communities, who were often seen by others as 'backward and prerational' (Nadel-Klein 2003: 48–49).

Nadel-Klein described fishermen as 'veterans of a more extended or chronic kind of crisis' (2003: 134). What is the nature of this crisis? Subjected by both the logic of the market and the need to be a safe mariner, fishermen had to do things that they knew were unsafe to survive, like Findus who 'knew his boat was a bloody death trap but yet he persevered', or Alasdair who kept fishing on an uninsurable boat so he could keep 'going ahead'. 'The tradition of the oppressed teaches us that "the state of emergency" in which we live is not the exception but the rule', said Walter Benjamin (1999 [1968]: 248), a state of emergency which Michael Taussig characterised as having an 'irregular rhythm of numbing and shock' (1992: 15): the concussive shock of being woken by your boat ramming a familiar island at full speed, the numbing days of inconclusive searching for a friend lost at sea, of wondering what happened, and what or who might end up in the net as a result.

## Structural violence: a state of emergency?

It was not until I finished my time working on a fishing boat that I learned how dangerous the job was, statistically: UK fishing boat crew are 115 times more likely to die at work than the average UK worker, 24 times more likely to be killed even than those working in the dangerous construction industry (Roberts and Williams 2007). Filipino and Eastern European crew have a death rate over three times higher.[2] Slavoj Žižek identifies such violence as 'objective' or 'systemic', and as 'the often catastrophic consequences of the smooth functioning of our economic and political systems' which 'took on a new shape with capitalism' (2008: 1, 2, 10). Žižek contrasts this systemic violence with 'subjective' violence, like murder, which is 'performed by a clearly identifiable agent' and results in the 'perturbation of the "normal", peaceful state of things' (2008: 1).

Traditionally 'anthropologists saw, heard and reported no violence from the field' because 'violence was not considered a proper subject' for anthropology (Scheper-Hughes and Bourgois 2004: 6). Initial anthropologies of violence tended to focus on extreme situations such as war, but this has now shifted to encompass 'peacetime crimes' and 'everyday violence' that is 'implicit, legitimate, and routinized' and 'inherent in particular social economic and political formations' (Scheper-Hughes and Bourgois 2004: 19, 21). Studying 'the violences of everyday life ... offers an alternative view of human conditions that may give access to fundamental, if deeply disturbing, processes of social organization' (Kleinman 2000: 238).

Between 2003 and 2009 six men died at sea in the course of their work in the waters around Skye – out of a local population of only a few hundred fishermen and other maritime workers.[3] I cannot recall a single local murder being discussed during my research. However, many people had the experience of searching for bodies at sea, like the volunteer lifeboat coxswain who easily reeled off: 'The rule [in searching] for bodies is three hours, three days, three weeks. That's it, you won't get it after that.'[4] While it is often assumed that violent and traumatic experiences can be isolated from the 'normal' course of human life, fishermen who lose friends at sea must compel themselves to return to the same activity and frequently the same place of their loss, again and again, in order to continue their work. Like the *Kathryn Jane*, wrecks still lie on the seabed (Figure 39), and some bodies are never recovered. When the searching was done and the funerals were over, fishermen went back to working the same grounds, but this time with a boat missing from the ambling morning conversations. Now present was a dangerous new obstacle on the grounds, a new mark on the chartplotter, and a new potential for horror: like the east coast fishing boat that trawled up the body of a former crew who had been dragged overboard by fishing nets two weeks earlier (*Fishing News* 2009a: 7).

Living in their small workplaces and pushing themselves to the limit made fishing more dangerous than most jobs, particularly compared to other industries in the UK where workplace safety has significantly improved in the past 200 years. But the same fundamental contradictions between workers' 'task-orientation' and knowledge about the job, and the compulsion to produce is experienced, violently, by workers in industries around the world. At least 2.34 million people died from work-related incidents or diseases in 2008 (6,300 work-related deaths per day). A further 317 million workers were injured (ILO 2011: 10–11). These figures likely underestimate the actual problem. These deaths and injuries are growing – contrary to popular myths about the disappearance of the working class, the number of people 'who supply labor for the production of goods and services' has grown from 1.9 billion in 1980 to almost 3.4 billion in 2014 (World Bank 2016).

Through an ethnography of American product design and safety laws, anthropologist Sarah Jain shows that violence is so ingrained into processes of capitalist production that workers' compensation laws 'might be read as an attempt to codify how much of a worker's physical body may be spent in the process of production: "excess" wounding will count as injury' (2006: 18). A basic level of death and injury is expected. Jain concludes that 'accidents and human wounding provide a boost to the economy that is astonishingly undertheorised in economic and social theory' (2006: 154).

Workplace safety criminologists Tombs and Whyte estimate that it is more likely for a person to be killed through their work than much higher profile forms of violence, such as assault and murder (2007: 107). They show that 'key institutions that produce violence structurally and systematically in the context of work include labour markets, the occupational structure and the labour process, the uneven distribution of power in and around work relations, the corporate form *per se*, and the constituent parts of the state' involved with regulating work' (Tombs and Whyte 2007: 7). Their work supports the analysis by Scheper-Hughes and Bourgois that 'the most violent acts consist of conduct that is socially permitted, encouraged, or enjoined as a right or duty' (2004: 4). Modern forms of work and production normalise and obscure the deaths and injuries of workers, which are rarely prosecuted and almost never described as a crime. The death rate in the fishing industry is alarmingly high, and it should be considered a 'state of emergency'. Yet, as I will discuss, the structural causes of this violence are obscured by an ideology of 'accidents' and an ideology of 'nature' which is augmented by the autonomy of work on individual small boats that makes it harder to see the roles of broader economic and institutional structures in the industry.

## The ideologies that obscure the 'state of emergency'

On the pier and mending the net one sunny afternoon Alasdair told me that 'there is not a year goes by, I don't think, without somebody I know or know of killed at the job'. He stopped, lit a cigarette, and inhaled deeply:

> I don't imagine there's too many occupations where that's the case. In fact I very much doubt there's one. And one of the obvious next questions to that is 'What do you think should be done about it?' When you actually look at the involved statistics, were it any other job, then the number of fatalities would not have been tolerated. That number of fatalities would not be tolerated 100 years ago. If it was a land-based job – when mining was that dangerous, there was a drive to improve it, to introduce safety standards.
>
> There are cosmetic drives in the fishing industry to improve safety records. But the nature of the job will always make it dangerous.

But what is accepted as being 'the nature of the job'? The conventional understanding is that the dangerous 'nature' of the job is the overwhelming presence of the sea itself, yet as historian Marcus Rediker pointed out (Introduction), concentrating on this struggle between people and nature obscures the role of human exploitation and economic pressures on seafarers' lives.

After telling me about the dangerous 'nature of the job' Alasdair went on to explain that 'Very few people, crewing, skippering, whatever, die at sea in a genuine accident', and argued that the Marine Accident Investigation Board should really be named the 'Marine *Incident* Investigation Board'. He explained:

> I would have thought that their *raison d'être* would be to investigate incidents and separate what are accidents from what were avoidable. It strikes me as slightly odd that they start out from the standpoint, purely in their own name, of there being an assumption that there has been an accident.
>
> If someone deliberately disconnects, or knows that the brakes on their car aren't working, and goes driving, and crashes – they would be had up in court! There are parallels with that.

Alasdair moved from this example about car brakes to discuss much broader problems, like the pressure on 'top-notch skippers … to work in weather that nobody else will risk'. And he told me, again, about the death of his good friend Findus', whose boat was wrecked because 'it got into a state' and he was caught in a downward spiral, unable to catch enough to invest in his boat to be able to work more efficiently, as required by the continuously declining market prices.

Why were the number of fatalities in the fishing industry 'tolerated', as Alasdair described? Why was it not considered a 'state of emergency?' In his 30-year retrospective on studying violence, anthropologist Philippe Bourgois reflects that structural or 'invisible' violence is generally 'misrecognised' by both its victims and by those in positions of power, in a way that legitimates this violence (Bourgois 2009). First, the autonomy and isolation of fishing work processes obscured an understanding of other factors like market pressures and prices which structured and pressured fishermen's work. Second, where these pressures were recognised by regulatory agencies, they were treated and understood entirely separately from the issue of safety, and their tension with 'good seamanship' was never recognised or examined. Third, the intensifying class dynamics in the fishing industry centralised authority and decision-making about boat maintenance with owners ashore, leaving the hired crew working on the boat to cope with the consequences, like Graeme in Chapter 3, whose boat owner ashore refused to provide enough money to properly maintain the boat he was hired to skipper. Hired crew risked their lives at sea but had the least control over the maintenance of the tools, machines and boats they relied on.

The key characteristic of the organisation of labour under capitalism is the way in which decisions about what is produced, how it is produced, and who produces it are separated from those actually performing this work. Fundamentally, these are class relationships (Part III). Control of working processes is shifted and alienated – directly, through boat ownership structures and indirectly, by 'inhuman' market pressures, as Schacht describes. Anthropologist Sarah Jain argues that 'wounding and inequality are inextricable, the former is an expression of the latter' (2006: 18). But when it comes to bodily safety, the critical form of inequality is not financial, but the differential ability to control one's own body and labour, and the tools, machines and boats that people relied on to do their work and get home safely. As Elaine Scarry argues, class is not just about 'the haves and the have-nots' – the 'concussiveness' of class relations mean that 'what is had and had not is the human body' (1985: 263). Yet these class relationships of control and lack of control of people's own bodies and own labour are obscured by two deep-running ideologies that Alasdair alluded to, the ideology of 'accidents' and of 'nature'.

## The ideology of nature

Alasdair said that the 'nature' of the job will always make it dangerous – but here, Alasdair is not just referring to the 'nature' of the sea itself, but the whole 'nature' of the job' as it is currently organised. The idea that the sea is a naturally dangerous wilderness is deeply ingrained in the broader ideology of capitalism and class society. Yet fishermen did not see the sea in this way – they saw it as a humanised environment, extended from the shore, and which they made productive through their work (Chapters 1 and 2).

Geographer Neil Smith has outlined how an 'ideology of nature' arose with the development of capitalism, and here I will explore how his analysis applies at sea. Smith argues that the ideology of nature arose in Europe with the separation of the majority of the population from the ability to meet their own needs on the land, and the creation of waged labour in urban centres. In parts of Scotland, peasants were uprooted from the countryside and forced to become full-time fishermen, or urban factory workers, or to emigrate like Bodach's family (Introduction). It was the separation of people from resources that could sustain them on land that led to the creation of full-time fishermen fishing for the market, whereas fishing was previously practised as part of a varied and partly subsistence livelihood: the 'crofter-fisherman' who worked on land and at sea.

If the development of capitalism led to the separation of town and country (Smith 2008: 60), did the development of commercial fishing lead to the conceptual separation of 'humanised' land from the 'wilderness' of the sea, an understanding that fishermen contest yet are continuously subjected to? An urban-focused class-divided society meant that 'nature appears accessible to some individuals, indeed to entire classes, without the performance of labor but through "pure contemplation"'. The relationship to nature for those now working full-time at sea and selling fish to a market is also changed, 'for though they related to nature directly through their labor-power, they are alienated from their own product' because fish are sold and not used by them, and because they produce fish and grounds not according to their own needs, but those of the market. In a different way, the person who buys and consumes fish caught as commodities is also 'alienated from any direct, practical relation with nature' (all Smith 2008: 63). Thus the economic separation of town and country, and of land and sea, also separated the vast majority of people from the practical experience of working and engaging with the sea and meant their experiences of the sea were largely limited to the contemplation of it on television programmes, as a holiday destination, and their general understanding of it as a wilderness.

As Smith describes, the resulting 'ideology of nature' consists of two mutually dependent but contradictory conceptions of nature: as both external to human activity, and as universal, something of which humans form an essential part. The external conception of nature is manifest in the way in which nature is seen as simply as a resource, as an ingredient to be used in the process of industrial production. The universal conception of nature is manifest in the scientific understanding of humans as determined by biology and the romantic notion that humans are a part of the unity of nature. The universal conception of nature also has an important ideological function as it invests 'certain social behaviours with the status of natural events', with the implication 'that these behaviours and characteristics are normal, God-given, unchangeable' (Smith 2008: 29).

Although the external and universal conceptions of nature seem logically incompatible, they rely on each other. The authority of an appeal to universal nature rests partially on an understanding of nature as something external which has an irresistible power *over* humans. The crux of the ideology of nature is that both conceptions exclude the role of human labour in nature: according to this ideology, humans cannot develop the affordances of their environment because it is external to them *and*, as a biological given and a universal, it has power over them (Smith 2008: 30). This is in plain contradiction to the productive relationships between fishermen and their environments I described in Chapters 1 and 2. Yet under such an ideology, the sea could be seen as the ultimate external *and* universal nature: something which is dangerous, hostile and which must be battled as part of a timeless and natural struggle, and which consists entirely of wilderness and must be preserved in that way.

The prevalence of this 'ideology of nature' in Scotland and internationally is manifest in several ways. First, a hostile and dangerous sea naturalises the deaths of those working upon it, no matter what the real cause. Second, it is manifest in the endless high profile discussion, legislation and marketing strategies concerned with the sustainability of the seafood that fishermen catch. Yet fishermen and their families experienced a stark difference in the concern they heard expressed by government, industry and the media about fish as a resource, and about the well-being of people actually fishing. Most shocking was a conversation I had with a civil servant in the Scottish Executive's fishing department, who should have been familiar with the statistics produced about the industry by other government agencies. He told me that he was sceptical about the actual danger of fishing, and that he thought that fishermen often exaggerated the danger of their jobs for political gain.

The ideology of nature can be so overwhelming that it blocks any mutual understanding between fishers and those who seek to regulate their activities. I watched this mutual incomprehension unfold at a panel discussion on 'Sustainable Seafood Sourcing' that discussed Marine Stewardship Council (MSC) 'eco-labelling' of fish at the annual Fishing trade conference in Glasgow. A woman stood up and challenged the speakers' strict focus on the environment, and lack of discussion about fishing as a social process:

> As a fisherman's wife I worry greatly about the social and economic effects of MSC choices within the industry, particularly in small inshore vessels in small inshore coastal communities and that goes right across all our shores. I wonder if the MSC could comment on that please?
>    It's just that the only reference in fact to socio-economic has been very low ... I just wondered in the whole the broad issues as outlined by MSC, not once was it mentioned, and it does actually worry me ... in the MSC presentation, there was very little, in fact, I don't think it was any.

Clearly worried, she was almost apologetic about interrupting the cosy dialogue about seafood 'sustainability' that had been taking place. Unfortunately her concerns were so far from the minds of the presenters that they could not even understand her question. A representative from Sainsbury's supermarket assured her that 'there were other routes to green on our decision tree' apart from MSC certification. The Marine Conservation Society (MCS) representative just corrected her to say that the MSC and the MCS were different organisations, utterly missing her point. Unfortunately, the fisherman's wife apologised and the next question was taken.

This contrast between concern for workers safety and concern about the products they produce is not unique to fishing. As Pine points out, 'workers subjectivities are shaped by alienation in the workplace and the fact (articulated or not) that the health of their bodies is worth less to capital than their product' (2008: 159). Fisheries researchers Symes and Phillipson argue that social objectives in fisheries have 'all but disappeared from view ... subsumed under the goals of economic growth and wealth creation' (2009: 1). As fisherman Iain angrily commented in a discussion about a new fisheries management proposal:

> They [the government] don't understand that when they talk about sustainability that also means the people and the boats - not just the environment. And that

takes money. Other countries in the Common Fisheries Policy have protected and supported their fisheries and they are in much better shape now. And they could have put that in this [pointing to a document outlining the proposal], but there was nothing in there for people. They could have done a lot to support us. But they didn't.

In the case of fishermen, the mainstream ideology of nature subordinates their health and well-being not only to their seafood 'products', but to the whole environment they work in and have made productive (Chapter 1). Government agencies and others frequently claim to know this environment better than fishers, and believe that they must protect it from fishers. Fishers found such assumptions utterly infuriating – particularly in the context of the contradictory pressures they were already subjected to and required to juggle.

### The ideology of accidents

Alasdair questioned why the Marine Accident Investigation Branch (MAIB) was not called the 'incident' investigation branch to 'separate what are accidents from what were avoidable' because in his view 'very few people, crewing, skippering, whatever, die at sea in a genuine accident'. Agencies were aware of the market pressures on fishermen. For example, a review of fishing vessel safety conducted by the MAIB pointed out that 'intensified commercial pressures' led to 'higher exposure to risk' (2008: 36). Yet not a single recommendation in the report went on to address these pressures. Instead the report commented that 'tragic accidents will continue to occur' unless there was a change in the 'deep rooted fatalistic attitude to safety among many fishermen' (MAIB 2008: 40). Another safety review criticised fishers' 'perception of risk ... and negligence' (Roberts and Williams 2007: 18). The report on the sinking of the *Kathryn Jane* spent considerable time documenting that the boat was in a poor state of repair (MAIB 2005). But it carefully avoided an investigation of what led to the poor state of the boat and Findus' decision to keep working as the weather deteriorated. An official ideology of 'accidents' isolated each death and prevented an analysis of the broader causes. Instead, government agencies routinely berated fishers for their lack of a 'safety culture' at the same time as they supported a market and management system that ratcheted up the pressure on fishers. Safety was often reduced to wearing a lifejacket in case of an 'accident'. This ideology also drew on the trope of the backward and prerational fishermen (Nadel-Klein 2003) to maintain a complete separation between fishing safety and the pressures of the market that fishers relied on. For government agencies to wring their hands about the 'safety culture' on fishing boats, while allowing these pressures to increase, or even by instituting policies that intensify them (like the EU market-based management systems), as Alasdair pointed out, is not much different than driving a car with the brakes disconnected. The perverse effects of the market on fishermen is illustrated by the fact that poor weather can become a cause for celebration: by owners and skippers looking for better prices for their catch, and by their exhausted crew hoping that it might finally mean that they will get a day off.

International safety regulations for ships (made at the UN agency the International Maritime Organisation) are likewise framed entirely in the language of 'human error' and the problems of 'the human element', and focus on regulating the behaviour of individual workers. This focus on individual behaviour has its origins in the 'vague but highly functional' concept of the 'accident-prone worker', used to deflect blame from corporate responsibility for dangerous workplace conditions onto the individuals who find themselves working in those conditions (Tombs and Whyte 2007: 74). For this reason, the *British Medical Journal* has said it would no longer use the word 'accident' as 'most injuries and their precipitating events are predictable and preventable'. Defining injuries as 'accidents' significantly reduced the support available to people who experienced them (*British Medical Journal* 2001). The focus on 'human error' as the source of 'accidents' is incorporated into maritime safety administrations. In a study of marine incident investigation reports in three countries, Mohamed Ghanem found that the 'operational level' was described as a cause of the incident in 98.2 per cent of the instances in which causal factors were mentioned, with supervisory, managerial, and beyond organisational causes receiving only cursory mentions (2009).

If the violence experienced by fishers and workers is obscured and normalised as an accepted consequence of activity in a 'dangerous' environment, and individual accidents are seen as exceptions which can be blamed on 'human error' or 'the human element', then 'increased discipline rather than structural change will be the answer' given by those in positions of power (Pine 2008: 165). In the fishing industry, this means lecturing people about wearing lifejackets, with the implication that this simple 'cosmetic' solution was all that was needed to prevent 'accidents'. Already under pressure to constantly juggle contradictory demands, almost always from sources who appeared to care little about their welfare, fishers paid little heed to such suggestions. The ideologies of nature and of accidents kept discussion of economic and other systemic pressures entirely separate from a discussion about dangers at sea, obscuring both the depth of the problems that fishermen faced and a proper discussion of the solutions.

By any measure, the death rate of fishers is at crisis levels, and completely out of proportion to the small size of the industry. Yet the deaths of fishermen were obscured and normalised by an ideology of nature that constructed such deaths as a natural and inevitable consequence of working in a dangerous wilderness like the sea. This was neatly complemented by the presentation of each death as a 'tragic accident' which irresponsible fishermen could have avoided, if only they wore a lifejacket.

## Coping with the 'state of emergency'

I asked Alasdair how people coped and kept fishing despite losing so many at sea, and his response was ambivalent: 'It is not so regular that statistically it frightens you. You can't count them disappearing. Unless you … [long pause] well you can't. It's not that frequent. It would have a massive effect if it were that frequent.' We went on to discuss the wreck of the *Brothers*, which had taken place only two weeks before, and of the *Kathryn Jane*, and of several people lost in harbours, and then Alasdair stopped.

> I honestly don't like keeping score. I consciously don't keep score because I just know the numbers just wouldn't, you know …
>
> It's not … [long pause] I was going to say it's not a touchy subject. It is to an extent a touchy subject. I suspect that, I know myself, if I was to seriously start keeping score, I would think, hey-ho, is this worth it? […]
>
> You don't look too closely at it, I know that is true.

I asked 30-something skipper, Graeme, about his experiences of losing people while fishing. He took a few minutes and counted up his friends who had been lost while working at sea: someone and his son, Findus, the *Brothers*. Over 20 years of work there were about five good friends he had lost to fishing, but there were plenty of others too. He shrugged uncomfortably. 'People don't keep track', he said.

Despite the assertions by skippers that they did not 'keep score', they were clearly upset and unsettled by each incident. At the Old Inn in Gairloch, a cosy wood-panelled pub a few hundred metres from the pier, Alasdair pointed out a few pictures stuck in the frames of the mirrors behind the bar. One was of the *Brothers*, and the other two were of her skipper, Neil, and crew, Davey. A year and a half before they left this pub, went out to sea and were never seen alive again: Davy's body washed up on a nearby beach, and Neil's body was never found. 'This would have been their pub', said Alasdair, 'Last summer they were sitting on these stools'. He paused. 'I want you to see how close it is.' It was not the statistics that unsettled people. It was the shattering impact of each incident, the person lost, and the extent to which that tragedy could have been you. But each incident was carefully isolated from the last, lest anyone 'think, hey-ho, is this worth it?' Skippers caught in the most dangerous situations frequently had no alternative but to keep trying to 'go ahead'. Findus tried: on the day that the *Kathryn Jane* disappeared, he was up at 2 a.m. and worked until at least 9 p.m. before his mobile phone cut out – and in bad weather that had sent other fishermen to port many hours before.[5]

Fishers lived between the logics of seamanship and the market, and knew they could not be separated. They kept fishing by avoiding 'keeping score' of their lost friends and work mates, and instead focused on moments of spectacular success by people who were in the right position at the right time to take advantage of profitable new markets or techniques. Skippers and crew lived in hope and anticipation of these opportunities: one crew explained 'sometimes you can make it big, there is always that potential, and that excitement, wondering. Some people like steady jobs, they just want to be paid. But not me!' 'I guess you get the bug', another young fishermen explained. 'There is all this strategy, things to figure out, how to do it better, always trying to get that big one, trying to get the best catch. And you do; sometime it works out! And that's the best feeling.' This perpetually anticipated potential was also mixed with the reality that such periods, although vividly remembered and continuously re-told, were rare in the context of the continually increasing pressure on fishermen. Thus, this perpetually hoped-for potential was mixed with a grim fatalism, or chronic sense of crisis. The hope that the big catch and a good price might be just around the corner kept fishermen going when times were tough.

Ultimately, fishing relies on hope. Huge amounts of money and effort are invested in the hope that fish will be caught in the future, but there is no guarantee that labour will be productive of fish, or that investment will produce the hoped-for returns. As increasing investments were made and pressure ratcheted up, these hopes could become increasingly fantastical – like Alasdair's description that he was 'going ahead' even in a situation which soon sent him far backwards. The thin line between hope and desperation is captured in a Newfoundland folk saying in communities relying on cod exports: 'We must live in hopes, supposing we die in despair' (Sider 2003: 260). Hope and crisis co-existed in an inextricable 'tense complementarity' (Sodikoff 2004: 371), and the fact that the rare potential of 'making it big' was structured into the share system facilitated fishers' acceptance of the difficulty and danger of their jobs.

'Not keeping score' kept people fishing, although it did not necessarily keep them happy. We sat in a pub near my flat in Glasgow. Alasdair got quite emotional as he told me 'I don't keep track of the number of people I have lost. I guess I have been close to only a few of them.' He banged on the table, tears starting in his eyes. 'But why do we accept this?! Why do I accept it? Why does every other bastard accept it? That is what is written for me in ten-foot high letters in this chapter that you gave me to read.' He paused. 'I believed what I said to you then, what you have quoted me as saying about the "nature of the job". But I believe it even more now. I feel even more strongly about it.'

### Angus: recognising the emergency

Most working fishermen coped with the danger they faced in their work every day by carefully avoiding acknowledging it. Those who did had frequently already sold up and left the industry, like Donald who was 'not interested' in the 'vicious cycle' of 'not taking a day off' that killed his friend and his six crew north of Orkney. Angus had worked on Skye and Lochalsh fishing boats, around the world in 'deep sea' cargo shipping, and now in the North Sea oil and gas industry. Angus was unusual in being both fully aware of the danger he faced each day at work, and in somehow finding a way to keep going back.

When we first met in a west coast pub, Angus had been dismissive of my experience of working on board trawlers and sailing boats:

> And are you a professional? No, I don't think so. No. What you did was fun. I could do what you did but you can't do what I did. And out on a trawler? Anyone can go out on a trawler for a week. Try two years, two-and-a-half years. You were just having fun.
>
> What I do is not fun, it is the opposite of fun. When I come back I am just glad to have survived. What you do and what I do are two completely different things. You haven't tried to feed your family at it, at trawling, never knowing what you will bring home.

Angus did not see working at sea as simply a matter of practising proper seamanship and developing skills and techniques for making grounds productive and
being oriented in them, as I described in Chapters 1 to 4. Even if we worked alongside each other on exactly the same boat performing exactly the same tasks, he felt
an important subjective difference between us. Angus' whole existence depended
on what came up in the net, the prices in different markets, the honesty of the
buyer who took it there, the owner's divisions of expenses and shares, and his own
ability to stay in employment and to avoid being killed by it. It was a precarity
that ran deep, a precarity that made my own work seem 'fun', and his seem 'the
opposite'. It was a precarity that could not be understood simply by examining
the techniques of working at sea, and required a more holistic understanding of
the economic context of both Angus' own life and the industry he worked in.

Angus had a very particular understanding of seamanship. I met up with him
one January afternoon in the bar of the Aberdeen train station as he waited for the
train to take him home after a four-week shift on board an oil platform supply boat
in the North Sea. He described the skills he brought to the job and the respect he
had from the supply boat skippers he worked with. 'What do they respect you for?'
I asked. 'For being brave, for doing things that other people wouldn't. For our seamanship', he replied. 'What is seamanship?' I asked. Angus replied: 'It is defending
yourself. Self-defence, paying attention. Knowing the knot that won't come undone.
Carrying a knife. I always tell the young guys they need to carry a knife, they usually
just laugh and don't believe me, but that has saved me a few times, believe me. And
it has to be sharp, in a sheath so you can pull it out and ...' In the middle of the small
train station bar he dramatically mimed cutting himself free, grimacing with struggle and effort as he made sharp cutting motions around his neck and body. Angus
experienced and practised the skill of seamanship as defending oneself, under constant pressure, in a workplace he could be skilled enough to cope with, but could not
control. It was as if he was under constant attack. Like Graeme, he saw an important
part of his work as being 'brave' – of openly recognising and defying the dangers he
faced. He experienced work as 'a state of siege' (Taussig 1992: 10), requiring skills of
'self-defence' in order to survive. In this state of siege, 'order is frozen, yet disorder
boils beneath the surface. Like a giant spring slowly compressed and ready to burst
at any moment, immense tension lies in strange repose' (Taussig 1992: 10).

I got to know Angus quite well over about four years. He always seemed
delighted to see me, with a twinkle in his eye and a story to share. He was expansive, open and generous, and loved his family, especially his mother and daughters,
fiercely and proudly. He had a keen sense of justice: 'I am not a violent man, but
if I see someone treating someone wrong I just won't let it pass.' Angus was also
proud of his work at sea, his skills, his ability to make a decent livelihood, and the
richness of his life experience. Through his work, he saw himself as a strong and
capable man, worthy of the respect of others. 'At least if you are working at sea you
get some respect for the skills you have', he told me one day. 'Even if the captain is
an asshole, he has to respect you, and he needs you.' Work at sea also gave Angus
the opportunity to travel, to make new links and through it he gained a cosmopolitan openness and generosity (Howard 2012a).

When Angus was on leave from the ship he spent most of his time in the pub, 'I want to see people and speak to them. I'm not just going to sit around the house by myself!' he explained. One young man told me about how he consciously avoided Angus because 'he's just always on edge'. Every four weeks, as he prepared to return to work, he would become even more agitated, days spent in anticipation of the phone call that would tell him the exact day and time he was to join the ship. He would call all his friends and family, and latterly, myself, to say goodbye because 'you never know if you are coming back'.

Twice I took the six-hour train journey with Angus from the west coast to Aberdeen where he was joining his ship. As the train left Inverness and approached the rolling farmland near Elgin, Angus got increasingly tense. It was 11 a.m. and he was on his third tin of Tennants lager, gripped tightly, aluminium crumpling in his hands. 'I hope you don't mind, but I am not allowed to drink anything for the next four or five weeks', he apologised. 'This is the part I hate!' he said, 'On my way to join a ship. I feel it in my stomach. I start to feel ill. I'm over 50! I'm a grandfather, and the work I do is insane, it is lunatic!' 'You'll be all right', I said, weakly, knowing that I couldn't assure him of any such thing. 'Thirty-eight years now I have been doing this, and I've been all right', he replied, 'Lucky. I'm supposed to do all kinds of brave things'. The train's refreshment cart trundled by and he bought another mini-bottle of whisky, and reflected: 'Ah well, I guess no one makes me do it, no one is forcing me to go.' He would alternate between looking at me intently and scowling out the window, and then started again: 'I don't like this countryside, it's so boring. Flat and farmed to death. I hate this part of the country because it means I am about to join a ship. It's all right when you are going the other way.' For Angus, going back to the ship meant danger, fear and a radical loss of control over his own life.

The subjective consequences of Angus' state of siege were immense. More than once, Angus began to cry as we sat together in the pub. I would return home, shaken, unsure how to reconcile my responsibilities as friend, ethnographer and sympathetic listener. 'I've seen men hurt, killed right in front of me', he told me, 'Men with no legs or missing an arm'. The stories would be told with gaps and silences, in which I would go and get him a glass of water because it was all I could think of doing. He seemed to have a compelling need to share these stories, to sit, to talk, and it seemed to be important to him that I was willing and interested in listening.

In the summer of 2009 Angus told me about a helicopter crash that had taken place a few months earlier in the North Sea. The men and women working on the offshore oil platforms arrived for their shifts and left again in these helicopters, but in April one had crashed into the sea. All 16 persons on board were killed. The supply boat that Angus worked on had been near the site of the wreck and had assisted in the recovery effort. Angus explained:

> When people think about a helicopter crash in the North Sea, about picking up the bodies, it is not like you are picking up someone who just looks like they are asleep. They are in pieces. You are picking up a leg here, a head there, and then trying to put them back together, for the family. It's awful, but you have to do it for the family, they want their man back, not someone else's arm or leg.

> A lot of the young guys were traumatised, they were sick, literally sick, they couldn't speak. A lot of them got sent home. We didn't, we just had to keep going. They think you get used to these things, but you don't.

'Why didn't they just send the boat back to Aberdeen and give you all a week off?' I asked, stunned. Angus replied: 'We had a job to do. There was cargo waiting to go to other platforms: we just kept on. A lot of the young guys got sent home, but we stayed on.'

Such catastrophes seemed a regular feature of work in the North Sea. The explosion of the Piper Alpha platform in 1988 killed 167 people and was regularly remembered and discussed in hushed tones. One fisherman who worked offshore at the time of the explosion spent an evening describing to me how men had jumped 61 meters off the burning platform into the North Sea, and how he often contemplated what it would be like to do that himself. As I walked home across the Skye Bridge that night he sent me a text: 'It's still just 45 metres from the primary if you can stand the height.' Another man still working in the North Sea told me that now the pressures are now far greater and the volumes of gas much larger than at the time of Piper Alpha. 'It's like a timebomb', he explained. 'If something ever happens it will be deadly serious.'

Angus lived in a world where what should be abnormal became normal as even off work, in the pub, with friends, or on the train he relived these experiences, not yet 'used to these things' after 38 years working at sea, in 'a state of siege', always on edge, 'ready to burst at any moment', jittery in the pub, waiting for the phone call to go back, draining his glass while the young men kept their distance. Alasdair and Graeme coped with similar experiences by refusing to make lists or keep track, aware at the same time that every year 'somebody I know or know of [is] killed at the job'.

Structural violence experienced through work, over the course of a person's life, can build to an increasingly traumatic 'state of emergency' that people must 'get used to' in order to maintain their livelihood. The effects of the global annual 2.34 million work-related deaths are multiplied through their workmates, families, friends and sometimes even further (McFarlane and Bryant 2007). Anthropologist and psychotherapist Rebecca Lester describes how traumatic incidents can bring people 'face to face with the limits of our own existence' and 'sheer ... us off from our expected connections with others, from our perceived social supports, from our basic sense of safety, however locally construed'. Lester therefore describes trauma as a 'relational injury' (2013: 754) – an injury that Angus saw 'them' regularly inflicting on workers just like himself. Angus had his own analysis about why 'they' did this. He described the most dangerous part of his job as dragging oil platforms from place to place, sometimes in a hurricane. Why in a hurricane? I asked, puzzled. 'Money', he replied, 'If they want the rig shifted then you had better shift it. Human life – it means nothing. Money, money, money, that's what it is in the oil, and it means that you have to do things in hurricanes and horrendous conditions.'

It was not only the people who were killed or injured in the Piper Alpha explosion or in the helicopter crash who were deeply affected by it. Other workers watched shocking and traumatic events kill people just like them, and they were expected to return and keep carrying out the same tasks. Such experiences are part of class experiences in contemporary production systems: of workers knowing that they do not have control of their own bodies and bodily safety, of knowing that it easily could have been you, and that your managers expected you to 'get used to these things'. But ultimately, as a human being, 'you don't'.

Lester suggests that recovery from trauma involves 'the rebuilding of social connection' in a process of 'retethering' and 'remaking one's world'. Where existing connections are exploitative, a 'revisioning' of the world that 'allows for a different ending' may be needed (Lester 2013: 758–760). Such a process 'may give rise to new ways of being-in-the-world' and possibly to 'collective agency and political engagement' that may be required to challenge the situation (Hinton and Kirmayer 2013: 617). At the same time as Angus seemed shattered by his experiences, he also had a political framework through which to understand and potentially challenge them, and a degree of potential industrial organisation through the union he was a member of. For Alasdair and others in the fishing industry, the regularity of traumatic events combined with the fragmented structure of the industry to isolated fishermen from each other, and from discussion and analysis of the problems they faced. Unfortunately, I saw little evidence of collective structures developing within the fishing industry that might have the capacity to support fishers and to challenge and change the structures of the industry they worked in.

Anthropologist Gerald Sider describes how after centuries of subjection to the international cod market, Newfoundland fishermen lived 'lives defined by ruptures', which left husbands and wives in Newfoundland unable to speak to each other about their deteriorating position and growing potential for catastrophe, and the fear and isolation that both lived in as a result. The 'coherence – the solidity and speakability of social life' had become impossible (Sider 2003: 322–323). Scottish fishers' ability to keep fishing likewise relied on not 'keeping score'. Although many people told me about their fears and traumatic experiences, I always felt these were unusual discussions that were provoked my presence. These ruptures were present in the challenges put to me by Donald and John (Introduction) about my inability to understand the tragic results of the pressures they found themselves caught in, the suicides of bank managers and deaths of friends that were both extraordinary and ordinary. The experience of these ruptures and the attempts to speak about them were also present in Angus' heartbreaking explanation that 'They think you get used to it but you don't', and in Alasdair, banging the table, eyes burning, demanding to know 'Why do we accept this?! Why do I accept it? Why does every other bastard accept it?'

## The nature of the job (revisited)

The ecological relations I have explored in this chapter extend well beyond the boat, the sea and the net to markets throughout the world, each extending into and reproducing each other. Neil Smith argues that the environment around us, even what appears as 'nature', is now produced by capitalist relations of production (2008). The alienation of people's labour and 'own purpose' in it is also an alienation of their relationship to their environment (Burkett 2009). We cannot properly understand environmental relations or crisis without including the capitalist relations that currently produce this environment. The exploitation of the sea's resources and of the people at the sharp end of extracting them are two sides of the same dynamic: the 'inhuman power' of a market whose competitive dynamics mean that people often need to catch more and more fish just to stay even, and where the consequences of not being able to keep up can be deadly. Fishermen's subjectivities were caught by and conditioned by the two contradictory logics of the market and of seamanship, and for those who kept fishing 'you don't look too closely at it, I know that is true'. The potentially deadly and frequently traumatic nature of the job was obscured by the ideology of nature and the ideology of accidents which blamed fishermen, seafarers and the sea for these deaths, letting the broader systems that shaped their interactions off the hook. The risk to fishers and seafarers was rarely acknowledged and they were left to cope in their own isolated ways.

The wrecks of fishing boats and helicopters at sea have the potential to expose the violence of whole systems and ecologies, and to reveal a more complete understanding of 'the nature of the job'. Anthropologist Yael Navaro-Yashin says that ruins, like the wreck of the *Kathryn Jane*, are 'abject objects', which may be ignored for ideological purposes that are revealing of the whole system. 'We will act as if the abject is only "there" (or about "that"), and not elsewhere, everywhere, and about everything' (Navaro-Yashin 2012: 151). Angus' helicopter crash revealed the constant violence he and other workers were expected to endure with indifference. The wrecks and deaths described here were about 'everything': about whole systems and their violence, a violence many would prefer not to acknowledge. State authorities and maritime agencies tried to re-present each wreck as the isolated result of irrationally poor judgement by individual backward and irresponsible fishermen or 'accident-prone' seafarers. Fishermen also protected themselves by focussing on the tragic details of each wreck, while avoiding 'keeping score' in case it lead to thinking 'hey ho, is this worth it?' As Navaro-Yashin explains: 'Some spaces have to be left filthy or wounded so the whole system does not appear to be so' (2012: 160).

The Scottish fishing wrecks are of boats that were squeezed between and could not keep up with impossible pressures. Amid ecological and relational approaches to the environment (e.g. Ingold 2000), wrecks and violence invite a consideration of 'dis-resonance or non-harmony' in these relations (Navaro-Yashin 2012: 21). They illustrate the contradictory and ultimately violent logics maintained within capitalist ecologies, and burst through the ideologies that obscure this violence. What these wrecks reveal is not a failure of the system, but the violence built into its normal and inexorable demands. The structural violence present in contemporary ecological systems, and in the capitalist relations that currently produce them, is made visible in these wrecks.

## Notes

1 Although fishermen's organisations in Scotland claimed to represent all fishermen, the membership dues for most organisations were based on the boat's revenue, meaning that they actually represented fishing boat owners. Leading members tended to own substantial numbers of fishing boats.

2 The fatality rates are: migrant fishermen: 350 deaths per 100,000 workers averaged between 2008 and 2009 (calculations in Chapter 5, note 12 of this book), all fishermen: 102 deaths per 100,000 workers, cargo shipping: 11 deaths per 100,000 workers, and the general workforce 0.9 deaths per 100,000 (Roberts and Williams 2007: 5, 16). Rates are averaged between 1996 and 2005 except where noted.

3 Jan MacLeod died on 23 January 2003 when his fish farm boat capsized east of Skye near Raasay (see Introduction). Lance Wiltshire-Butler and Allan 'Findus' Naylor died when the *Kathryn Jane* sank west of Skye on approximately 28 July 2004. David Davidson and Neil Sutherland died when the *Brothers* sank just north of Skye on 1 June 2006. Young skipper David Docherty was found dead in his bunk in 2009. A seventh man, skipper Charlie McLeod, was killed in a car crash on his way to his boat in 2007.

4 This well-known saying was explained as follows: after a person drowns their body sinks in three hours. When the body 'relaxes' it comes to the surface after three days. After three weeks it will become waterlogged and sinks again until the stomach contents 'gas'. The process is said to take longer in winter.

5 At 3.30 p.m. to 4 p.m., the *Friendly Isle* and the *Bellatrix*, both fishing near the *Kathryn Jane*, headed to port due to the poor weather (MAIB 2005: 7–8).

# Conclusion
## Labour, class, environments and anthropology

In this book I have taken up a labour-centred Marxist approach to human–environment relations, place and language, human–machine relations, technique and technology, political economy and violence. Despite Donham's observation that 'production is the privileged point of entry' for understanding societies (1999: 58) such an analysis goes against the grain of much anthropological analysis of the past 30 years. Harris observes that:

> The shift in anthropological attention away from work and production to what is produced and how it circulates, to objects – 'things' in Appadurai's (1986) formulation – and to exchange, was consonant with broader shifts in the global political economy away from the productivism of the socialist bloc to the dominance of neoliberalism, and away from labour to post-Fordism and consumption. (Harris 2007: 156)

As banks and economies have collapsed leaving ongoing crises, unemployment and real suffering in their wake, neo-liberal capitalism's claims to offer solutions to historic problems of inequality and exploitation look increasingly hollow. Perhaps, then, it is time for anthropologists to return the focus of our analysis back to work and production, and away from what Jackson describes as the 'enchantment of things' (2007: 77). Marx made a strikingly similar criticism of the materialism of a different era when he argued that 'the chief defect of all previous materialism ... is that things, reality, sensuousness are conceived only in the form of the object, or of contemplation, but not as human sensuous activity, practise, not subjectively' (1998 [1845]: 572). Throughout this book I have taken up this emphasis on the role of sensuous activity and practice in constituting environments and people's subjectivities.

Lukács described the 'enchantment of things' as reification: when things are experienced and understood simply as commodities that can be obtained by exchange, and the human labour and social relations which objects embody are forgotten or obscured. 'Contemplation' or observation of things in their 'immediacy' is illusory, because all we see are these objects, rather than the dynamic processes which brought them into being, and which will continue to transform them. Lukács emphasised that *things should be shown to be aspects of processes* and that the world should be understood as 'the unbroken production and reproduction of those relations, which when torn from their context and distorted by abstract mental categories can appear to bourgeois thinkers as things' (1972 [1922]: 179). Human societies have continuously developed new tools, new techniques and new forms of social and economic organisation, with the past 200 years in particular being a time of extraordinary changes. An understanding of the processes of production and reproduction can provide considerable insight into social organisation, technologies, and environments.

In addition to the reification promoted by commodity exchange, widespread but static understandings of 'labour' and 'class' have tied them to particular forms of work (especially factory work). As the dominant forms of work in Europe and North America have changed, some have dismissed the usefulness of a labour or class analysis altogether (Kasmir and Carbonella 2008: 5; Smith 1999: 172). This is despite the fact that identifying labour and class with only factory work is 'in stark contrast to [the views] of Marx, who believed that "labour" was synonymous with social life', and took on different forms in different societies and historical periods (Smith 1999: 172). These obstacles to a serious labour or class analysis are no doubt also symptomatic of the broader shifts Harris identified in academia away from Marxist analysis to post-modernism and post-structuralism, and a generally triumphant period of neo-liberal capitalist expansion. Nonetheless, the number of people in the world 'who supply labor for the production of goods and services' has in fact increased by more than seventy per cent from 1980 to 2014, numbering 3.4 billion people, not including informal workers (World Bank 2016). Things are shifting: the economic crisis may facilitate a revival of 'economic anthropology with a critical agenda' (Hann and Hart 2011: 164).

In this conclusion, I would like to re-examine the wider implications of the labour-centred approach I have taken for the study of the sea and for anthropology more generally. The 'ritualised forgetting' of labour that Jackson referred to (2007: 76) is doubly the case at sea. First, there is the impact of the generalised 'ideology of nature' produced through the divisions of labour and class in capitalism (Smith 2008; Chapter 6). 'Nature' is seen as both a powerful force external to human society and as a universal governing human society – but in both cases evacuated of human labour and interaction. Activities at sea are undertaken by a tiny group of specialised workers, far from places where they can be seen by others. The products of their labour are bought as commodities in contexts far removed from their original sources. For the majority, there is little evidence that the sea is a place of work: old city harbours are transformed into leisure areas, old fishing boats and ships are scrapped or sunk out of sight. Work at sea is generally seen as old-fashioned: the role of shipping in moving over 90 per cent of global trade (Rodrigue 2006) and of fishing as a global market worth $163 billion US is not widely known (Food and Agriculture Organisation 2011). The enormous bulk cargo and container terminals that form the basis of global trade are hidden from public view in outlying areas behind fences and in security zones and industrial parks. Fish simply appear in supermarkets.

Ethnographies of labour at sea must examine the experience of that labour and attend to the importance of its material results, rather than contemplate the commodities that are produced, or resort to trite metaphors about watery 'flow' and 'immersion' (Helmreich 2011; Introduction). If we allow the sea to be understood only through the commodities produced from it, or through contemplation of it as a wilderness or as sheer 'materiality', then we allow the sea to appear as empty of human labour, as colonisers represented Aboriginal country. Anthropological accounts of labour at sea can contribute to undermining these appearances and highlighting the significance of people's labour and lives at sea and the enormous metabolisms they are a part of.

Recognising the role of labour in producing the seascape can help us to understand how fishermen understand their own labour, and why they regularly come into conflict with management bodies. Fishermen see their own labour as productive, yet they felt 'under siege' due to the majority view that the sea was a wilderness that fishermen's labour was destroying. Humans have undoubtedly damaged marine and planetary ecologies (Angus 2016). But addressing these challenges requires a proper understanding of what has caused these changes. Explaining the decline of fish stocks as caused by the greed of individual fishers, or even through the 'tragedy of the commons', is not good enough – the whole economic and political system of capitalism is responsible (Angus 2016, Campling *et al.* 2012).

Human society has developed in a metabolism with marine (and terrestrial) ecosystems and altered them as we developed affordances in this metabolism to make this planet our home. Through metabolisms of labour, humans have actually produced nature as it currently exists (including our own bodies): humans 'change their own nature as they progressively deprive external nature of its strangeness and externality, they mediate nature through themselves, and ... they make nature itself work for their own purposes' (Schmidt quoted in Smith 2008: 35). As ecological psychologist Reed argues:

> The human environment is neither a made environment nor a found environment. It is a selected and transformed environment. The human environment is not the environment of one individual, nor is it identical for each and every one of us. The collectivizing of efforts by humans has been so deep and widespread that our environment itself is a populated one, heavily influenced by the peculiarities of the people we live among. (1996: 125)

The selections and transformations of environments produced by humans are regulated by human labour and organised through broader economic and political processes. But how are the selections, transformations, alterations and productions of our environment chosen? What is acceptable? To what ends? How can we ensure that the human production of the sea and other ecologies contributes to the maintenance of life (both human and marine)? Humans have created an 'inhuman power', in the form of capitalism, with profound effects on both ourselves and our planet (Chapter 6). Scientists have already determined that the stable planetary conditions that supported human life on this planet for the past twelve thousand years have come to an end due to human activities organised through capitalism (Angus 2016). While political theorists argue that it is possible to re-organise human society and economics on a sustainable basis, this requires profound, and revolutionary, changes to human work and production systems (Angus 2016, Burkett 2006).

In this book, I have argued that a labour and class analysis informed by a political economy of capitalism can make an important contribution to understanding the sea, human–environment relations, human–machine relations, and human societies more generally. Several implications follow for anthropological and other research:

1. We must give careful consideration to what extent the destruction of marine ecologies is connected to the exploitation of people working at sea. Marx described how for the agricultural worker the soil is 'the objective body of his subjectivity' (1964 [1858]: 92) and that capitalism simultaneously alienates people from both their own labour and their relations to their environment, creating rifts and degrading metabolisms (Burkett 2009). What is the relationship between increasing exploitation, marginalisation and market pressures in the lives of workers, and the state of the sea itself? The importance of political economy and the interlocking role of markets, labour relations, and states to a proper understanding of fisheries has been demonstrated (Campling *et al.* 2012), but much more work is needed in this area, particularly detailed ethnography that examines how systemic rifts articulate with individual alienations.

2. More broadly, studies of human–environment relations should consider the effects of political economy in structuring human–environment relations. A new focus on 'materiality' may obscure such relations, and even human experience, by focusing tightly on the environment itself.

3. There is a need for ethnographically informed understandings of people's relationship to their own labour and its productions. The relationships between humans, their labour and their environments is a practical and historical question, 'not an abstract philosophical puzzle' (Smith 2008: 51). This should contribute to 'new anthropology of labour' and a 'decolonised anthropology [that] dispenses with the disciplinary emphasis on the "outside" of capitalism and encompasses the dynamism and interconnections of global society' (Kasmir and Carbonella 2008: 21, 24). Such analysis of labour needs to incorporate the structuring effect of class and political economy, the material results of this labour, how environments are produced, and the subjectivities of persons in relation to their own labour and purpose.

4. Analysis of ecological systems tends to emphasise their holism and unity. Yet when environments are organised through capitalist relations of production, they can also be violent. Anthropologists should examine this possibility and be aware that this violence may be obscured or misrecognised by its victims and those in power, or by structural aspects of systems.

5. An understanding of labour and the environment at sea must consider the forces and pressures on that labour. The nature of work at sea means that notwithstanding the development of electronic navigation and communication

systems, a crew isolated on a boat is radically, immediately, responsible for all aspects of each other's lives. However, on commercial vessels, work is organised for the purpose of generating a profit in a global market. Living and working on a boat in such a situation means that capitalist market and waged labour relations significantly affect not only people's working time, but all aspects of their lives: when they wake, when they sleep, what they eat, and when they see their friends and family. Unlike on shore, there is no division between work and leisure time: you are living in your workplace 24 hours a day. Therefore understandings of work at sea need to carefully consider to what extent the distinctive aspects of seagoing work are due to the pressures of capitalism itself, rather than the environment of the sea as is more commonly imagined.

6. Political economy must be integrated into considerations of how skills and techniques are developed, adopted and practised, and who controls them. This is important for understanding, first, existing practices, second, the systematic obstacles to developing and practising skills that people face in capitalist relations of production.

7. A class analysis can play an important role in examining the contradictions and dynamism in skill and many other topics of anthropological research. I have discussed the intimate relations that could develop out of people's skilled interactions with machines in the process of feeling, sounding and maintenance, as long as they remained in control of them. But I also discussed the situation of structural violence that arose for people who were not able to exert this control. A class analysis of similar contradictions in many other areas of human practice can assist with understanding the complexities of 'Western' societies and avoid projection of the contradictions that can arise within capitalism onto the relations between the 'West' and others. This is particularly important given the geographic spread of capitalist relations.

Capitalism has vastly expanded the forces of production and the ability of human society to intervene in, transform, produce, exploit and even destroy the environment we live in and rely on. Yet capitalism also involves a division 'between the capacities of the whole person, inseparably mind and body, and the agency that puts those capacities to work' (Ingold 2000: 300). Thus it is important to identify who, or what forces, actually control metabolisms of production and their relation to the people who must actually carry out this work. The pressures of particular capitalist markets must be understood, including competing pressures and dynamics. The practical work of 'capitalism' is carried out by individual persons who are organised by it, who survive through its wages and are also exploited through this process – a situation that was so contradictory that Marx and Engels identified these people as the potential 'grave-diggers' of the system (1998 [1848]: 50).

Through their work, people living on the west coast of Scotland today have direct and inside experience of huge corporations like BP, Shell and Qinetiq and the many contractors that work for them. They have seen and carried out the work of global trade, and seen its dark underside too,[1] and they have worked alongside, lived with and shared food with people from every continent. They know, first-hand, the extraordinary investment of labour and machines it takes to pump oil out from deep under the seafloor; they have helped build the massive oil platforms, they keep them running, they keep them supplied. They can talk, knowledgeably and with personal experience, of the 'cock-ups' [amusing and embarrassing errors] of the UK Ministry of Defence. They have seen how nature can be made abundantly productive and then transformed, suddenly, with the rise and fall and new rise and new fall of entire fishing industries. They track seafood prices in markets all over Europe, and speak knowledgeably of the seafood eating habits of the various countries they keep supplied. They live everyday with the debris from world wars that their fathers and grandfathers fought in, monumentalised on street corners, and still lying on the seafloor. It is their whole environment that they are a part of cajoling, producing and working.

People from the Inner Sound and millions of other working people around the world have experienced being a part of a metabolism of labour on a massive scale. They have played crucial roles in it, and they know how it works. They make it work. At the same time, they are subjected to it, they must choose the roles that are available within it, and play by the rules if they are too keep food on the table and keep up with payments on the house, the boat and the car. They live continuously with the 'painful negotiation' between what they know, what they can do, what they want to do, and what they have to do. They oscillate between pride and frustration, skilled attention and anger, camaraderie and isolation, resignation and determination, passion and alienation. Such contradictory experiences of work are part of the everyday experience of workers in capitalism.

Earlier in this book I argued that the relational use of the term 'work' by fishermen could not be interpreted as a remnant of some kind of idyllic, pre-capitalist unalienated relationship to work. Now I would like to make a stronger claim: that the very real experience of alienation in work under capitalism exists in 'tense complementarity' (Sodikoff 2004: 371) with the experience of a relationality that ties together persons and organisations, and produces commodities – and nature – on an extraordinary scale. The future of the planet depends on understanding these relations – and acting on them. Anthropologists should play a role.

## Note

1 One man worked as deck crew on a cargo ship he later found out was secretly carrying weapons from Los Angeles to Indonesia for use in the occupation of East Timor. The cargo was officially listed as 'chandeliers' and 'washing machines'.

# References

Amith, J. (2005) 'Place making and place breaking: Migration and the development cycle of a community in colonial Mexico', *American Ethnologist* 32(1): 159–179.

Anderson, J., H. Curtis, R. Boyle and K. Graham (2007) *2005 Economic Survey of the UK Fishing Fleet Short Report*, Edinburgh: Seafish.

Angus, I. (2016) *Facing the Anthropocene: Fossil Capitalism and the Crisis of the Earth System,* New York: Monthly Review.

Aporta, C. and E. Higgs (2005) 'Satellite culture: Global Positioning Systems, Inuit wayfinding, and the need for a new account of technology', *Current Anthropology* 46: 729–753.

Árnason, A., A. Nightingale, R. Macintyre and J. Lee (2005) ' "So the wind won't blow it all away": Field(s) and ethnography in the glocal ecumene', Unpublished.

Barber, P., B. Leach and W. Lem (2012) *Confronting Capital: Critique and Engagement in Anthropology*, New York: Routledge.

Beare, G. (1987) 'Heath Robinson: The illustrator', in *The Inventive Comic Genius of Our Age: W. Heath Robinson (1872–1944) Exhibition Catalogue*, pp. 9–43. London: Chris Beetles.

Bender, B. (1993) *Landscape: Politics and Perspectives*, Oxford: Berg.

Benjamin, W. (1999 [1968]) 'Theses on the philosophy of history', in Hannah Arendt (ed.), *Illuminations*, pp. 245–255. London: Pimlico.

Bernstein, H. (2010) *Class Dynamics of Agrarian Change*, Halifax: Fernwood.

Blaeu, W. (1964 [1612]) *The Light of Navigation*, Cleveland: World Publishing Company.

Blanchard, W. (2010) 'Decca's corporate highlights'. Available at http://jproc.ca/hyperbolic/decca_corporate_highlights.html, accessed 16 January 2011.

Bourgois, P. (2009) 'Recognizing invisible violence: A thirty-year ethnographic retrospective', in B. Rylko-Bauer, L. Whiteford and P. Farmer (eds), *Global Health in Times of Violence*, Santa Fe: School of Advanced Research Press.

Bray, F. (2007) 'Gender and technology', *Annual Review of Anthropology* 36: 37–53.

*British Medical Journal* (2001) 'BMJ bans "accidents" ', *British Medical Journal* 322: 1320–1321.

Brooks, C. (2009) 'Salmond fears over Filipino ban', *Press and Journal*, Aberdeen, 12 June 2009.

Brown, A. (2009) *UK Fleet Financial Performance 2009 Mid-Year Review*, Edinburgh: Seafish.

Burkett, P. (2006) *Marxism and Ecological Economics: Towards a Red and Green Political Economy*, Chicago: Haymarket.

Bynorth, J. (2008) 'Slaves of the loan sharks', *The Sunday Herald*, Glasgow, 9 August 2008.

Callinicos, A. (2004 [1987]) *Making History: Agency, Structure and Change in Social Theory*, Leiden: Brill.

Campling, L., E. Havice and P. M. Howard (2012) 'Political economy and ecology of capture fisheries: Market dynamics, resource access and relations of exploitation and resistance', *Journal of Agrarian Change* 12(2–3): 177–203.

Carrier, J. and D. Kalb (2015) *Anthropologies of Class: Power, Practice and Inequality*, Cambridge: Cambridge University Press.

Clarke, W. (n.d.) Highlands and Islands Immigration Society (HIES). Available at www.angelfire.com/ns/bkeddy/HIES/3.html, accessed 7 November 2015.

Clausen, R. and B. Clark (2005) 'The metabolic rift and marine ecology', *Organization & Environment* 18: 422–444.

Clausen, R. and B. Clark (2008) 'The oceanic crisis: Capitalism and the degradation of marine ecosystems', *Monthly Review* 60: 91–111.

Cohen, A. P. (1987) *Whalsay: Symbol, Segment and Boundary in a Shetland Island Community*, Manchester: Manchester University Press.

Coull, J. (1996) *The Sea Fisheries of Scotland: A Historical Geography*, Edinburgh: John Donald.

Cregeen, E. (1970) 'The changing role of the House of Argyll in the Scottish Highlands', in N. Phillipson and R. Mitchison (eds), *Scotland in the Age of Improvement: Essays in Scottish History in the Eighteenth Century*, pp. 5–23. Edinburgh: Edinburgh University Press.

Crehan, K. (2002) *Gramsci, Culture and Anthropology*, London: Pluto Press.

Crighton, R. (2008a) 'Memorial service to four fishermen: Hundreds pack church to remember foreign workers who died in two fishing boat accidents', *The Press and Journal*, Aberdeen, 15 September 2008.

Crighton, R. (2008b) 'UK accused of complicity in issuing temporary visas: New storm rages over Filipino fishermen', *The Press and Journal*, Aberdeen, 10 December 2008.

Curtis, H., C. Brodie and E. Longoni (2010) *2008 Economic Survey of the UK Fishing Fleet*, Edinburgh: Seafish.

Curtis, H., S. Metz and C. Brodie (2009) *2007 Economic Survey of the UK Fishing Fleet*, Edinburgh: Seafish.

De Ste Croix, G. E. M. (1981) *The Class Struggle in the Ancient Greek World from the Archaic Age to the Arab Conquests*, London: Duckworth.

Desjarlais, R. (1997) *Shelter Blues: Sanity and Selfhood Among the Homeless*, Philadelphia: University of Pennsylvania Press.

Dobres, M.-A. (1999) 'Technology's links and chaînes: The processual unfolding of technique and technician', in M.-A. Dobres and C. Hoffman (eds), *The Social Dynamics of Technology: Practice, Politics and World Views*, pp. 124–146. Washington, DC: Smithsonian Institution Press.

Donham, D. (1999) *History, Power, Ideology: Central Issues in Marxism and Anthropology*, Berkeley: University of California Press.

Draper, L. and P. Draper (2005) *The Raasay Iron Mine: Where Enemies Became Friends*, Dingwall: Lawrence and Pamela Draper.

Feld, S. and K. Basso (1996) *Senses of Place*, Santa Fe: School of American Research Press.

Feld, S. and D. Brenneis (2004) 'Doing anthropology in sound', *American Ethnologist* 34: 461–474.

*Fishing News* (2009a) 'Fishermen dies after going overboard', *Fishing News*, London, 27 November 2009, p. 7.

*Fishing News* (2009b) 'Stop prawn days-at-sea transfers', *Fishing News*, London, 4 December 2009, p. 3.

*Fishing News* (2009c) 'More skippers back non-transfer of days', *Fishing News*, London, 11 December 2009, p. 2.

Food and Agriculture Organisation of the United Nations (2011) 'Appendix II – World fishery production: Estimated value by groups of species', Rome: Food and Agriculture Organisation of the United Nations.

Foster, J. B. (2000) *Marx's Ecology: Materialism and Nature*, New York: Monthly Review Press.

Frake, C. O. (1985) 'Maps of time and tide among medieval seafarers', *Man, New Series* 20: 254–270.

Gell, A. (1985) 'How to read a map: Remarks on the practical logic of navigation', *Man, New Series* 20: 271–286.

Ghanem, M. (2009) 'Investigating and reporting accidents at sea', *Seafarers International Research Centre Symposium Proceedings (2009)*, pp. 25–46.

Gibson, J. J. (1979) *The Ecological Approach to Visual Perception*, London: Houghton Mifflin.

Gladwin, T. (1970) *East is a Big Bird: Navigation and Logic on Puluwat Atoll*, Cambridge, MA: Harvard University Press.

Glen, D. (2008) 'What do we know about the global labour market for seafarers? A view from the UK', *Marine Policy* 32: 845–855.

Goodwin, C. (1995) 'Seeing in depth', *Social Studies of Science* 25: 237–274.

Gordillo, G. (2004) *Landscapes of Devils: Tensions of Place and Memory in the Argentine Chaco*, Durham, NC: Duke University Press.

Gramsci, A. (1971) *Selections From the Prison Notebooks*, edited by Q. Hoare and G. Smith, London: Lawrence & Wishart.

Grigor, I. F. (2000) *Highland Resistance: The Radical Tradition in the Scottish North*, Edinburgh: Mainstream.

Hann, C. and K. Hart (2011) *Economic Anthropology: History, Ethnography, Critique*, Cambridge: Polity.

Hardy, K. and C. Wickham-Jones (2002) 'Scotland's first settlers: The Mesolithic seascape of the Inner Sound, Skye and its contribution to the early prehistory of Scotland', *Antiquity* 76: 825–833.

Harris, O. (2007) 'What makes people work?', in R. Astuti, J. Parry and C. Stafford (eds), *Questions of Anthropology*, pp. 137–165. Oxford: Berg.

Harvey, D. (2006) *Spaces of Global Capitalism: Towards a Theory of Uneven Geographical Development*, London: Verso.

Hastrup, K. (1987) 'Fieldwork among friends: Ethnographic exchange with northern civilzation', A. Jackson (ed.), *Anthropology at Home*, pp. 94–108. London: Tavistock.

Helmreich, S. (2007) 'An anthropologist underwater: Immersive soundscapes, submarine cyborgs, and transductive ethnography', *American Ethnologist* 34: 621–641.

Helmreich, S. (2011) 'Nature/culture/seawater', *American Anthropologist* 113(1): 132–144.

Highland Shellfish Management Organisation (2004) *Highland Shellfish Management Organisation Management Plan*. Formerly available at www.hsmo.org.uk, accessed 15 March 2005.

Hinton, D. and L. Kirmayer (2013) 'Local responses to trauma: Symptom, affect and healing', *Transcultural Psychiatry* 50: 607–621.

Hoeppe, G. (2007) *Conversations on the Beach: Fishermen's Knowledge, Metaphor and Environmental Change in South India*, Oxford: Berghahn.

Holborow, M. (2006) 'Putting the social back into language: Marx, Vygotsky, Volosinov and Vygotsky reexamined', *Studies in Language and Capitalism* 1: 1–28.

Howard, P. M. (1998) 'Projecting place: The cartography of colonisation, and the navigation of resistance', *Hinge: A Journal of Contemporary Studies* 4: 15–35.

Howard, P. M. (2012a) 'Workplace cosmopolitanisation and "the power and pain of class relations" at sea', *Focaal* 63: 55–69.

Howard, P. M. (2012b) 'Sharing or appropriation? Share systems, class and commodity relations in Scottish fisheries', *Journal of Agrarian Change* 12(2–3): 316–343.

Howard, P. M. (2016) 'What wrecks reveal: Structural violence in ecological systems', in J. Marshall and L. Connor (eds), *Environmental Change and the World's Futures: Ecologies, Ontologies, Mythologies*, pp. 196–213. London: Routledge.

Hull, J. (2005) 'Rainfall and the blind body', in C. Classen (ed.), *The Book of Touch*, pp. 324–327. Oxford: Berg.

Hutchins, E. (1995) *Cognition in the Wild*, Cambridge, MA: Massachusetts Institute for Technology.

ICES (2015a) '5.3.24 Norway lobster (Nephros norvegicus) in Division VIa – FU 11 (West of Scotland, North Minch)', in *ICES Advice on Fishing Opportunities, Catch, and Effort: Celtic Seas Ecoregion*.

ICES (2015b) '5.3.25 Norway lobster (Nephros norvegicus) in Division VIa – FU 12 (West of Scotland, South Minch)', in *ICES Advice on Fishing Opportunities, Catch, and Effort: Celtic Seas Ecoregion*.

ILO (2003) *Conditions of Work in the Fishing Sector: A Comprehensive Standard (a Convention Supplemented by a Recommendation) on Work in the Fishing Sector*, Geneva: International Labour Office.

ILO (2011) *ILO Introductory Report: Global Trends and Challenges on Occupational Safety and Health*, Geneva: International Labour Office.

Ingold, T. (2000) *The Perception of the Environment: Essays in Livelihood, Dwelling, Skill*, London: Routledge.

Ingold, T. (2002a) 'Communication and communion', *Behavioural and Brain Sciences* 25: 627–628.

Ingold, T. (2002b) 'General introduction', in T. Ingold (ed.), *Companion Encyclopedia of Anthropology*, pp. xiii–xxii. London: Routledge.

ITF (2008) 'Migrant workers in the Scottish and Irish fishing industry: Forced or compulsory labour or just plain modern day slavery', London: International Transport Workers' Federation. Available at www.ictuni.org, accessed 15 January 2011.

Jackson, M. (1989) *Paths Toward a Clearing: Radical Empiricism and Ethnographic Inquiry*, Bloomington: Indiana University Press.

Jackson, M. (2002) 'Familiar and foreign bodies: A phenomenological exploration of the human-technology interface', *Journal of the Royal Anthropological Institute* 8: 333–346.

Jackson, M. (2007) *Excursions*, Durham, NC: Duke University Press.

Jain, S. L. (2006) *Injury: The Politics of Product Design and Safety Law in the United States*, Princeton: Princeton University Press.

Jedrej, C. and M. Nuttall (1996) *White Settlers: The Impact of Rural Repopulation in Scotland*, Luxembourg: Harwood.

Johnson, M and M. Johnson (2013) *Advances in Marine Biology: The Ecology and Biology of Nephrops norvegicus*, London: Elsevier.

Kasmir, S. and A. Carbonella (2008) 'Dispossession and the anthropology of labor', *Critique of Anthropology* 28: 5–25.

King, T and G. Robinson (eds) (Forthcoming 2017) *At Home on the Waves: The Human Habitation of the Sea from the Mesolithic to Today*, Oxford: Berghahn.

Kleinman, A. (2000) 'The violences of everyday life: The multiple forms and dynamics of social violence', in V. Das, A. Kleinman, M. Ramphele and P. Reynolds (eds), *Violence and Subjectivity*, pp. 226–241. Berkeley: University of California Press.

Kleinman, A. and E. Fitz-Henry (2007) 'The experiential basis of subjectivity: How individuals change in the context of societal transformation', in J. Biehl, B. Good and A. Kleinman (eds), *Subjectivity: Ethnographic Investigations*, pp. 52–65. Berkeley: University of California Press.

Knipe, E. (1984) *Gamrie: An Exploration in Cultural Ecology*, Lanham: University Press of America.

KPMG and Sea Fish Industry Authority (2004) *Seafood Industry Value Chain Analysis: Cod, Haddock and Nephrops*, Edinburgh: Seafish.

Kroeber, A. and C. Kluckhorn (1952) *Culture: A Critical Review of Concepts and Definitions*, Cambridge, MA: Harvard University Press.

Latour, B. (1987) *Science in Action: How to Follow Engineers and Scientists Through Society*, Cambridge, MA: Harvard University Press.

Lauer, M. and S. Aswani (2009) 'Indigenous ecological knowledge as situated practices: Understanding fishers' knowledge in the western Solomon Islands', *American Anthropologist* 111(3): 317–329.

Lawson, C. (2008) 'An ontology of technology: Artefacts, relations, and functions', *Techné* 12: 48–64.

Leakey, R. (1974) *Modern Inshore Fishing: A Guide for Beginners and Experts*, Settle: Leakey's Books.

Lemonnier, P. (1992) *Elements for an Anthropology of Technology*, Ann Arbor: University of Michigan.

Lester, R. (2013) 'Back from the edge of existence: A critical anthropology of trauma', *Transcultural Psychiatry* 50(5): 753–762.

Linkie, D. (2006) *Fishing Vessels of Britain and Ireland 2006*, London: Fishing News/ Informa.

Lockley, P. (2009) 'Weather lifts prices at new Brixham market', *Fishing News*, London, 4 December 2009, p. 5.

Lukács, G. (1972 [1922]) *History and Class Consciousness: Studies in Marxist Dialectics*, Cambridge, MA: MIT Press.

MacDonald, S. (1997) *Reimagining Culture: Histories, Identities, and the Gaelic Renaissance*, Oxford: Berg.

MacKenzie, D. (n.d. [1852]) 'Letter written by Donald MacKenzie', in *Penifiler and Heatherfield Recollections*. Self-published.

MacKenzie, D. (1996) *Knowing Machines: Essays on Technical Change*, Cambridge, MA: MIT Press.

MacLeod, C. (2007) *Fàsachadh An-Iochdmhor Ratharsair: The Cruel Clearance of Raasay*, Dunfermline: Clò Àrnais.

MacLeod, G. (2005) *Muir is Tìr*, Stornoway: Acair.

MAIB (2005) *Report on the Investigations of the Foundering of the Kathryn Jane*, Southampton: Marine Accident Investigation Branch.

MAIB (2007) *Report on the Investigation of the Grounding of fv Brothers*, Southampton: Marine Accident Investigation Branch.

MAIB (2008) *Analysis of UK Fishing Vessel Safety 1992 to 2006*, Southampton: Marine Accident Investigation Branch.

Marine Management Organisation (2010) *UK Sea Fisheries Statistics 2009*, London: Marine Management Organisation.

Marks, B. (2012) 'The political economy of household commodity production in the Louisiana shrimp fishery', *Journal of Agrarian Change* 12(2–3): 227–251.

Martin, A. (1981) *The Ring-Net Fishermen*, Edinburgh: John Donald.

Martin, A. (2004) *Fish and Fisherfolk of Kintyre, Lochfyneside, Gigha and Arran*, Isle of Colonsay: House of Lochar.

Marx, K. (1964 [1858]) 'Pre-capitalist economic formations'. Marxists Internet Archive. Available at www.marxists.org/archive/marx/works/1857/precapitalist/ch01.htm, accessed 12 November 2015.

Marx, K. (1971) *Capital Volume III*, Moscow: Progress.

Marx, K. (1973) *Grundrisse*, Harmondsworth: Penguin.

Marx, K. (1976 [1890]) *Capital: A Critique of Political Economy, Volume I*, London: Penguin Books.

Marx, K. (with Friedrich Engels) (1998 [1845]) 'The German ideology', in *The German Ideology including Theses on Feuerbach and Introduction to the Critique of Political Economy*, pp. 27–568. Amherst: Prometheus Books.

Marx, K. and F. Engels (1998 [1848]) *The Communist Manifesto: A Modern Edition*, London: Verso.

Mason, J. (1987) 'Scottish shellfish fisheries', in R. Bailey and B. Parrish (eds), *Developments in Fisheries Research in Scotland*, pp. 88–98. Farnham: Fishing News Books.

Massey, D. (1994) *Space, Places and Gender*, Minneapolis: University of Minnesota Press.

Mauss, M. (2006) *Marcel Mauss: Techniques, Technology, Civilisation*, Oxford: Berghahn.

Mauss, M. (2006 [1927]) 'The divisions of sociology', in N. Schlanger (ed.), *Marcel Mauss: Techniques, Technology, Civilisation*, pp. 49–54. Oxford: Berghahn.

Mauss, M. (2006 [1935]) 'Techniques of the body', in N. Schlanger (ed.), *Marcel Mauss: Techniques, Technology and Civilisation*, pp. 77–95. Oxford: Berghahn.

Mauss, M. (2006 [1935/1947]) 'Technology', in N. Schlanger (ed.), *Marcel Mauss: Techniques, Technology, Civilisation*, pp. 99–140. Oxford: Berghahn.

McFarlane, A. and R. Bryant. (2007) 'Post-traumatic stress disorder in occupational settings: Anticipating and managing the risk', *Occupational Medicine* 54: 404–410.

Menzies, C. (2002) 'Work first, then eat! Skipper/crew relations on a French fishing boat', *Anthropology of Work Review* 23: 19–24.

Menzies, C. (2011) *Red Flags and Lace Coiffes: Identity and Survival in a Breton Village*, Toronto: University of Toronto Press.

Metz, S. and H. Curtis (2008) *Scottish Fleet Financial Performance 2008 Mid-Year Review*, Edinburgh: Seafish.

Money, R. (2008) 'Working conditions cited in boat fire deaths', *The Sunday Herald*, Glasgow, 2 August 2008.

Nadel-Klein, J. (1991) 'Reweaving the fringe: Localism, tradition and representation in British ethnography', *American Ethnologist* 18: 500–517.

Nadel-Klein, J. (2003) *Fishing for Heritage: Modernity and Loss along the Scottish Coast*, Oxford: Berg.

Nader, L. (1996) *Naked Science: Anthropological Inquiry into Boundaries, Power, and Knowledge*, New York: Routledge.

Narotzky, S. and G. Smith (2006) *Immediate Struggles: People, Power, and Place in Rural Spain*, Berkeley: University of California Press.

Navaro-Yashin, Y. (2012) *The Make-Believe Space: Affective Geography in a Postwar Polity*, Durham, NC: Duke University Press.

Neis, B., M. Binkley, S. Gerrard and M. Maneschy (2005) *Changing Tides: Gender, Fisheries and Globalization*, Halifax: Fernwood.

Nicolson, A. (2004) *Seamanship: A Voyage Along the Wild Coasts of the British Isles*, New York: HarperCollins.

Nightingale, A. (2011) 'Beyond design principles: Subjectivity, emotion, and the (ir-) rational commons', *Society and Natural Resources* 24(2): 119–132.

Orlove, B. (2002) *Lines in the Water: Nature and Culture at Lake Titicaca*, Berkeley: University of California Press.

Pálsson, G. (1991) *Coastal Economies, Cultural Accounts: Human Ecology and Icelandic Discourse*, Manchester: Manchester University Press.

Pálsson, G. (1994) 'Enskilment at sea', *Man* 29: 901–927.

Parman, S. (1990) *Scottish Crofters: A Historical Ethnography of a Celtic Village*, Ft. Worth: Holt, Rinehart, and Winston.

Patterson, T. (2009) *Karl Marx, Anthropologist*, Oxford: Berg.

Pine, A. (2008) *Working Hard, Drinking Hard: On Violence and Survival in Honduras*, Berkeley: University of California Press.

Povinelli, E. (1993) *Labor's Lot: The Power, History, and Culture of Aboriginal Action*, Chicago: University of Chicago Press.

Rapport, N. (2003) 'The computer as a focus of inattention: Five scenarios concerning hospital porters', in C. Garsten and H. Wulff (eds), *New Technologies at Work: People, Screens and Social Virtuality*, pp. 25–43. Oxford: Berg.

Rapport, N. (2009) *Of Orderlies and Men: Hospital Porters Achieving Wellness at Work*, Durham, NC: Carolina Academic Press.

Rediker, M. (1989) *Between the Devil and the Deep Blue Sea: Merchant Seaman, Pirates, and the Anglo-American Maritime World, 1700–1750*, Cambridge: Cambridge University Press.

Reed, E. (1996) *Encountering the World: Toward an Ecological Psychology*, Oxford: Oxford University Press.

Rees, J. (1998) *The Algebra of Revolution: The Dialectic and the Classical Marxist Tradition*, London: Routledge.

Retsikas, K. (2007) 'Being and place: Movement, ancestors, and personhood in East Java, Indonesia', *Journal of the Royal Anthropological Institute* 13(4): 969–986.

Roberts, S. and J. Williams (2007) *Update of Mortality for Workers in the UK Merchant Shipping and Fishing Sectors*, Southampton: Maritime and Coastguard Agency.

Rodrigue, J.-P. (2006) 'Ports and maritime trade', in Barney Warf (ed.), *The Encyclopedia of Human Geography*. London: Sage.

Russo, J. and S. Linkon (2005) *New Working-Class Studies*, Ithaca: ILR Press/Cornell University Press.

Scarry, E. (1985) *The Body in Pain: The Making and Unmaking of the World*, Oxford: Oxford University Press.

Schacht, R. (1970) *Alienation*, London: George Allen and Unwin.

Scheper-Hughes, N. and P. Bourgois (2004) *Violence in War and Peace*, Oxford: Blackwell.

Schlanger, N. (1998) 'The study of techniques as an ideological challenge: Technology, nation, and humanity in the work of Marcel Mauss', in W. James and N. Allen (eds), *Marcel Mauss: A Centenary Tribute*, pp. 192–212. Oxford: Berghahn.

Schlanger, N. (2006) 'Introduction. Technological commitments: Marcel Mauss and the study of techniques in the French social sciences', in *Marcel Mauss: Techniques, Technology and Civilisation*, pp. 1–29. Oxford: Berghahn.

Scottish Fishermen's Organisation (2011) 'Crewing – available to vessels fishing outside the 12 mile limit'. Available at www.scottishfishermen.co.uk, accessed 10 September 2011.

Scottish Government Statistician Group (2010) *Scottish Sea Fisheries Statistics 2009*, Edinburgh: Scottish Government.

Searle, J. (1983) *Intentionality: An Essay in the Philosophy of Mind*, Cambridge: Cambridge University Press.

Searle, J. (1993) 'Response: The background of intentionality and action', in E. Lepore and R. Van Gulick (eds), *John Searle and His Critics*, pp. 289–299. Oxford: Wiley-Blackwell.

Sider, G. (2003) *Between History and Tomorrow: Making and Breaking Everyday Life in Rural Newfoundland*, Peterborough: Broadview Press.

Sigaut, F. (2002) 'Technology', in T. Ingold (ed.), *Companion Encyclopedia of Anthropology*, pp. 420–459. London: Routledge.

Slocum, J. (2001 [1900]) *Sailing Alone Around the World*, Mineola: Courier Dover.

Smith, G. (1999) *Confronting the Present: Towards a Politically Engaged Anthropology*, Oxford: Berg.

Smith, N. (2008) *Uneven Development: Nature, Capital, and the Production of Space*, Athens: University of Georgia Press.

Smout, T. (1970) 'The landowner and the planned village in Scotland, 1730–1830', in N. Phillipson and R. Mitchison (eds), *Scotland in the Age of Improvement: Essays in Scottish History in the Eighteenth Century*, pp. 73–106. Edinburgh: Edinburgh University Press.

Sodikoff, G. (2004) 'Land and langour: Ethical imaginations of work and forest in northeast Madagascar', *History and Anthropology* 15: 367–398.

St Martin, K. (2007) 'The difference that class makes: Neoliberalization and non-capitalism in the fishing industry of New England', *Antipode* 39: 527–549.

*Stornoway Gazette* (2007) 'Top fishing skippers', *Stornoway Gazette*, 18 December 2007.

Strang, V. (2006) 'Introduction: Fluidscapes: Water, identity and the senses', *Worldviews* 10: 147–154.

Subramanian, A. (2009) *Shorelines: Space and Rights in South India*, Stanford: Stanford University Press.

Suchman, L. (2007) *Human-Machine Reconfigurations: Plans and Situated Actions*, 2nd edition, Cambridge: Cambridge University Press.

Symes, D. and J. Phillipson (2009) 'Whatever became of social objectives in fisheries policy?', *Fisheries Research* 95: 1–5.

Taussig, M. (1992) *The Nervous System*, London: Routledge.

Therborn, G. (1980) *The Ideology of Power and the Power of Ideology*, London: Verso.

Thomas, J. (2006) 'The trouble with material culture', *Journal of Iberian Archaeology* 9/10: 11–24.

Tilley, C. (1994) *A Phenomenology of Landscape: Places, Paths, and Monuments*, Oxford: Berg.

Tombs, S. and D. Whyte (2007) *Safety Crimes*, Cullompton: Willan.

Trower, S. (2008) 'Editorial: Vibratory movements', *Senses and Society* 3: 133–136.

Tyrrell, M. (2006) 'From placelessness to place: An ethnographer's experience of growing to know places at sea', *Worldviews* 10(2): 220–238.

UK Border Agency (2008) *Accession Monitoring Report May 2004–September 2008 A8 Countries*. Available at www.nesmp.org.uk, accessed May 2011.

UK Border Agency (2010) *Warning to Employers of Non European Fishermen*. Issued 4 August 2010. Available at www.ukba.homeoffice.gov.uk/sitecontent/newsarticles/2010/275292/14-warning-to-employers, accessed May 2011.

Ungfors, A., E. Bell, M. Johnson, D. Cowing, N. Dobson, R. Bublitz and J. Sandell (2013) 'Nephrops fisheries in European waters', in M. Johnson and M. Johnson (eds), *Advances* in *Marine Biology: The Ecology and Biology of Nephrops norvegicus*, pp. 247–306. London: Elsevier.

Volosinov, V. (1986 [1929]) *Marxism and the Philosophy of Language*, Cambridge, MA: Harvard University Press.

Walley, C. (2004) *Rough Waters: Nature and Development in an East African Marine Park*, Princeton: Princeton University Press.

Whitehouse, A. (2004) *Negotiating Small Differences: Conservation Organisations and Farming on Islay*, St. Andrews: University of St. Andrews.

Widlok, T. (1997) 'Orientation in the wild: The shared cognition of the Hai||om bushpeople', *Journal of the Royal Anthropological Institute* 3: 317–332.

Widlok, T. (2005) 'Comments', *Current Anthropology* 46: 750–751.

Wolf, E. (1997) *Europe and the People Without History*, Berkeley: University of California Press.

World Bank (2016) *Labor Force, Total*. Available at: http://databank.worldbank.org/data/home.aspx, accessed 10 May 2016.

Žižek, S. (2008) *Violence: Six Sideways Reflections*, London: Profile Books.

# Index

Note: Entries beginning in 'fish' are not cross-referenced to each other, only to entries that do not begin with 'fish'.

CPSIA information can be obtained
at www.ICGtesting.com
Printed in the USA
JSHW021625191219
3103JS00004B/18

9 781526 143693